The Transformation Imperative

Achieving Market Dominance through Radical Change

THOMAS E. VOLLMANN

Harvard Business School Press ■ Boston, Massachusetts

Library of Congress Cataloging-in-Publication Data

Vollmann, Thomas E.
  The transformation imperative : achieving market dominance
through radical change / Thomas E. Vollmann.
    p. cm.
  Includes index.
  ISBN 0-87584-676-9
  1. Organizational change—Management. 2. Organizational
learning. I. Title.
  HD58.8.V645 1996   95-43826
  658.4'06—dc20   CIP

Contents

Acknowledgments

Much of the insights for this approach to integrated strategic transformation has been developed and tested in the field through working with member companies and through other research initiatives of Manufacturing 2000 (M2000), a major collaborative research project between industry and IMD—International Institute for Management Development in Lausanne, Switzerland. Over its five-year work to date, the following firms have participated:

Andersen Consulting
Australian Manufacturing Council
Bally
Bell Packaging Corporation
BP Chemicals
CMB Packaging
Digital Equipment Corporation
Du Pont De Nemours International
Exxon Chemical International
GKN Automotive
Heineken
International Business Machines
Johnson & Johnson
KNP BT
Mandelli
Nestlé
Nokia Mobile Phones
Omega
Philips
Siemens
Sony Europa
Volkswagen/Audi

The Manufacturing 2000 project has as its primary mission "to continuously redefine the nature of manufacturing activities and enterprises by identifying the changing requirements for manufacturing excellence and the appropriate organizational responses."

This mission statement has served the project well over its history. The primary or overriding research project that has driven Manufacturing 2000 is in fact enterprise transformation. The titles have changed, the approaches and understanding of this critical concept have shifted, but there has never been any doubt that it is indeed enterprise transformation that will determine which companies survive in the long run. Other research topics in Manufacturing 2000 include: change management, benchmarking and performance measurement, information technology and management, marketing and manufacturing convergence, commercialization of new technology, and supply chain management.

This book has taken a long time to complete, and it has been thrown away on several occasions as my thinking changed. I am indebted to many people in the companies where the bulk of the Manufacturing 2000 work has taken place, and many of their experiences are reflected in this book. At the same time, the ideas have been presented and refined in our classrooms at IMD, in other assignments, on trips to the United States and Asia, by numerous conversations with colleagues around the globe, and of course by reading the literature. The examples in the book are not exclusively based on Manufacturing 2000 companies.

There have been many people who have helped me change my thinking, and some of them deserve mention. Jeffrey Miller at Boston University has been a constant source of inspiration—often with a special irreverence that cuts through fuzzy thinking. Jinichiro Nakane at Waseda University worked with me on an earlier version of this work—at several sites in Japan—and he provided more key insights than can be acknowledged here. Mark Brazas also was very helpful in some of the early research. Michael Oliff and I worked together on the Manufacturing 2000 project for four years, and he played a key role in the early development of my thinking. Robert Collins has been a great friend and colleague for more years than either of us likes to remember and he has also helped crystallize my thinking. Donald Marchand is another colleague with whom I have worked closely in recent times, particularly on the linkages between enterprise transformation and the resultant changes required in information systems. Carlos Cordon has helped to extend the transformation ideas—especially to supply chain management. Several people from

Andersen Consulting, most notably Guy Vanderbrouck and Fabio Mercandetti, also helped in development of the ideas. Peter Bonnici at Quadrant has served as a foil for idea generation, the ways in which they can be generalized, and how those idea can best be expressed. Peter Lorange read a version of the manuscript and provided some helpful insights. Finally there have been a series of deans that have encouraged me over time, including George McGurn, Robert Leone, and Douglas Hall at Boston University, and Juan Rada and Peter Lorange at IMD.

The Transformation Imperative

Introduction

"Let us look at the matter thus: May we not conceive each living being to be a puppet of the Gods? Affections in us are like cords and strings, which pull in opposite and different ways, and to opposite actions. . . . According to the argument there is one among these cords which every man ought to grasp and never let go, but to pull with against all the rest, and this is the sacred and golden cord of reason. There are others which are hard and of iron, but this one is soft because golden. . . .
Now we ought to associate with the lead of the best, which is law. For inasmuch as reason is beautiful and gentle, her rule must have ministers in order to help the golden principle in vanquishing other principles."
—Plato, *Laws*

Like the puppets described by Plato, present enterprises are subject to many and powerful forces pulling them in all sorts of directions and compelling all sorts of actions. Some pulls are rigid and hard and appear to be impossible to ignore, such as downturns in the marketplace or corporate mandates. But in too many cases, the connections among these pulls—and the sense of a unifying direction—become unclear. The search is now on for the golden cord of reason by which the enterprise can steady itself, sort out priorities, and make a united stand for the future.

Challenges have changed since Henry Ford introduced the first production lines in 1913. So fundamental is the change that some call this the "third industrial revolution." The first industrial revolution, coinciding with the invention of the power loom at the end of the eighteenth century, can be characterized by the surrender of some craft skills to machines. The second industrial revolution, following the invention of the production line, saw the role of machines increase and ushered in the age of mass production. Today's revolution is characterized by a massive explosion of information and a technological quantum leap, with consequent increases in power and flexibility of manufacturing technology and processes. The number of new patents, inventions, and products is proliferating at a breathtaking rate, thus raising the stakes and increasing the competitive pressures.

Not only must companies now do different things, but in the third industrial revolution they must also do things differently. Gone are the days when the enterprise had the luxury of establishing and securing a base by being first in market with a new product. In the past decades the battle between PepsiCo and Coca-Cola, for example, it took just three weeks between the launch of the first clear cola drink and the appearance of its rival product—not enough time to establish market presence. Similarly, when the time between design and launch of a new car drops from eight years to two, what chance is there to build barriers to entry against competitive products? What chance does any company have when its approach to competition is to match the production costs of competitors—while they are delivering new levels of service and competing on time as well?

How does the manufacturing company respond to:

☐ the greater power of retailers?

☐ the emergence of "Eurobuyers" or global purchasing?

☐ increasingly unique bundles of customer product/service requirements?

☐ foreign "dumping" in its market at prices 20 percent below its cost?

☐ targeting by the "greens" for its environmental practices?

Tearing Up the Rule Book

The rule book for competitiveness used by second industrial revolution companies has been rendered obsolete by these sorts of challenges. The old rule book for enterprise management—based as it is on Adam Smith's pin factory model—should now be torn up as well.

The mass production model has been largely responsible for the present standard of living enjoyed in industrial countries. But when conditions have altered beyond recognition, new principles of production and management models need to be found. The last ten years have witnessed an increasing intensity in this search. Many remedies have been tried. While some are quite successful, few are standing the test of time. Anyone who believes in a one-time change to some new steady state will be woefully disappointed.

One explanation for the failure of so many recent change programs has less to do with the change tools than with the organizational environment in which they are being applied. The problem is that third-wave tools are being used by managers wedded to second-wave business notions. Whatever the tool, a mass market, mass production mentality will result only in "better sameness," rather than fundamental improvement that will allow the enterprise to achieve and sustain an influence in its industry—*to dominate.*

Why Transformation

Domination requires companies to grasp present-day cultural and technological reality and let go of yesterday's. No amount of fine-tuning will allow them to do this. To be successful in navigating toward becoming a third-wave player, the enterprise requires deep, broad, fundamental change in operational paradigms, practices, and outputs. *This level of change is what we call enterprise transformation.* Enterprise transformation implies change in the overall company, in its business units, in its factories, and in its other organizational units. It also implies coordination among these units and a shared overall objective.

Paradigm shifting—a transformation of fundamental assumptions—has been a feature of change theory for some time now, and yet the desired results are far too rarely realized. This book proposes that the reason for this failure has less to do with the tools for change and more to do with the process.

Four Essential Features of Transformation

For change to be truly transformative—creating a dominant third industrial revolution enterprise—the change agenda must be:

□ *integrated* from the strategic intent of the transformation down to the detailed processes and other infrastructure requirements to achieve it.

    ☐ *consistent* in terms of all activities leading to the same goal and all employees having a clear sense of priorities.

    ☐ *feasible* from the point of view of resources and corporate performance.

    ☐ *desirable* because it matches both enterprise and individual objectives.

Without integration and consistency across every facet of the enterprise, the outcome is likely to be mixed signals and confusion rather than fundamental transformation—like a car that has one wheel going faster than the others. Even the integration and consistency of strategy, with the resultant necessary changes in processes and other infrastructure, is not sufficient on its own. Two more features are required for success. Without feasibility and desirability, carrying out a program of change will be like trying to get up a hill with the brake on and with a driver who has no interest in reaching the top of the hill.

These four features—integration, consistency, feasibility, and desirability—ensure that the likely outcome of a change program is fundamental enterprise *transformation* (and not just "better sameness").

This book describes the golden cord of reason that links these four features of change, thus significantly enhancing the probability of successful enterprise transformation—which leads to dominance. The golden cord ensures that enterprise transformation is based on a definitive linkage between a well-defined strategic intent, closely coupled strategic response or action programs, the necessary competencies to carry out these responses, and the detailed processes and other infrastructure to enable the competencies. Fundamental enterprise transformation is the only way to achieve dominance in today's business environment.

Being Pragmatic About Change

Our approach to enterprise transformation is pragmatic. It recognizes that different enterprises enter the change process from different points—some start with strategy, some with processes, others with competencies. Moreover, in most companies change is occurring in all these components—at the same time—but far too often in an uncoordinated fashion. We hope to show that the entry point into the change process is less important than making sure that the golden cord is unbroken and that it be followed upward and downward to ensure that it is not snagging at any point. Enterprise transformation requires both top-down and bottom-up efforts to achieve consistency and integration. The classic hierarchical or deductive approach to determining change and its associated action programs is just not sufficient for the task.

The process model for transformation we have developed links the various entry points to change—eight in all.

☐ Strategic intent

☐ Competencies

☐ Processes

☐ Resources

☐ Outputs

☐ Strategic response

☐ Challenges

☐ Learning capacity

The golden cord integrates these eight change facets, ensuring consistency and integration. Built into it are points at which one can check for feasibility and desirability. Being pragmatic, we have not attempted to invent a new semantic to describe change. Instead we use existing terms and apply the model for transformation to shed light on their relevance.

The goal is dominance. The vehicle is strategically driven enterprise transformation. The process requires integration, consistency, feasibility, and desirability. *Transformation begins when the enterprise embraces change.*

The Connections with Reengineering and Core Competencies

Two important contributions to the improvement of business practices in recent times are business process reengineering and the focus on core competencies. Enterprise transformation is complementary, building upon both sets of ideas, and more importantly developing a key synthesis. Enterprise transformation provides both a model and a concrete approach for explicitly linking the detailed process and systems changes associated with business process reengineering with the critical aspects of strategy that are reflected in core competencies and the concept of "strategic intent." The result is a better integration, where specific reengineering efforts are channeled to be explicitly consistent with overriding strategy. In doing so, priorities can be better managed, transformation efforts can be targeted in specific business units, continual updating is facilitated, and there is a greater understanding of how a firm's strategic intent plays out in an overall context.

Journeying to Transformation

Our approach is largely built on a model for transformation. The model sees transformation as constituted of two closely related sets of activities. The first is strategy formulation, where the challenges facing the enterprise are evaluated, summarized, and ranked in terms of importance. Thereafter, strategic responses to the challenges are formulated in a way that is consistent and integrated with the strategic intent or mission of the company.

The other set of activities to implement transformation is to create the necessary changes in infrastructure to make the strategy a reality. The link between strategy and infrastructure is competencies—fundamentally, the new competencies required to support the strategic responses. The infrastructure necessary to enable the new competencies consists of detailed processes and systems, as well as the resources to support them. The way in which the new infrastructure is to be achieved becomes the change agenda for the enterprise.

The book develops the model as it explores several other sets of ideas: the process of *using* the model (i.e., the transformation journey), the experiences of companies undergoing transformation, and a set of lessons for managers.

 □ Chapter 1 provides the backdrop to enterprise transformation, under the imperative: Dominate or die. The basic message is that in today's world, it is simply not sufficient to continue to do the same things a bit better.

 □ Chapter 2 describes eight facets or viewpoints for thinking about transformation. True transformation requires fundamental changes in all of them: Strategic intent, competencies, processes, resources, outputs, strategic response, challenges, and learning capacity.

▢ Chapter 3 develops the model in some detail, linking it to the eight facets of transformation, some other enterprise transformation concepts, and a specific method for applying the model.

▢ Chapter 4 focuses on the drivers for transformation, or challenges. These are the internal and external "discontinuities" (incorporating the major shifts, rather than only the usual forces and constraints); and the changes in expectations of customers, customers *of* the customers, and other stakeholders.

▢ Chapter 5 is devoted to strategic intent and strategic response—and to the necessity that these two concepts are integrated and consistent, first one with another, then each with the resulting competencies and infrastructure. It is imperative to have a well-developed set of objectives for enterprise transformation, and it is equally important that the set of action programs reflects this intent.

▢ Chapter 6 is focused on the detailed infrastructure requirements for transformation. The basic tool used is "competency mapping," by which the detailed set of processes and resources to achieve the desired new competencies is determined.

▢ Chapter 7 is concerned with developing learning capacity. Transformation is not a one-time activity, and the company that develops its ability to implement transformation faster and better than its competitors will dominate.

▢ Chapter 8 comes back to "people transformation," a topic we consider throughout the book, but now with the overall set of transformation concepts in place. In the last analysis, it is the capacity of a company's people to carry out transformation that determines its ultimate survival and health.

▢ Chapter 9 asks "So What?" At the end of it all, the need is for a set of clear managerial lessons for implementing transformation. This chapter tries to provide this summary and conclusions.

1 Dominate or Die

When the Manufacturing 2000 project at IMD was first started, the "Dominate or Die" message was our provocative description of what was happening in the world of manufacturing. We took delight in using this outrageous semantic to challenge groups of managers out of a sense of complacency. The sense of urgency in the phrase raised the creative level of executives' thinking. In short, it got people's attention!

Now, in the '90s, with global economies and industries being devastated by deep recession, there is little dispute that this is "how it is" in business. Today the sentiment of "Dominate or Die" is as common in the boardroom as computer games are in teenage bedrooms. Many firms once dominant in their industries or on the list for *In Search of Excellence* are now, if not "dead," at least among the walking wounded.

Every Company Is Vulnerable

Figure 1.1 depicts the issue quite well. Who would have thought that the market value of Intel and Microsoft would come to rival that of IBM—which basically put the other companies in business? How could Wal-Mart—a little discount operation in Arkansas—overtake the giant Sears? How did General Motors lose so much market share to the Japanese? Finally—and most important—what company is invulnerable to this kind of change?

> □ Bill Gates and Paul Allen, founders of Microsoft, are well aware of the company's vulnerability. Gates says: "The Internet is the seed corn of a lot of things that are going to happen, and there are so many parallels to when Paul and I were involved in the beginnings of the P.C. We said back then, 'Don't DEC and IBM know that they are in deep trouble?' Here we are, staring at that the same kind of situation."[1]

Figure 1.1

The Changing Game

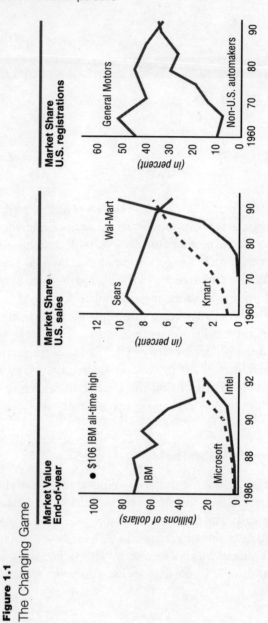

Source: Joshua Mendes, "Dinosaurs?" *Fortune*, May 3, 1993, 33, 34, 36. © 1993 Time Inc. All rights reserved.

□ Another view comes from Lou Gerstner of IBM: "One of the great things about this industry is that every decade or so you get a chance to redefine the playing field. We're in that phase of redefinition right now." It will be interesting to see how it plays out.[2]

□ And industry leader Boeing is equally clear about the need for major improvements to retain their position. Says Philip Condit, president and chief operations officer: "Our choice is either we change or we will not be successful, so let's do it."[3]

Many of today's leading enterprises and leading management thinkers agree that the stark choice facing companies in the light of massively changed environments and customer expectations is to dominate or die. Yet far too many businesses treat this warning with a large pinch of salt and continue pursuing strategies aimed at improving "the way we do business around here." Domination of their industry or sector is rarely on the agenda in reality (although many mission statements, with words like "pre-eminent," "leading player," "world class," might have you believe that dominance is in fact a common goal).

The acid test is: Who really believes such claims? What we say to the companies that pay lip service to the concept of industry leadership but continue to pursue second wave thinking is: Open your eyes, or you will not see that there are others in serious training to take your place. We know this is true, because we are working with many of them—across sectors and covering a range of sizes. They have definitely taken on the challenge and are doing something about it.

What is more, there seems to be a growing appreciation that the fundamental nature of challenges has altered the competitive environment to such an extent that what once constituted a profile of a winning organization does not necessarily apply any more. All around us we hear the thuds of dinosaur organizations hitting the deck, and even the Japanese giants show signs of wobbling, but we need to be alert to notice that a new species has come to life. Its ways are catching hold, and its performance is allowing it to seize the initiative.

□ In Brazil, Ricardo Semler's manufacturing company, Semco, is peculiar in that no one in the company knows exactly how many people it employs. Workers are either full-time, part-time, self-employed Semco satellites, or self-employed contractors using Semco facilities. The CEO position and budgets last just six months (but not the same six months, requiring the incoming CEO to pick up midway through the budget period). All meetings are open, and information is shared with workers. Workers set their own hours and salaries and are required to complete evaluations of the managers. Semler finds that the only functions that need to be kept in-house are: top management, applications engineering, some R&D, and some hi-tech, capital-intensive skills. He does not care how the rest gets done. If this seems like outright lunacy, some figures attest to the viability of this type of organization: Since 1990, 28 percent of capital goods manufacturers in Brazil have gone bankrupt, and capital goods output has fallen to pre-1970 levels, but in the same period Semco's overall sales and profits have remained intact. This is no one-day wonder—Semler has been at it since the early '80s.

❑ Call British Airways' reservation desk at twelve noon, and the call might be taken by a pleasant woman at London's Heathrow. At two 'oclock, you can dial the same number, and your call could be answered by a pleasant woman in Boston or Belfast, or anywhere in the world, made possible by telecommunications. The traditional notion of organizational configuration has been thrown out of the window.

❑ At Connecticut Mutual Life Insurance Company (a successful firm), a "mentality of deliberate and calculated chaos" has been introduced. Every job is being redefined in terms of its contribution to "client service," and all employees must reapply for their current jobs or some other job for which they feel most qualified. All jobs are open to competitive bidding.

❑ One European airline's accounts are processed in Bombay. Another U.S. airline's passenger data input is handled by people in Barbados, miles from corporate headquarters. Where are the borders of these enterprises?

The rules governing third-wave companies such as these are fundamentally different from those governing their struggling predecessors. It is also clear that they did not arrive at their current position through a process of slow evolutionary steps. At one time a transformative leap gave them a profile for dominance. This new profile will not only equip them to survive in the present environment, but will also provide a platform for the next leap. And they will need to make the next leap—there is no room for complacency in the third industrial revolution.

Because, even more important than viewing the "dominate or die" imperative as acceptable theory is identifying the actions required to make it a reality. It is absolutely imperative that dominance be seen not as more of the same—only better—but as requiring fundamental transformation, based on new underlying assumptions. Devising the strategies to transform an enterprise for dominance in whatever its sphere of influence or niche—as a proactive, rather than reactive step—has thus become the key management challenge. It will be these actions, rather than words, that will decide tomorrow's leaders.

Before any strategy can usefully be identified, however, it is important to have the target clearly in sight. If the target is domination, and missing it means death, then what are the characteristics of domination, and what are the signposts to death?

Characteristics of Dominance

The reason that people in Western companies in particular have a problem with our challenge is that the notions about domination conjure up pictures of "Big Brother" or aggressive, bullying nations with megalomaniacs for leaders. To dispel some of these notions it is important to first establish what we do not mean by the word "dominance":

□ *Size:* General Motors may be the biggest automotive company, but it certainly does not dominate the industry. Companies like Honda or Toyota, which are a lot smaller, seem to be the ones that are calling more of the shots, forcing GM to scramble to keep up.

□ *Monopoly:* The dominant company does not need artificial barriers to entry into its business. It is periodically undergoing fundamental transformation, as well as learning at such a fast rate that others just will not be able to catch up.

□ *The bottom line:* There are many firms that make excellent financial returns that just cannot be considered as dominant—and vice-versa. Financial returns are obviously an objective of dominance, but there are always time lags, as well as confounding influences. Financial returns are the passengers; dominance is the driver.

Dominant firms lead their industry, sector, or niche by not only attaining but also *sustaining an influence* in an area while remaining intensely customer-focused. The key words in our description are "sustaining an influence." Any number of companies have managed to attain excellence or leadership—at least in some of their business units. Few, however, manage to achieve dominance in every business unit and sustain it.

IBM, for example, dominated the computer industry for decades by offering a full product line, providing service, and helping its customers solve problems. In due course, its bundle of goods and services was duplicated by others, and customers became able to do their own integration, picking and choosing the parts needed. Moreover, the battle went from hardware to software—and currently it is Microsoft that dominates this 'industry'. Similarly, in steel there was a time when "big was beautiful," until Nucor changed all that with its minimills. Now there is intense competition here as well, with a new shakeout of the industry coming. Those firms and business units that manage to keep on sustaining an influence are what we call dominant.

This qualification dispels another notion of dominance. It is not a single steady state. Influence can be seen or measured on any number of scales, and it depends as well on the way each enterprise measures success. Some may choose market share; others may choose quality or innovation, or whatever they feel allows them to exert an influence on the customer. And there are changes in priority over time. Nor is there a single entity called 'the market' any more. With a proliferation of products comes the proliferation of niches. There is the beer market, for example, which includes the lager market, which in turn includes the imported brands of lager, which in turn includes German brands. Companies can be dominant on any of these levels.

■ In the grand piano market, in terms of quality, Steinway is dominant because every Steinway grand is a unique item—beautifully crafted, with a unique sound that is all its own. At the same time, we can also say that on the same scale of quality Yamaha dominates in the grand piano market, because, wherever you happen to find a Yamaha, it will sound exactly the same as any other Yamaha grand piano. Similarly, in terms of market penetration, Steinway dominates; in 80 percent of the world's leading concert halls, you will find a Steinway grand. The plot thickens . . . because on that same scale of market penetration, Yamaha also dominates; it sells more grand pianos than anyone else.

The key here is that the moment the influence of Steinway can no longer be sustained—concert artists start preferring the sound of Baldwin, for example—it will lose its position of dominance. Equally, the moment another manufacturer starts outselling Yamaha, Yamaha will not be dominant any longer.

OBSERVABLE CHARACTERISTICS OF DOMINANCE:

- Anticipation of and quick response to changes in marketplace conditions
- Proactive, opportunity-seeking atmosphere
- High rate of learning
- Flexibility, responsiveness, and speed
- Internal sense of urgency, nonbureaucratic
- Team spirit
- Setting of standards that competitors try to follow
- Changing the rules
- Growth of capabilities and competencies
- Growth in market share
- Pipeline of new products and services

The important lesson here is that any definition of dominance as a one-time steady state is not useful. The strategies for domination need to be goal-oriented and process-oriented in equal measure. That is, as we will constantly emphasize, the dominant firm has good strategy and matching good infrastructure. Good strategy without matching infrastructure will lead to frustration and confusion; good infrastructure not integrated with a consistent strategy leads to false security and chaos.

The two key questions are: "What does the enterprise need to aim at to become the dominant player?" and "What does the enterprise need to be like to keep hitting the target consistently—particularly when it is a constantly moving target?" Winning may be seen as analogous to the restaurant that is only as good as its last meal.

Characteristics of Death

When we speak about companies dying, we are talking about companies that do not exhibit any of the characteristics of dominance. A dying company does not lead; it follows. It is losing market share, it is losing capabilities, it has the wrong set of competencies, it is demoralized, its activities and responses have little impact. In fact, all around us we can observe companies that are in a state that is worse than death—they have joined the living dead, aware (or not) that whatever they do makes little difference to their situation, and yet they feel compelled to keep on acting, producing, carrying on.

Death is most often a long drawn out affair. Even with inept management (or managers very capable at the wrong things), it still takes a long time to destroy a large company with once strong, if currently obsolescent, capabilities.

Death is no stranger to the ranks of once powerful manufacturing companies. Every industry has its share of the dead (former companies or divisions), as well as the terminally ill and the walking wounded. For example, Pascale notes that five years after the publication of *In Search of Excellence,* only fourteen of the forty-three companies this widely read book identifies as "excellent" were still considered to be so.[4] Similarly, eleven of thirteen U.S. industry leaders in 1962 had fallen from that position by 1982.

DEATH NEEDS TO BE SEEN AS:

- staying level with or falling behind the competition
- risk aversion
- bureaucracy
- losing capabilities
- erosion of what were once distinctive competencies (everyone has them now)
- focusing the major attention of the company internally, instead of on the customers
- limited knowledge of how customers use the company's products and services, of the customer's basic problems, and of their customer's problems
- making panic decisions to reduce short-run costs
- not developing people
- not "unlearning" obsolete concepts and practices
- not aggressively pursuing desired business scenarios
- gradual, if any, improvement of "business as usual"

Death does not necessarily imply fifth place in sales volume among five competitors. General Motors is still, by far, the biggest automotive assembler in the world, but Figure 1.1 suggests a death trend. Relative size is not the only issue. Death is more closely tied to shrinking market share and to competitive underperformance. Death is also strongly associated with downsizing and retrenchment; companies going through these phases rarely have the ability to take on the proactive changes necessary to win the competitive battles at the same time. While GM is going through the agony of closing twenty-one plants, and laying off 74,000 employees, how is it going to gain the capabilities necessary to compete aggressively in the automotive world marketplace? During this downsizing, the company is even more vulnerable to competition. Researchers are forced to stop work on exciting projects that could make a difference. People try to hang onto their jobs until retirement or redundancy gives them their golden parachutes.

To sharp observers, the signals of death in a company are evident long before the enterprise hits crisis mode: shrinking market share, reduced growth, unsatisfactory new product development, employee disaffection, management shuffles, underestimation of the competition's capabilities, and the like. In too many cases, the early signals are ignored; even when death symptoms start tickling the bottom line, excuses and palliatives, rather than fundamental transformation, get produced.

Death Signals

Dying may be slow, and the dying enterprise may even be profitable on the road to the graveyard. But there are unmistakable signs of impending doom—"weak signals" at first, which become clearer and grow louder until there is no ignoring them.

Beginning or weak signals include:

- □ loss of key marketable staff

- □ underestimation of competition

- □ loss of niche markets

- □ failures or delays in new product development

- □ few people visiting the customers

Next come clear signals:

☐ shrinking market share

☐ reduced growth

☐ little new product development

☐ key customer exodus

"Louder" manifestations are in:

☐ employee dissatisfaction

☐ turnover at all levels, especially management

☐ serious bottom-line problems

☐ management rationalization

☐ reactive knee-jerk responses

Until the crisis signals:

☐ major cutbacks

☐ deep financial crisis

☐ redundancies.

Examples of Dying—and the Response Imperative

Firms need to be attuned to all of the death signals and take the appropriate action, rather than cursorily respond to one or two symptoms. It is just too easy to transmute customer dissatisfaction or a lack of new products into a need to reduce prices—just as it is too easy to underestimate the real causes of employee morale problems.

There are many examples of firms exhibiting death symptoms, and the responses are too often questionable. One has only to pick up the paper any day to read of yet still another firm announcing some massive restructuring, with attendant layoffs and accounting adjustments that allow problems to be written off against the past. In many cases, the restructuring results in a fundamentally weaker firm. A major chemical company trying to reduce costs announced a voluntary retirement program. It was chagrined to find far more people leaving than anticipated. Even worse, the best people left to take new jobs (some with competitors).

Other cases of "death symptoms" while competitors are doing better:

- ☐ A recent article bemoaning the fate of American automobile manufacturing and poor sales figures points out that Honda, Toyota, and Nissan "transplants" in the U.S. are running overtime.

- ☐ The computer business is tough, yet Dell and Compaq seem able to compete, while IBM and DEC appear unable to "unlearn" their approach to the market. NEC, the long-time dominant firm in personal computers in Japan, is losing 7 percent of market share per year to Compaq, Dell, and IBM in the Japanese market.

- ☐ Philips institutes one labor force reduction and plant closure after another, while Sony in Europe increases market share and wins awards for its products and factories. At the present time all consumer electronics companies are facing hard times—but there are degrees of hard times and degrees of response. Sony is not in as much trouble as many other firms. But Philips is also not sitting idly by. It's Centurion transformation process is a fundamental response to its problem, is achieving results, and there is a growing feeling of accomplishment and hope for the future in the company.

- ☐ At the extreme, we have Wang (one of *In Search of Excellence*'s forty-three excellent in 1982), which sold everything in sight to raise cash—including recently its corporate headquarters for about one-tenth of its initial value—and Honeywell, then Honeywell/Bull, now just Bull, which announces loss after loss, each necessitating another downsizing, but each time with a prediction of profits next year. Whether any of these responses will produce the desired result is highly questionable.

- ☐ Nestlé, on the other hand, is engaged in a fundamental restructuring of the company before it is in financial trouble. Its response focuses on the marketplace and new ways of doing business—not downsizing or cost reductions.

- ☐ Similarly, Siemens has created a fundamental transformation process for revitalizing its business units. The results to date are very impressive, and transformation is accelerating.

We do not intend to pick out winners and losers. In fact, there may be no permanent winners or losers. The game is constantly changing—at an ever faster pace—and there are many games.

What Makes the Difference?

What is going on inside the death versus dominance companies? What are the differences in long-run strategic objectives, and how are they being implemented in the firm in all its activities? How do successful managers lead transformation? How does enterprise transformation play out in different divisions or business units? What are the distinctive competencies—those that will make a real marketplace difference? How are resources—throughout the enterprise—being deployed in the dominant firms and in the dying firms? What is happening to the culture and morale of the employees? What do the customers think?

Who, for example, wants to buy a computer system from a company that has a good chance of not existing in a few years—or at least a very good chance of not having state-of-the-art hardware, software, and service? How long can Bull live on its "installed base"? How can General Motors compete with Toyota and Honda when it takes GM at least twice as long to bring out new models? The much vaunted Saturn has only recently reached break-even volume—with many clouds on the horizon for increasing output. But the Honda Accord, started only one year earlier, has been through several model changes and is much farther down the learning curve.

What explains these differences? No company is so irresponsible or blind to the competitive environment as simply to sit around doing nothing. Everyone is on the change bandwagon, on the improvement bandwagon. Some are "returning to core business," some are restructuring, some are reengineering. Few serious players doubt that the management of change has moved to the top of the corporate agenda. Change theories and tools proliferate. Change consultants criss-cross the globe spreading pearls of wisdom. Executives are bombarded with remedies that promise everything.

Yet companies like IBM, which have been advised by the best and the greatest, which are into all the change tools on the planet, seem to be on the death spiral. Why? They dominated. Now they appear to be dying. IBM has at least raised the percentage of its employees who visit customers from 30 percent to 70 percent. Moreover, those who know the company believe it still has first class competencies that can be focused with the right management. It remains to be seen how effective their efforts will be. From the executive office to the shop floor, the question is: How are companies to escape the death spiral?

Some Dying Responses

Clues that indicate an answer to this question seem to lie in the way firms view change and how they respond to it. Below we examine the most commonly observed responses to faltering performance. They need to be considered alongside the characteristics of dominance—third-wave companies—and those of death—companies stuck with the old operational notions. How will these responses lead to the characteristics of dominance?

Improvement Programs: Necessary, but not Sufficient to Forestall Death

Improvement programs are a part of every manufacturing company's daily life. Manufacturing companies have been bombarded with so many change programs in recent years that it is wearisome to recall all the three-letter acronyms (e.g., MRP, JIT, SPC). Beyond the particular programs are the more general necessities such as speed, responsiveness, time-based competition, quality, and flexibility. Clearly all these are important; the firm that does not achieve them does so at its peril. The fact is that these change programs and more general imperatives are necessary but not sufficient conditions for meeting the challenges facing manufacturing firms today.

"Improvement" is usually not enough in itself to achieve dominance. Increasingly, the capabilities generated by TQM, JIT, and other "world-class manufacturing" techniques are only the ante to play in today's manufacturing competitive game—not the winning cards. Such improvement programs might have contributed to dominance in the past, when they were revolutionary. And even now, some companies are achieving excellent payback from implementing these techniques. But increasingly, they can no longer be the sole basis of dominance. They are "commodities of process," analogous to product commodities—necessary, but not sufficient.

Think of the European cities with central cathedrals and plazas where hundreds of pigeons congregate, looking for food from the tourists. It is easy to flush the pigeons, as most children know. A loud noise or quick movement will send them airborne. But then it is usually one time around the cathedral, only to land pretty much in the same place. Far too many change programs are little more than flushing the pigeons—a loud noise from on high, a flurry of activity, and then a return to more or less the status quo.

The key point is that enterprise transformation requires more than change initiatives and general condition imperatives. Some authors are now calling for "reinventing the corporation," or, as Roger Martin recently put it: "To compete, companies must burn themselves down every few years and rebuild their strategies, roles, and practices."[5] This is what is implied by dominance. Included are all the latest change programs—as reflections of the general imperatives in the overriding strategy of the company.

Enterprise transformation requires consistency and integration. It is not enough to tackle many improvement programs simultaneously. There needs to be a common focus, a sense of unity to the programs and impera- tives, a widely shared understanding of the overall strategy—why the efforts are required and the resulting impacts on the organization and its people, a transparent process for achieving the changes, appropriate measures for evaluating progress, and a true commitment to making the changes. Moreover, change efforts need to be targeted.

Business process reengineering, for example, is a popular improvement process. It is even more popular when connected to benchmarking, where the objective is to study the attributes and characteristics of the processes that create best-in-class performance. But indiscriminant use of these tools can lead to a perception of great progress, when in reality there is no "golden thread of reason" to prioritize or integrate the efforts.

Enterprise transformation has to be much more than flushing the pigeons. In order to dominate, companies must institute far-ranging change. Change needs to be consistent in terms of its objectives and efforts. It also must be integrative; the entire organization needs to be actively involved, so that the individual change efforts are pieces of a puzzle, and the puzzle box lid (the road map for change) is in everyone's mind. Moreover, the sequence of efforts needs to be understood; priorities need to be set, and efforts need to be concentrated on key targets, not dissipated on generalities that are hoped to pay dividends in the future (such as quality programs that focus on the number of training sessions, rather than on concrete results).

Financial Restructuring: Looking Good to Outsiders but . . .

Financial restructuring is usually a response to crisis. The slide toward death has become bad enough to be seen repeatedly in the financial statements. When the excuses run out, the balloon goes up, top management issues a press release, and "financial restructuring"—too often a Band-Aid on a serious wound—begins. Unfortunately, news of this kind of restructuring is usually welcomed by the financial community. The company's stock price rises on the news, and management is thus falsely encouraged.

Far too many manufacturing companies respond to death signals by focusing on head count reductions in an effort to reduce costs. This will certainly reduce costs, but will almost as certainly reduce the firm's capabilities. And in the end, it is capabilities that decide dominance or death. Developing new capabilities and leveraging existing capabilities are the drivers of dominance.

The question rarely asked in these financial restructurings is: "How are fewer hands to do the same jobs?" The result: burned-out employees with zero time to work on any type of proactive responses to the competitive marketplace. In fact, the organizational energy required to adapt to the reduction might better be expended on proactive improvement and redeployment of capabilities. The latter is more likely to deliver a better result than applying an ax that inevitably hits the organization's nervous system and brain as well as its fat. IBM, for example, recently announced a major reduction in its research and development budget to save money.

At the outset of the Manufacturing 2000 project in 1989, we used the term "restructuring" to encompass what we now call enterprise transformation. The change in terminology is important; restructuring has become a pejorative term, with the emphasis on shutting factories, reducing head counts, and downsizing. In far too many cases, these are reactive responses made when the firm is on the death path, not proactive changes made to dominate—and to continue to do so.

Downsizing is not always undesirable or unavoidable. But companies often grossly underestimate the true cost of it. Conventional cost measurement metrics and managerial ideologies encourage the delusion. It is comfortable and "decisive" to get behind the "concrete numbers" of x heads times y average salary, divided by one ax. It just takes more imagination and creativity to generate alternatives that redeploy human resources to add value to the business, than to label them as waste and put them into the "out" tray. Napoleon said, "The morale is to the physical as three is to one," on his battlefield. But as the physical is easier to measure, it is too often believed to be more "manageable."

In reality, many firms have had to face up to downsizing: They have had no choice. This has been the only way to survive—and fight again another day. Interestingly, the executives we see at IMD are moving away from the "slash and burn" mentality. These actions are behind them, and they are now thinking more proactively. The focus is on customers and markets, not just costs.

■ A good example of the real but "intangible" costs of cutting heads can be seen in a major European airline that recently downsized. The firm was not in serious financial difficulties at the time, but managers could see the potential for it in the future. Their approach, however, was fundamentally cost-driven as opposed to customer value-driven. The focus was head count reduction.

Management did an excellent job of communicating the strategic reasoning and urgency of the downsizing. These were readily understood by the managers who were left, but those made redundant felt betrayed, as did many of their colleagues who remained. To many, the restructuring was a double cross to some people who had devoted their lives to the company, and they felt that more attention to improving customer-perceived value could have achieved better results.

Morale did not just go down—capabilities suffered. Specifically, customer satisfaction levels dropped. The cabin crews did not have the same degree of enthusiasm, and this was noticed by the customers—and communicated by their choice of a different air carrier. Many of the managers who remained were at first quite surprised; the logic of the action was so clear to them—and the benefits were so concrete. Their consultants presented such a clear picture of how well things would all work out. But the true costs associated with capability loss and re-energizing the remaining employees are now becoming apparent.

Companies can sometimes improve their circumstances with a reactive downsizing. The result might also be viewed as constructive inside the company, if the employees sense that all is not well and that management needs "to do something." But it is imperative that real improvements take place that impact the competitive advantage of the company in the marketplace, as opposed to simply "taking fat out of the system." Lean and mean can lead to anorexia instead.

The challenge is to cut costs and increase revenues and capabilities at the same time. There are many ways to reduce costs as well as ways to increase capabilities and/or revenues. Doing both at the same time, or at least significantly increasing the ratio of revenues and capabilities to cost, is indeed the challenge. It can be achieved only by concerted actions directed toward fundamentally changing the way the firm operates.

If this is not done, sooner rather than later, employees catch on to the fact that management is trying to get something (improved productivity) for nothing (no change in the way business is done, but fewer resources with which to do it). Cynicism sets in concerning the motives and competence of management, the long run prospects of the firm, and the chance of ever being allowed to do the job one is capable of and earn just advancement. The most capable (marketable) employees begin to pursue opportunities away from the death ship, which continues to ply the same waters under the illusion that something important has changed—when it has not.

Management Shuffles: . . . or, Rearranging the Deck Chairs on the Titanic

Another misguided "improvement" is the organizational reshuffle. Job titles are changed, job descriptions are rewritten, boxes are regrouped on the organization chart. There are winners and losers in the game of office politics, and life—or rather death—goes on, because what is really important in the company has not changed—it is still business as usual. As with the financial restructuring charade, cynicism is a likely by-product, because people are not easily fooled. Without a well-developed and communicated new mission that clearly justifies a reorganization—and that focuses on capability development and increasing customer value—the result is far too often a major expenditure of resources inside the company instead of their deployment toward competitive dominance.

■ The European division of an international computer systems firm reacted to headquarters directives to increase profits and to double fee-earning staff in a short period by looking first at its organization chart.

Managers created five divisions, each headed by a "business manager." But the managing director still holds all the reins; the business managers were selected on the basis of "reward" and convenience; no distinction is made between value-adding outputs for the customers and new business development or internal support services. Headquarters was suitably impressed. But less than six months after the changes were instituted, tensions have mounted, and the system is on the point of breakdown.

Any organizational form can be made to work. Conversely, no organizational model is a guarantee that proactive restructuring will take place. This is not to say that organizations should not change; in fact, many of the best run enterprises are breaking out of the organizational constraints that artificially separate activities that need to be "seamless." But these companies care more about substance than form—about getting the (new) job done, rather than passing out new business cards. Teams are put together to tackle projects with a clear business purpose, and then disbanded. Permanent linkages are established between functional areas to support delivery of particular customer product or service "bundles." Organizational forms are generally changed to reduce the time for information to travel to where it can be used for decision making, and decision making becomes more and more decentralized. When there is genuine empowerment, there is achievement. Without it, however, information is worthless, and so are organizational reshufflings that do not restructure the company toward dominance.

The traditional structure may impede fundamental transformation in many companies. Hierarchy and "command and control" management do not relate to getting the job done. Reducing the levels of hierarchy in this type of organization will create frustration for employees who have modeled their professional lives around traditional career ladders—and now see fewer opportunities for advancement. Breaking out of the fundamental constraints of hierarchy allows employees to develop individual career patterns, based on the ever-changing set of problems and opportunities in a company. The focus is less on vertical career ladders and more oriented to assignments where employees grow in their capabilities: a form of "horizontal" career ladder.

Instead of hierarchical progression, a new model is required. Perhaps it will be one where employees act as owners of the business—instead of as hired hands. Bob Ogle, Johnson & Johnson's Director of Worldwide Quality Assurance, speaks of empowering "process owners" to drive improvements in business processes as one of the most powerful sources of energy in a company.

Some leading manufacturing enterprises, such as Oticon in Denmark, Semco in Brazil, and Trenton Foods in the U.S., are attempting to achieve dominance by significantly reducing hierarchical organizational forms—and, more important, hierarchical practices. These firms are attempting to gain better use of all people in the organization, increase the "knowledge work" done by everyone, better identify with customers, solve customer problems (rather than selling products that are becoming low-margin commodities), form project teams to solve particular business problems and then disband them, eliminate many traditional forms of management control that deliver little customer value, and implement new technology faster and more effectively by bringing all those affected by it into the implementation process. In all these cases, there have been very positive results, both in terms of traditional financial criteria and in others such as new product introduction times.

We have seen these examples in small enterprises, or, in the case of Trenton Foods, in an operating unit of a large corporation (Nestlé). For the large multinationals, the best practice in enterprise transformation has (1) some central direction or focus, (2) detailed efforts in the individual business units or operating companies, and (3) a means of sharing results and fostering joint learning. The corporation in total has a shared sense of urgency, a spirit of joint helping and learning with sister business units, and an outward-focused approach—based on developing one combined learning curve.

Siemens provides a good example of how this can work. The firm has always been organized in divisions and business units, and also by geography. In the past, each of the individual business units tended to focus on functional excellence, but at the expense of overall process optimization (see Figure 1.2). Decisions had to progress up hierarchical ladders before conclusions could be reached, with interfunctional decisions made at higher levels. Siemens, at a corporate level, decided to develop an approach to enterprise transformation, which managers call "TOP." The result is shown in the bottom half of Figure 1.2. Processes are integrated—they overlap—and management is based on networks instead of hierarchies—all with the overriding focus on maximizing customer benefit.

But achieving the results requires more than diagrams or edicts from headquarters. The approach in Figure 1.2 was applied to a few business

Figure 1.2
Siemens TOP Initiative

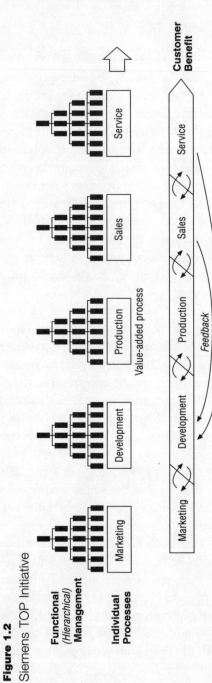

Source: Franz Holzwarth, Director of the Productivity Centre at Siemens A.G. Presented at a Manufacturing 2000 meeting, IMD, Lausanne, Switzerland, May 1994. Reprinted with permission.

units, starting with ones where the need for fundamental change was well-understood. When excellent results were achieved, the ideas and approach spread to other divisions and business units. The TOP process is now well-institutionalized at Siemens, with results and lessons shared widely.

Achieving the results gained by Siemens and other leading-edge companies requires proactive change of the basic company culture—a much more difficult task than changing organizational forms. The former defines "why we do things the way we do," while the latter addresses one of the "ways we do things." Culture change toward less hierarchy is a key aspect of enterprise transformation—but only if the result is better competitive advantage. If not, it is no more than rearrangement of the deck chairs on the Titanic.

Compare the characteristics of a dominant response to change with dying responses. They show companies that have managed to develop an internalized, pervasive ability to challenge and modify their fundamental assumptions in a constructive and dynamic fashion—continuously.

Some Dominant Responses

Enterprise transformation is much more than change programs, three-letter acronyms, organizational reshuffling, or financial restructuring. A fundamental change in world view is a prerequisite.

Paradigm Shifting

The word paradigm is largely associated with the work of Thomas Kuhn. His book, *The Structure of Scientific Revolutions,* explains how certain thought patterns, models, or rules of behavior develop on the basis of some underlying theory—as Newtonian physics redefined physical phenomena as well as religious beliefs, art, and language, for example. At some point, a new theory—e.g., quantum mechanics—is required, because the old one does not adequately explain, or is contradicted by, newly observed phenomena. At a more mundane level, we all have a "paradigm" for what happens when we drive an automobile in traffic. If the paradigm is based on experience in Switzerland or Los Angeles, the basic assumption is that other drivers are disciplined and obey the law. That paradigm is not adequate to govern driving in Italy or Boston.

A paradigm shift is necessary when an old set of operating assumptions is no longer valid. When a manufacturing enterprise adopts a philosophy of quality- or time-based competition, a different set of operating practices needs to be implemented in the company. Old concepts have to be unlearned, and new ones learned. New performance measures have to be adopted to guide actions, and old ones discarded, because behaviors must change profoundly. Implementing the TOP program at Siemens has required all these changes. A fundamentally different culture prevails when a network or process approach replaces one based on hierarchy.

Proactive transformation usually starts with a paradigm shift aimed at dominance rather than fine-tuning. Concrete action plans, a well-articulated process for implementation, and periodic reviews of progress are also essential. But fundamentally, the transformation needs to be integrated, consistent, feasible, and desirable.

Transformation necessarily requires a clear strategy. Without it, we too often find the "salami slicing" approach to restructuring, which does not work. In the oft-quoted words of a Polish politician, "One cannot leap a chasm in two jumps." On the other hand, although strategy is necessary, it is not a sufficient condition for proactive restructuring. Changes in competencies and capabilities, as well as adaptation in the marketplace must follow. Unfortunately, too many firms underestimate the necessary changes, with the result that the transformation is incomplete.

Symptoms are treated when, instead, underlying problems need to be eliminated. Wang is a good example. Wang had fundamental problems for several years—that were well understood by many employees, and even discussed in the business press—but the firm was unable to face up to them until crisis conditions were reached. The results were massive layoffs, serious morale losses, and a company so weakened that it may not survive.

This phenomenon—when many people in the company clearly see the need for change, yet the company is *unable* to do it—is far too frequent an occurrence. Changing the paradigm as well as the underlying culture requires leadership as well as follow-through. Both are required. It is not enough to have a good plan; the underlying processes, systems, resource allocations, measurements, and priorities *all* need to change to sustain the new paradigm. As Jan Timmer of Philips so nicely puts it: "The trouble with Total Quality Management is that you have to *do* it."

A number of European consumer products companies have clearly recognized the requirement and are tackling the changes they are finding by instituting fundamental change. Companies such as Nestlé, Unilever, Johnson & Johnson, and Nabisco have traditionally maintained organizational forms based on geography, with individual country managers evaluated on bottom line results. The post–1992 paradigm, however, requires cross shipping between countries, fewer factories, more specialized plants, new physical distribution systems, new partnerships with customers and suppliers, regional profitability metrics, and other enterprise linkages that argue against "every tub on its own bottom" paradigms.

Solutions cannot be found merely by tinkering with the status quo. But at the same time, true "solutions" are not achieved by executive fiat—or in short time periods. Making the detailed changes in infrastructure takes years. For many companies, the difference between dominance and death will be the extent to which all the efforts are integrated and consistent.

■ A major European packaging company was created through the merger of two companies—each with its own national culture as well as its unique company culture. It has been necessary to establish a new culture fundamentally different from that prevailing in either of the former companies. The new culture simply could not be based on some minor mutation of the culture in either of the former companies. An entirely new set of organizational forms and managers was required—a "paradigm shift" from national to regional orientation. To achieve this new orientation, an overall plan was necessary—coming from the top—that produced the vision, resolved the fundamental issues, provided the road map and directions, and established a mechanism for achieving the desired results in the shortest possible time.

■ Ikea, the Swedish furniture retailer, has profoundly changed the furniture industry in the geographic markets it has entered—by satisfying demand immediately, by designing furniture that can be assembled at home, by increasing the self-service component of the sale through the use of "live displays" of the furniture, and through its attractive catalogues. Supporting this sales concept are a myriad of processes and systems to design furniture, work with furniture manufacturers, coordinate logistics, manage inventories, use show room floor space effectively, design catalogues, and manage mail order service.

■ Alps, a Japanese electronic components producer, was experiencing reduced growth rates in its traditional markets. A set of scenarios was generated based on different assumptions about the future and associated company restructuring plans, and the most desirable was implemented.

Fundamental change in manufacturing was the point of departure. The number of batches was expected to increase fifty times, with a corresponding increase in customer deliveries. The scenario also called for penetrating a major new market area (automotive electronics), and competing on the basis of satisfying all customer delivery requests—whatever they might be. The cultural change was profound: The company defined its restructuring paradigm shift as "the elimination of mass production." Implementing this change required a monumental change in infrastructure.

Table 1.1 presents a list of new business paradigms. At the top of the list is the rejection of "either/or" decisions: The new paradigm calls for "and." Table 1.2 lists the trade-offs common to second-wave companies. These either-ors are so deeply embedded in the corporate mind-set that they are taken as common sense, as "business reality." For an enterprise to be dominant, the trade-off mentality needs to go. This means that leading-edge firms become mass customizers, achieve both high quality and low cost, high customer service and low inventories, and a host of other combinations that are summarized in Table 1.2. The domination paradigm is "greedy." It calls for "both," and "all"—not "one or the other," or "some." All these paradigm shifts have the same demand for massive change in the underlying support systems or infrastructure—to make change a reality.

Table 1.1

New-Wave Paradigms

From	To
"Either/or" decisions	"And" conclusions
Command and control	Coaching and teamwork
Making products "for"	Creating value "with" customers
Satisfying requirements	Exceeding expectations
Efficiency	Effectiveness/opportunity-seeking
Financial measures as drivers	Financial measures as passengers
Functional excellence	Distinctive competency
Cost cuts	Capability enhancement
"Flavor of the month" programs	Sustained change
Bureaucracy	Vision
Complacency/reaction	Urgency/proaction

Table 1.2

False Trade-offs

Either	Or
Changing in small steps	Changing in strategic leaps
Mass producer	Customizer
Low delivered costs	High perceived value
Minimum-cost focus	Maximum-quality focus
Productivity	Responsiveness
Short-term orientation	Long-term orientation
Day-to-day activities	Strategic actions
Product development	Process development
Local/regional	Global
Enterprise transformation	Business unit change program
Existing customers	New customers
Products	Services
Manufacturing	Marketing
Physical capital	Intellectual capital
Technology-driven	Customer-driven
Low component price supplier motivations	Vendor partnerships
Throughput time	Flexibility
Low inventories	Customer services

What sort of changes are needed in order to navigate from "trade-off" to "dominant"? Can you fine-tune your company toward the dominant paradigm, or will it require a more fundamental change?

Table 1.1 also lists a shift from "command and control" to "coaching and teamwork." This shift recognizes that controls often add very limited value to the final customers. Furthermore, command and control makes pejorative assumptions about the motives of employees, and presumes that only managers should do the thinking. Domination requires every employee to do better things continually—as well as do things better, achieving the general direction or overarching strategy, and anticipating customer requirements.

No one leaves his brain at the door, and everyone is expected to work in teams as needs dictate. Value is added with customers—rather than for customers—implying partnership development and nurturing. Expectations are exceeded, not just met. This requires a hard set of paradigm shifts that many executives view with suspicion, but they are still valid.

■ The Lexus automobile entering the United States market is a good example. A totally new approach to providing after-sales service has completely changed the industry—and customer expectations. A computerized data base is maintained for each automobile and customer, and whenever a car needs service, it is picked up at the customer's home, a new Lexus is left to drive, and the car is returned full of gasoline and washed. When this policy is first described, many people express amazement—and think it wasteful. But the Lexus has taken a much greater share of the U.S. luxury car market than anyone could have guessed.

Each of the other paradigm-busting challenges needs to be considered. The company that ignores any of them does so at its peril. Moreover, each of these challenges needs to be examined in the context of particular business units—prioritizing them, sharing best practices, and developing overall company support for faster improvement.

Proactive, not Reactive, Change Makes the Difference

The dominance-bound company embraces change proactively, as an opportunity to respond to where the market is heading, rather than as a defensive response to crisis conditions. Head count reductions to boost the short-term bottom line do not create dominance; they are probably more symptomatic of death. The *Harvard Business Review* World Leadership Survey found 70 percent of the companies surveyed in twenty-five countries with more than 10,000 employees had undergone a major restructuring in the last two years. The same is true for 54 percent of companies with fewer than 10,000 employees.[6]

But how many of these restructurings—with all their disruptions and risks—were proactive attempts to achieve competitive dominance, rather than reactions to cost-containment pressures? Perhaps the financial community needs its own paradigm shift: To view restructuring as an admission of management failure—instead of a decisive action.

Change can be more or less proactive, and will require organizations to dig very deeply into their values, attitudes, and beliefs in order to produce the appropriate response. Three levels of adaptation through transformation have been identified:

□ *Responsive/flexible:* Many companies are overhauling their manufacturing systems to cope with unexpected change, unpredictable demand, new customer preferences, and other vagaries of the present marketplace—with minimal inventories. The intent is to transform operations so that the company can respond like McDonald's: When two bus loads of Boy Scouts pull up unexpectedly, everyone gets lunch, and no one waits in a line for long.

☐ *Anticipatory/forecasting:* Whenever possible, it is better to anticipate required changes and shrink response time. Transformation assuming closer linkages with customers and suppliers, electronic data interchange, and strategic alliances based on information integration are some of the approaches being taken. Key Xerox suppliers, for example have detailed knowledge of both the Xerox build schedules they will support and the Xerox new product developments in which they are actively participating.

☐ *Proactive/causing change:* Proactive responses on the part of leading-edge companies can dictate the terms of competition by changing the rules of the game. Creating new forms of physical distribution such as that put in place by Wal-Mart; bringing products to the marketplace that people did not even know they needed, such as the Sony Walkman; seeing environmental issues as a way of defining the competitive agenda; creating a genuine learning organization; retaining workers before their skills are obsolete; and cultivating a competitively superior culture are examples of more proactive transformation.

Proactive transformation often begins with the definition of some desired "scenario" or description of a competitive state. Thereafter, the major changes required to achieve it are identified and put in place. Proactive transformation also implies a never-ending process of change, not a one-time adjustment to solve some particular problem. It is essential to implement a number of periodic paradigm shifts—as listed in Table 1.1.

Figure 1.3 depicts dominance and death. The X axis is time, and the Y axis is capabilities. Two hypothetical companies, A and B, are both losing (or failing to gain) capabilities relative to competitors up to point 1 on the X axis. At point 2, Company B engages in a reactive restructuring, which initially is viewed as a positive step by the company, its customers, and the business community at large. But thereafter, no real efforts are put into developing the new sets of capabilities required to compete in the marketplace. Rather, we see business as usual, with fewer hands to do the work. The net result is a further loss in relative capabilities (no time for draining swamps when one is up to one's neck in alligators!). Company B then arrives at time point 3, with poor financial performance,

Figure 1.3
Dominate or Die

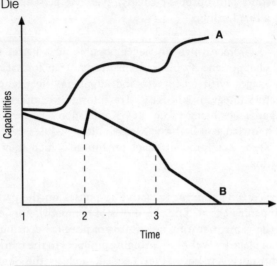

and a need to restructure again. This time the impact is totally negative, with a faster downhill slide.

Company A, on the other hand, lives by proactive transformation. Its goal at each phase is an improvement in capabilities, and paradigm shifts are made before the firm is in any serious trouble. Perhaps the first is implementation of total quality management, a decision taken before reaching point 1. An "S" curve results; TQM capabilities are developed, slowly at first, then rapidly, then slowly again as the program nears completion and diminishing returns set in. Before time point 3, a new proactive transformation is initiated, perhaps time-based competition. Again the "S" curve results, with still another transformation (perhaps market focus) after point 3. (Also shown is the potential dip in capabilities that can result when paradigms are shifted.) The difference in capabilities between companies A and B is the difference between dominance and death.

■ The approach used by company A is not a figment of our imagination. Sony, NEC, and Toshiba, for example, have used this method to revitalize their company operations continually. Every three or four years, top management dictates a proactive transformation, with a desired scenario in mind. Each of the subunits in turn develops its own scenario consistent with the overall scenario. Thereafter, every person in the company is mobilized to achieve the new vision, using the classical "small steps" approach of Japanese companies. There are numerous examples of Company B behavior. Bull and Wang appear to be increasingly worst cases.

Figure 1.3 conceptualizes another related issue. Capabilities must be seen as relative to those of competitors. Leading-edge capabilities today, like quality, are "base" requirements—everybody's property—tomorrow. Firms need to ask what rate of improvement in capabilities needs to be achieved—and sustained. Over what time period does your company need to be twice as capable as it is now? We believe that many leading-edge manufacturing enterprises will answer "something like three to five years." That is, whatever base one chooses, it will be necessary to double the effectiveness of competitive competencies in a three- to five-year period. For this, a series of proactive transformations—where major changes take place—will be required.

Enterprise Transformation

As we embark on what people are calling the third industrial revolution, the lessons of the past are so inadequate that what is mandated is fundamental transformation of the organization. When we use the term transformation, we do not intend to create another synonym for restructuring, or reengineering. We are talking of a process: A firm enters through one door, and a different firm exits at the end.

There is nothing magical about transformation. In fact, worldwide recession has resulted in several corporate transformations—some proactive, others forced by factors beyond management control. In the successful ones, the very shape and structure of enterprises have had to change. Their competencies and capabilities have changed, their resources have changed, their outputs have changed, their attitude to customer service has changed, and their fundamental *raison d'être* has shifted. In the unsuccessful, corporate mission has reverted to "doing core business," crisis management has replaced strategy, and passengers (such as costs) replace drivers (such as customer satisfaction). These certainly are not the companies they once were—they have indeed been transformed—but nobody was steering the change toward dominance.

Crisis is a good launching point for transformation. When old ideas about what running a business is about hold sway, however, management reaction will too often gravitate toward fine-tuning the old, when instead managers are presented with a genuine opportunity to shape the new.

Transformation Is Not a One-Time Fix

Transformation as an idea can also be seen in Figure 1.4 Here a two-by-two matrix shows the scope of change on one axis and the speed of change on the other. When change has a relatively narrow scope, and speed is fast, "reengineering" may be appropriate. When change must be speedy but on a broad scope, this may well be a turnaround, requiring downsizing and tough decision making. When conditions allow a relatively slow speed and narrow scope, the classic Japanese approach of continuous improvement, *Kaizen,* is descriptive. It is in the upper right-hand corner, where the scope of change is broad, and the time frame for achieving the change is long, that the term "transformation" seems most appropriate.

Figure 1.4 is useful in that it allows each change situation to be examined as to the goals of the intended change, as well as the expected time period during which the change is to take place. The approach can be applied to individual business units. At Siemens, there were great differences in the extent to which fundamental changes were required—which in turn dictated differences in the scope and approach of enterprise transformation.

Figure 1.4

Dimensions of Change Programs

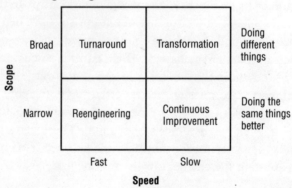

Restructuring, reengineering, and the like might well be effective in cutting out waste—human, material, and time—but if by the end of the process of disruption the fundamental operational paradigm remains untouched, it is unlikely that the changes will stand the test of time. In today's world, doing the same things better is necessary, but not sufficient. When the next crisis hits, some other action might well be required to dig the company out of its hole. In the third industrial revolution, the old notion of what constitutes a winning combination is just not sufficient; alternative product and service bundles must be created, bundles that come from a different starting point. The past approach to employees, the past relation with suppliers, the past notion of customers—all these need to be brought in line with third industrial revolution reality. In the third industrial revolution, employees, suppliers, and customers are different creatures, capable of delivering different skills and demanding different products and services.

Most firms more than ten years old are feeling the bite of intense forces and constraints. Even some newly established enterprises are struggling, because their founding mission is now obsolete. Then there are those that have embraced today's paradigms—they are growing by leaps and bounds, while others in their industry are retrenching. They are a bit like children who have the new electronic gadget up and running before their parents have managed to decipher the model diagram on the first page of the instruction manual.

Old established second-wave companies, particularly those that have managed to amass considerable assets and huge customer bases, might shrug at these ideas. They are a bit like the man falling off the top of the Empire State Building and shouting into each window he passes: "Haven't hit the pavement yet! Haven't hit the pavement yet!" These companies respond to problems by digging into the bag of tricks that produced a fix in the past. At some point, the best of tricks will not produce the goods. Vast sums will be spent, with little return. Ask IBM. Ask DEC. Ask Sears. Ask General Motors. Ask all those "excellent" companies that do not exist any longer.

This is a clear signal that the time is right for fundamental enterprise transformation.

The Double Objective

Figure 1.5 helps to demonstrate enterprise transformation. The difference between a firm's costs and its prices is its profits. The difference between

Figure 1.5

Enterprise Transformation: The Double Objective

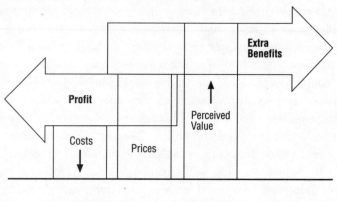

its prices and the value that its customers perceive in the overall set of goods and services that they receive is a set of "extra benefits," or an advantage that the company can exploit—either in the form of higher prices, greater customer loyalty, higher sales, or perhaps improved market share. In far too many restructuring efforts, the sole emphasis is on reducing costs; most companies today are better advised to focus their transformation efforts on increasing the perceived value they add in the marketplace. But, as we have previously noted, this should not be seen as an either/or trade-off. The objective is both lower costs and higher perceived value.

The higher perceived value objective has another critical benefit. In many firms, the focus on cost reduction leads inevitably to head count reductions—often for those who have made the improvements. This game of "you play ball with me—then I will hit you over the head with the bat" has dire consequences. Maintaining morale, nurturing a proactive change culture, and other dimensions of excellent human resource management practices can be seriously set back—undermining key competencies and capabilities.

An example of how to play the higher perceived value game may be seen in a packaging company that is developing a strategic alliance with a transportation company to provide a more targeted bundle of goods and services. In essence, there are a set of customers who want to receive just-in-time deliveries from their suppliers, but they have to carry extra stock to hedge against the arrival of damaged goods. Consider that damage is a function of the packaging as well as the shipping methods. By attacking both together, the damage can be significantly reduced. Moreover, the shipping company can take back the packages for recycling, thereby solving another customer problem (bringing in "raw material" for the packaging company).

A proactive attack on improving customer perceived values can provide the necessary "growth" mentality to the transforming company or business unit. This mentality can provide a driving force for further proactive change.

We often ask executives in our programs what they would do if they had an extra day per week. After getting over the responses about playing more golf, we settle into a more serious discussion. What could you do for your company if your present work done in five days could be accomplished in four? The answers will be usually in the customer perceived value arena, and most companies have no shortage of good ideas here. The problem is finding the time to do them. As soon as managers see this, they are likely to have a new understanding of the importance of business process reengineering and other techniques that simplify work. The new proviso is not to fire those middle managers who are freed up by the efforts. On the contrary, they should be retained, with work delegated from the top—to provide those days per week.

Viewing Transformation as a Proactive Strategy

At M2000, our focus has been to work with companies that are open to being proactive about transformation. They have chosen transformation as the valid response instead of fine-tuning. Some are transforming even though they have not been pushed into it by faltering corporate performance. Others are prepared to leap. For companies such as these, we have identified certain characteristics of the change process that ensure transformation will be the likely outcome.

The Four Characteristics
of Strategic Transformation

For change to be transformative it will need to be integrated and consistent across all organizational facets; it will also need to be feasible and desirable to stand any chance of success. If one of these ingredients is missing, it means that the end of the process is likely to be "better sameness" with its beguiling short-term injection of adrenaline and hope and improved bottom line.

□ *Integration:* Is the firm's transformation plan integrated? Is there a clear linkage from marketplace dictates to the overall strategic intent, down to the particular actions required, and the processes that need to be redesigned? We call this linkage "the golden cord." It is an approach founded on reason. It ties the key facets of the enterprise to each other, allowing them to be examined in order. But integration must be seen in a context. There is always a need to accelerate the change process driven from the top—but supported throughout the enterprise, always in search of new triggering mechanisms followed up by integrative actions.

□ *Consistency:* Do all the various actions lead to the same place—and are they mutually supportive? Does the management team have a clear sense of how things fit together? Do all people in the company see the same picture on the puzzle box top?

□ *Feasibility:* Is the transformation plan capable of being realized in the time allotted to it? Stretch goals are fine, but impossible objectives will surely lead to disillusion and cynicism. At the same time, there needs to be a perceived sense of urgency; transformation requires unfreezing and fundamental change in the status quo.

□ *Desirability:* Is the overall transformation effort desirable—both from the company's point of view and from that of the key players? At the company level, strategic business unit level, and individual level, everyone needs to believe in the need for acceleration of change and be ready to buy into the resulting need for "managed crisis."

So essential is transformation for the achievement of dominance—for the achievement of a position from which to exert and sustain an influence on the market—that we can restate the challenge that launched M2000. We now challenge companies to "transform or die."

Of much more importance, however, is for companies to appreciate the process orientation of the challenge and not to see dominance as a better steady state than the one they now find themselves in. Dominance is an organizational state in which change is no longer a major upheaval; it is a way of life. The process for getting there involves not just learning;

more critical is the ability to unlearn. Suppose IBM had been able to unlearn its attachment to mainframes. Compared to learning, unlearning is massively difficult. Compared to reengineering, transformation is massively difficult.

An executive in our Manufacturing 2000 program from a firm that has undergone some massive changes in recent years said that he now could easily tell which employees would not be able to make it over the long run. If anyone talked of things returning to normal—or of some steady state where rampant change would not be part of daily life—that employee clearly did not understand.

In 1989, M2000 embarked on research into the implications of a transformation strategy on the enterprise. We have developed tools and models that require both reason and innovation. The golden cord of reason links each step to the one that follows. Getting from one step to the next involves inventiveness and the occasional flash of brilliance. Sustaining transformation requires seeing it as an ongoing, never-ending process.

Transformation Examples

There are many examples of enterprise transformation to achieve dominance. There are also examples of failures, and instances where the results are not yet known. It is not our intention to crown winners, like *In Search of Excellence*. We believe the most fundamental issue is to acknowledge and respond to change—to do something, not sit idly by. Those who rest on their laurels will never dominate. It is better to try proactively, even unsuccessfully, than to assume a paradigm will endure forever.

■ A European brewer became an important regional player by buying up several other companies, merging with a major competitor, forming licensing agreements in other countries, bottling soft drinks and mineral water, and creating an overall distribution system that delivered important economies of scale and increased its market share. In some ways, this transformation can be seen as a series of changes. But there is more to it. To achieve this transformation, the company required major change in culture, new approaches to the marketplace, and the implementation of new technology.

■ Alps determined it would be futile to try to dominate consumer electronics. Instead, it looked at the rapidly growing market in automotive electronic and mechanical products ("mechatronics"). This market is a target for traditional automotive suppliers, by the automotive companies themselves, and by electronics manufacturers. Fundamental transformation by Alps meant new markets, new competencies, and new resource development. Alps devoted significant company engineering talents to automotive electronics, developed a new sales and marketing organization, built problem-solving partnerships with key customers, and transformed manufacturing operations to produce make-to-order products with much higher product variety.

■ GKN, a European automotive parts supplier, is also pursuing an aggressive strategy based on a paradigm shift. The company had previously enjoyed patent protection of its front-wheel drive technology. Demand had been so high that it was necessary to license others to manufacture. As the patents expire, the former licensees are latent competitors. GKN's proactive response has been to focus its factories, make fundamental changes in manufacturing, hire new engineers to drive performance improvement, and develop long-term contracts with major automobile manufacturers based on targeted price reductions that outweigh the productivity improvements these customers could obtain themselves. GKN uses the expression: "Dominate or die."

Summary

Chapter 1 describes the harsh reality of today's competitive world—and the responses that are being made—both good and bad:

□ The fundamental choice facing today's enterprise is basic: Dominate or die. Every enterprise needs to examine itself in the light of this stark reality—and accept the resulting set of imperatives.

□ An enterprise can be seen as an overall company or as an individual business unit. Companies with many dominating business units will in turn dominate.

□ Enterprises avoiding the death syndrome must not react to tomorrow's challenges with yesterday's remedies: improvement programs that are necessary but not sufficient, financial restructuring and head count reduction, and management reshuffles. All along, the basic paradigms for running the ailing enterprise must not be the last thing questioned.

□ Dominant enterprises must be continually transformed through periodic paradigm shifts—augmented with constant improvement in all parts of the enterprise. They must be responsive and flexible; they must anticipate and forecast. They must challenge the rules, and raise the stakes.

□ Transformation must be integrated, consistent, feasible, and desirable—if it is truly going to work. It is imperative to have both good strategy and good supporting infrastructure.

It is all very well to put forward some war stories that identify past performance, good and bad, but future forecasts of winners and losers are a lot tougher. By the time this book is published, there will undoubtedly be examples of companies shown here as good that are in trouble—and vice versa. There *is* no certainty; all one can do is to take the actions to increase the probability of dominance. In the next chapters we hope to help identify future-oriented actions—those that in fact allow the enterprise to be continually transformed to meet the dominate or die imperatives.

2 Enterprise Transformation Facets

Dominate or die is a colorful phrase. Beyond that, what more precisely is enterprise transformation? How is it different from other kinds of change programs? Is there a way to be sure that mere activity is not substituted for fundamental paradigm shifting (we may be just flushing the pigeons)? How do we align the efforts in individual business units with overall transformation objectives? How does a company know if it is in fact examining the relevant dimensions of transformation—and not overlooking something essential?

To help answer these questions, it is useful to dissect the terms "enterprise" and "transformation." This chapter focuses on the first of these terms, enterprise. An enterprise (a company or a business unit) can be described in terms of eight facets. Examining each of these facets—and the changes in them—allows us to develop a diagnostic for enterprise transformation.

□ *Strategic Intent.* An enterprise needs to have a true mission, vision, overriding set of objectives, or strategic intent that drives its actions. This is not necessarily what is written in the annual report, published in press releases, or touted in speeches.

□ *Competencies.* An enterprise can also be viewed in terms of its collective competencies and capabilities. These enable the enterprise—and constrain it—both in terms of the activities in which it can engage, and the extent to which it can achieve a strategic input.

□ *Processes.* The infrastructure of an enterprise largely consists of various processes and systems that enable capabilities and competencies. Processes, by definition, can be clearly identified, flow-charted, evaluated, benchmarked, and reengineered.

□ *Resources.* The fundamental resources in an enterprise are its people, information, and technology. The way these resources are deployed in

47

various processes is the only way an enterprise can add value to raw materials.

□ *Outputs.* An enterprise can be seen in terms of the bundle of goods and services it is producing—and the customers for whom these goods and services are being created. This view also encompasses the match between the bundle of goods and services and the customers' perceived value of that bundle.

□ *Strategic Response.* An enterprise can be observed in terms of the action programs, improvement efforts, or strategic responses it is taking. That is, what is the company doing, and what are its relative priorities?

□ *Challenges.* The most difficult view of the enterprise to understand is the company or business unit seen in terms of its present set of problems, challenges, or opportunities. But this view is indeed critical to comprehend the enterprise, its strategic intent, strategic response, and other dimensions.

□ *Learning Capacity.* An enterprise has an inherent capacity to learn. Moreover, the enterprise can be examined in terms of its "drivers" or "engines" for change, such as the change programs like total quality management (TQM), and how well these programs are working. The "learning organization" has a much better chance of achieving domination and building its intellectual capital. Related to this—and probably more critical—is an ability to unlearn. The fear of letting go of tried and tested past practices is what shackles organizations to second industrial revolution modes of operation. Learning means learning to measure different things as well. Learning needs to be rapid—as well as focused on the right objectives. The golden cord dictates that learning creates the competencies necessary to enable the strategic response to achieve the strategic intent to meet and exceed the challenges.

The Eight-Facet Viewpoint

These eight facets are not separate—they are merely different ways of looking at the same entity. One can look in from a different vantage point, but in the last analysis one is looking at one enterprise. Each viewpoint just gives a different perspective to the enterprise.

An Indian fable tells about a group of blind men presented with a new creature called an elephant. Each man took up a different position around the beast and used touch to explore what he faced. The man who felt the tusk described the elephant as a thin, smooth creature that ended in a sharp point. The one who felt the leg disagreed. He described the elephant as a creature like a tree, rough and round. The man who felt the tail came up with a totally different description, as did the man who felt the trunk. Experience may be insightful, but it is only when the whole picture is seen that wisdom replaces insight.

The lesson is that in order truly to understand the enterprise it is essential to see it from *all eight viewpoints.* This is even more critical when one is engaged in enterprise transformation. Enterprise transformation is in fact the summation of changes in all eight facets. The key issue is how to change all eight facets—in an integrated, consistent fashion.

The utility of these eight views is that they correspond to the various starting points for change that different enterprises adopt according to their different natures. Some start with strategic intent, some with competencies, some with processes, and so on. Of more importance than this, however, is appreciating that any of these starting points must lead into a process that affects the whole organization and not merely some small self-contained area of operation.

A change in strategic intent leads all the way to competencies, resources, outputs, and the rest. If strategic intent redefinition stops in the boardroom, then the view is flawed. It will lead to confusion for those who do not see corresponding changes in the other facets. Similarly, entering change through the business process facet should lead all the way to strategic intent and challenges. If reengineering stops at the process level, then the view of process is flawed. At the very best it is then only doing the same things better.

The eight-facet view is consistent with organizational reality. Of course it is desirable to have a well-developed strategic intent. But its lack should not preclude efforts in one or more other facets. Improvement in one can lead to more understanding of the need for work in others.

Another utility of these eight views is that they provide a checklist that ensures integration and consistency throughout the entire enterprise. The eight views of the enterprise can be used to examine whether the change program is transformative, consistent, and integrated—or if the end result is likely to be "better sameness." At the end of the day, all eight facets need to be unfrozen, changed, and redefined for the future. The eight facets of the enterprise—and the changes in those facets—need to be examined in order to assess the overall integrity of a transformation effort. All too often, an enterprise believes it is engaged in transformation, when in fact it is undertaking serious change in only one or two of its facets.

The Strategic Intent Facet

At its most basic level, an enterprise cannot be separated from its true mission or strategic intent. These words have been used interchangeably and so loosely that there is little agreement about what they actually stand for. As it is not our intention to create a new semantic, we will use the term "strategic intent" to indicate the impulse that informs and shapes all outputs, activities, processes, behaviors, and resources.[1] This is not the mission statement that graces the front page of the corporate brochure, which is usually a combination of a marketing gimmick and a vague "should say" statement of aspiration. Transformation, at its most basic, therefore, is the process of transforming this true mission—with all its ramifications for the rest of the organization.

Transforming the strategic intent means a fundamental shift in the overall driving force of the enterprise.

It may be useful to distinguish between "core values" and "strategic intent." In most companies, there is indeed a set of core values that dictate what strategic intents are permissible. In most cases, these are not well-articulated, but some are. Johnson & Johnson, for example, has its "Corporate Credo," which is not only very explicit but also shapes the company's product offerings, support of customers, and responses to unforeseen circumstances (such as its instant worldwide withdrawal of Tylenol after some capsules had been tampered with). The distinguishing point between core values and strategic intent is that the former rarely (if at all) changes, while the latter should be transformed to respond to current conditions and future opportunities.

Strategic intent also should be operational in that it is more than a vague desire such as "to be the supplier of choice," or "to exceed our customer expectations by helping them solve problems." There is nothing inherently wrong with these statements, but they do not set explicit targets so that strategic responses (and the other facets of transformation) can be evaluated, directed, and coordinated. Fundamentally, strategic intent needs to mean something to a large population of the employees, perhaps not all of them, but clearly those who lead and are role models.

For strategic intent to be operational, it is essential that the best brains in the company buy into it—and see it as influencing the ways in which they need to operate—and that they adopt a belief in the urgency of change. These people need to agree upon a window of opportunity and the necessary speed to achieve a transformation during this period.

One absolutely critical part of "strategic intent" is the measurement of performance. If transformation is to occur, inevitably new measures will be required and old ones discarded. How else is a transformation process to be evaluated? If quality is a key part of the strategic intent, quality needs to be measured, good quality practices need to be rewarded, and any measures that run counter to improved quality need to be eliminated systematically (and very publicly). Typical candidates are measures that focus on volume at the expense of quality, as well as financial measures, which now need to be seen as "passengers," rather than as drivers.

Transformation requires an explicit statement of what the true mission is, what the enterprise needs to become, and what determines when the true mission has been attained. This is easier said than done. Far too often, the current strategic intent is not at all what is stated. In other cases, the desired strategic intent requires a change so fundamental that it is quite unlikely to occur—the streetwise employees know when to duck and let this infeasible transformation just blow over their heads. Alternatively, the mission is so general that success cannot be measured. As we shall demonstrate, it is working on all eight facets that results in a truly workable strategic intent. An interactive process of top-down and bottom-up is essential.

Inappropriate Strategic Intent Transformation

Let us now examine a few examples of strategic intent or missions that are incomplete at best, and often lead to cynicism.

■ One of the new London Universities called in a group of auditors to identify opportunities for intellectual and technology transfer. The auditors conducted their survey on two levels: (1) an itemization of research projects, and intellectual property and patents held (i.e., the outputs), and (2) an examination of the institution's commitment and willingness to work with industry partners (i.e., its mission in terms of intellectual/technology transfer). The institution's mission statement spoke grandly of its proposed contribution to improving the knowledge base of financial institutions in the City of London and its interest in spearheading the regeneration of London's East End as a thriving craft center of excellence. But examination of the output and actions facets turned up no evidence of any excellence in research or any projects that could be of the remotest interest to the City clients. Analysis of the resources facet was equally bleak: Staff were demoralized, the buildings were run-down and dowdy, the enabling technology was poor. Everything pointed back to one governing influence—the financial department. The FD's goal was to achieve a balanced budget, so it placed hurdles down every track that led to the spending of money. The faculty were treated as financially naive and irresponsible (and they behaved accordingly). Everything indicated that the institution's strategic intent was to achieve a balanced budget. This led to a strategic response of "command and control," which in turn ultimately shaped the institution (both its infrastructure and its outputs). Transforming the mission was in fact essential to achieving intellectual/technology transfer. But anyone with any perception considered making this transformation a reality only a pipe dream.

■ One management consultant's paper mission was to supply the best consulting services and products to its market and be profitable at the same time. Right from the beginning, however, the founders' strategic intent was to sell the company in five years. This true mission required the speedy growth of capital assets and cash and an expansion of the client base. As a consequence, interaction with joint venture partners and suppliers were evaluated solely on low prices. There was little investment of cash or energy in excellence (the competencies, processes, and resources views) and a lot in growth through acquisition. The result was also a major mismatch in defining the challenges and appropriate strategic response facets. The inconsistency of strategy required to support each of these missions is that a number of camps have sprung up within the firm: those that criticize what they see as profligacy (they believe the actual strategic intent), and those that criticize thrift (they subscribe to the published mission statement); those that scorn a marketing approach (true mission), and those that despise the sales-led approach (paper mission); those that become inspired by innovative approaches (paper mission), and those that have no respect for "esoteric approaches" and want to go on creating product out of the tried and tested (true mission). This lack of consistency in mission—and the necessary transformation in strategic intent (and the other transformation facets)—makes it impossible for the full potential of either mission to be realized.

■ A company producing environmental pollution reduction equipment believed that in order to operate effectively in this market, it had to be very "environmentally friendly" itself. As a result, it had an environmental mission statement, signed by the top officers of the company, that was reproduced in the annual report and in many other publications. But in a work session on enterprise transformation with an executive group, a key dilemma came up. A frustrated executive finally stated: "This is all well and good, but let's face it: If we have to make a choice between the environment and making our numbers for the quarter, we have to make the quarterly numbers."

KEY QUESTIONS

- Is the stated mission consistent with reality?

- Does it include a set of well-defined stretch objectives that people can buy into?

- Is the change in strategic intent achievable?

- Who are those who will be most cynical about a change—and how do we get them to believe in (and commit to) it?

- How is the transformation personally desirable as well as desirable for the enterprise?

Enterprise transformation is hard work, and true transformation must encompass a consistent match among most if not all of the transformation facets. Moreover, the strategic intent facet of enterprise transformation is in many ways the most crucial, as it sets the drum beat for the changes that must take place in the other facets.

The strategic intent view of enterprise transformation is based on ensuring that one mission defines the direction for the entire enterprise, rather than the fragmentation that results from a plethora of different agendas. The strategic intent view also focuses on a consistent integration of objectives (and measures) and actions (and rewards). The transformation "journey" can start by identifying the behaviors that get rewarded (who the company role models are, for example), and from these intuit the true mission. Another test is to list the things the company measures, and from them intuit the true mission or strategic intent.

Transformation must address any gap between these perceptions of the true mission and the desired new strategic intent that is to drive the transformation. The company will then be in a position—perhaps for the first time—to ask itself where the existing mission will lead it, and if that's where it really wants to go. An acid test to determine whether a change program is truly going to be transformative, or just end up in better sameness, is to ask if it results in a transformed strategic intent—that is real.

True Mission Transformation

Let us now look at some cases where firms did indeed understand the necessary change in strategic intent, and thereafter made the concomitant changes in the other facets of enterprise transformation.

■ Alps, the Japanese electronics company referred to earlier, decided that its future prosperity depended upon a transformation to serving its existing and new customers (which required a new set of outputs—and challenges). Alps had been making large batches of electronic components to customer specification, with an emphasis on continuous cost reduction. The executives of the company became convinced that the firm could not prosper in the long run following this approach. Their resulting strategic response included entering a new market segment (automotive electronics), and developing customer partnerships both to offer much greater product variety and to provide much faster deliveries without carrying inventories. The new mission statement centers around "customer-oriented thinking," with an explicit mandate for manufacturing to "eliminate mass production." The subsequent changes in necessary competencies, processes for making products and serving customers, and the bundle of goods and services offered were profound.

■ The changes in strategic intent associated with several European consumer products companies as they implement strategic responses to achieve globalization/regionalization are equally serious. It has been necessary to develop new measures of corporate performance (e.g., abandoning country profitability metrics), and to adopt a strategy that recognizes the differences in particular geographic markets and particular large customers. A similar transformation has been required in automotive parts suppliers. The ways in which their customers (the major automobile manufacturers) have globalized/regionalized have to be factored into their ways of operating—as well as into the underlying missions for the companies.

■ SKF, the Swedish ball bearing manufacturer, went through a transformation of its business based on market segmentation. The after market was separated from the original equipment manufacturing market, and a separate strategic intent statement was developed for it. The fundamental change is summed up in the new mission statement as "providing trouble-free operations" to the customers—instead of selling them bearings. This implies a major change in the bundle of goods and services offered, new competencies, processes, and resources to provide them, and a major action plan to implement and refine the concept.[2]

Experience with companies in formulating mission statements suggests that the eight-facet view of enterprise transformation is very helpful. It is too easy to fall into the traditional approach of asking a senior management group to define a mission statement that thereafter will drive all actions in a top-down fashion. In fact, it is understanding the actions, changes in competencies, and new processes that helps formulate a true mission.

The Competencies Facet

Competencies are another facet of an enterprise. Competencies, as well as their supporting capabilities, enable the enterprise to accomplish certain things—and preclude it from achieving others. Moreover, it is the entire set of competencies/capabilities—and their consistency and integration— that is critical to fulfilling an objective or mission.

Several years ago, a major U.S. defense contractor, looking for new markets, decided to go into portable classrooms for schools. It saw a growing need for this product, and the company had excess manufacturing capacity that could be focused on this product line. It clearly had the necessary manufacturing competencies and capabilities. Unfortunately, the firm's defense department-oriented marketing competencies were wholly inappropriate for dealing with local school boards.

Figure 2.1 depicts competency in four degrees. It could be either "distinctive" (the competition cannot easily copy it, it provides a competitive advantage in the marketplace, and higher margins can be derived from it); it could be "essential" (common to immediate competitors but necessary to be in this industrial or business sector); it could be a "routine competency" (common to most organizations); and finally, it could be an activity more profitably outsourced. At the left-hand side of Figure 2.1, we find distinctive competency. Over time, what might have been a distinctive competency usually tends to fade, as others catch up—particularly if the competence is based on technology. Before long, the distinctive competence becomes an essential competence, one that is necessary to run the business. These in turn over time degrade into routine competencies—like preparing the paychecks—that a company can at least think about outsourcing (can someone else do this at least as well as we can?).

A critical question for any firm or business unit pertains to the "optimal mix" or portfolio of the four competencies. One would expect fewer distinctive competencies than essential, and fewer essential competencies than routine competencies, but it is more than a matter of counting. Are we renewing and strengthening our distinctive competencies? Are these the right ones for the future (e.g., main frame computers for IBM)?

It does not necessarily require management inefficiency for competencies to slide from being distinctive to becoming candidates for outsourcing. For example, before the introduction of the Apple Macintosh, graphic designers worked out their schemes on paper, painstakingly tracing letter forms, and drawing in parallel lines to indicate blocks of text. Some companies excelled in this art, which gave them a competitive edge. Then the first wave of designers started to use the new technology. It

---

Figure 2.1

Four Degrees of Competency

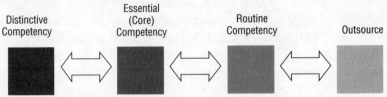

enabled them to produce five times the number of totally different designs in the time the most competent "old-wave designer" could produce one. These new designers thus seized the upper ground, and what for the old guard was a distinctive competency now became a core competency. With the proliferation of Macs, the picture has changed again. What once gave the new wave its edge has now become "the way things are done," and the "new" old guard are struggling to win contracts. Customer expectations of standards of presentation have risen immeasurably, particularly when many customers have basic design packages in their own offices. Now, as expectations have risen, quality of concept and the measurable impact on delivering business objectives through design have become the distinctive graphic design competencies—rendering any lesser skill merely "core."

But the movement in Figure 2.1 is not always from left to right. With the right kind of investment and commitment of resources, essential competencies can become distinctive. One key here, however, is to focus the resources in such a way so as to achieve distinction—and dominance—often by outsourcing activities that are more easily done by others.

An interesting example of new distinctive competency can be seen in the case of Sony. Its distinctive competence has been miniaturization. This implies design and manufacturing competencies, and indeed Sony has these. But Sony now sees "box building" as today's game, not tomorrow's. The firm that controls what comes out of the boxes will have the competitive advantage. Sony has made major investments in the entertainment business, and has talked of moving its corporate headquarters from Japan to the United States to develop a distinctive competency in entertainment production and distribution. Sony's intention to develop the new distinctive competencies has been difficult to achieve. It recently took a large financial write-off on this activity. At the same time, many box-building activities will probably be outsourced.

Thus we see that even a firm with a clear distinctive competency cannot achieve a steady state. The technology, the competitors, the expectations of customers will ensure that things keep moving. And, to make the picture even more complex, each organization will have a number of competency areas. "Brand management" may be one area, "information management" another; "order processing," "marketing," and others may also be appropriate. The result is that enterprise transformation requires Figure 2.1 to be rendered as Figure 2.2, where an enterprise is viewed as

Figure 2.2

Mix of Competencies

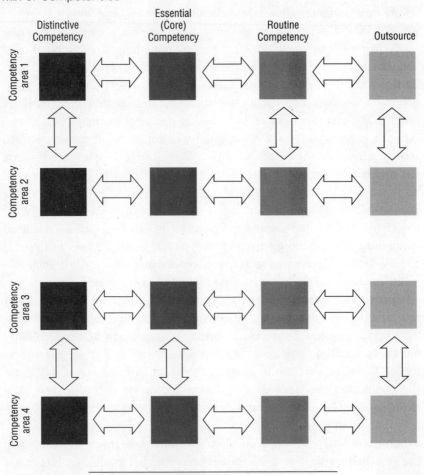

a mix of competencies—each of them capable of moving from left to right or from right to left. Figure 2.2 also shows the interrelationship among competencies.

The key point is that transformation of competencies is a complex process. The enterprise's need is to decide on what new competencies are required, and which existing competencies must be transformed—ideally guided by a well-defined strategic intent and strategic response.

Outsourcing is a critical activity in enterprise transformation, and it needs to be seen in terms of the desired set of competencies needed to achieve dominance. Some leading-edge firms are reviewing not only their competencies, but also the underlying processes and resources, asking whether these will make a difference in the marketplace—or if a different set will be required in the future.

An example is the European Hewlett-Packard group, which makes personal computers. The group recently decided to outsource all circuit board assembly operations, which includes the factory, people, and equipment. The decision is based on the fact that circuit board assembly is not a distinctive competence, and HP needs to have people, information, and technology resources focused on the marketplace of the future.

KEY QUESTIONS

- Do we have any distinctive competencies?

- If not, then what should they ideally be?

- What is the required transformation in competencies?

- And how is it achieved?

In the competency view of enterprise transformation, the change manager's task is to identify current competencies, assign them their status (distinctive, essential, and so on), and then ask whether these are the correct set of competencies required to support true transformation in the other seven facets of the enterprise. To determine whether a change program is transformative or not requires asking how the batch of corporate competencies is being transformed. If there is no explicit answer to this question, then the change program is unlikely to result in enterprise transformation.

Transformation in competency needs to be tied to the desired transformation in strategic intent. Let's return to some of the examples to see how this is the case.

■ The London university, management consulting, and environmental products examples all have a mismatch between their stated missions and the true missions. Until these mismatches are resolved, it is impossible to know what kind of transformation in competencies is required. In the case of the London university, if the strategic intent is truly to develop a transfer of technology to better support city activities, it is clearly necessary to "unlearn" the present financial control mentality. The management consulting firm also needs to decide which way it really wants to go. The competencies required for maximizing the worth of the company for sale are quite different from those required to develop long-term excellence. And the firm making environmental pollution reduction equipment needs to better resolve what is now seen as a conflict between objectives on the part of its key people.

■ It is easier to show the connection between transformation in strategic intent and competencies in the three manufacturing examples. For Alps, the focus on "elimination of mass production" means that the company needs new competencies in manufacturing responsiveness and flexibility, customer information systems, and logistics. The European consumer products and automotive parts companies will need "globalization," new sales and marketing approaches, and regionalized distribution. SKF needed to develop totally new competencies in supply chain management, customer-based information systems, and communication methods.

The Processes Facet

An even more detailed view of an enterprise is that it consists of a series of processes for accomplishing things—things as various as delivering products to customers, designing new products, paying invoices, training employees, or cleaning the rest rooms. While it is somewhat difficult to distinguish exactly between a competency and a capability, there is less problem in defining a process. A process is capable of being described by a flow chart. *If it cannot be flow-charted—it is not a process.* Employee attitudes, customer satisfaction, supply chain management, and design expertise may all be important issues for the firm, but they are not processes. On the other hand, they are *supported by* specific processes that can be carefully studied and improved, such as training programs, after-sales service activities, inventory control procedures, and computer-aided design systems. The latter can be flow-charted, reengineered, and compared to others in terms of both metrics and practices (i.e., they can be benchmarked).

A great deal of current activity in transforming processes comes under the heading of business process reengineering. But this activity needs to be focused: It needs to be consistent, integrated, feasible, and desirable. Business reengineering without guidance from the transformed mission—

and from the need for transformed competencies—runs a severe risk of being another "flushing of the pigeons." We read all too often about the poor payoffs many firms are receiving from business process reengineering.

■ In the Alps example, the new mission of "customer-oriented thinking" and "eliminating mass production" requires new competencies in customer partnerships and flexible manufacturing. These lead in turn to required capabilities in customer-based information and communication systems and rapid product changeovers. These new capabilities require supporting processes, including paperless invoicing, electronic data interchange (EDI), finite capacity scheduling systems, and machine setup time reduction.

■ In contrast, conflicts among mission, competencies, and processes can be illustrated by the largest CarnaudMetalbox production site for producing aerosol cans in Europe. The facility ostensibly was pursuing a somewhat similar avenue for meeting its competitive challenges. Features were a major reduction in throughput time (achieved by just-in-time and cellular manufacturing), quality improvements (supported by a total quality effort, worker empowerment, and a less hierarchical organization), and an overall focus on better delivery performance. All was going quite well, until a new manager arrived, with the old competence paradigm and the underlying systems and processes to support it. The new manager foresaw fewer problems in manufacturing with more buffer inventories— and implemented a material requirements planning system (MRP) so that inventory accuracy could be improved. But the prior work on just-in-time led to a deliberate focus on reducing work-in-process inventories to essentially zero, and with no inventories there certainly was no need for a system to keep track of them. The new manager's interventions, as well as implementation of the MRP system, seriously degraded employee morale, production quality, delivery performance, and customer satisfaction—and created a need to change many of the basic processes on the shop floor. In order to solve the resulting problems, it was necessary to go back to the roots—and make sure that the golden cord of reason was in place. Management was changed, the customer-oriented strategic intent was reinforced, work force empowerment was reactivated, and a series of other actions were taken. Furthermore, the key processes needed to support all this became quite obvious—as well as those that were counterproductive.

Figure 2.3 presents a "competency map" for the SKF example, showing as the new strategic intent for the after market "trouble-free operations." One key competency has been supply chain management, and Figure 2.3 explicitly shows the golden cord relationship between this competency and the related capabilities and processes. The overall competency, supply chain management, is supported by five major capabilities (or subcompetencies): procurement, customer partnerships, supplier partnerships, manufacturing planning and control, and logistics. Each of these capabilities requires detailed processes to support it. The processes in turn require resources.

Figure 2.3 takes one capability—"manufacturing planning and control"—and shows four key processes that are required to enable the capability. One of them, "final assembly scheduling," is also depicted with two subprocesses that have to be in place as well. The golden cord is that in order for this division of SKF truly to achieve its stated mission, it has had to redefine its outputs from bearings to kits of materials designed to solve particular problems—such as all the parts to replace a water pump in a 1986 Saab (including the castings, bearings, screws, gaskets, grease, and installation tools). The result is something like a hundred-fold increase in the number of part numbers that need to be planned and made

Figure 2.3

SKF Competency Map for Implementing "Trouble-Free" Operations in the After Market

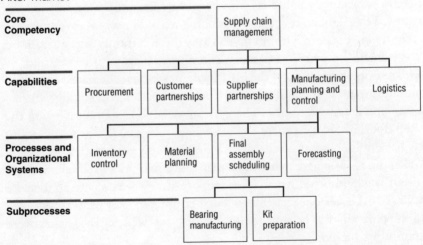

available. If the inventory control system is not absolutely excellent, the financial costs to the company could well exceed any customer derived benefits. The same degree of criticality exists for all the processes listed in Figure 2.3.

The detailed processes depicted in Figure 2.3 are relatively familiar to manufacturing executives. But in the less clearly defined capabilities, such as customer partnerships, the underlying processes are more complex, involving parts of the organization not formally linked. An example is a system for customer complaints. There are many places where a complaint might be registered—including order entry, field service, sales personnel, or even the president of the company.

All our experience indicates that the processes that cross functional boundaries in a company are the best candidates for significant improvement, i.e., reengineering. The potential is even higher when these processes cross organizational boundaries. The customer complaint system is a good example. A key issue is to define explicitly how complaint information is systematically collected, distributed through the organization, measured, and acted upon. Complaints can come from wholesale dealers or from the ultimate customers. In the latter case, they might be passed through dealers—or maybe not passed through. The responses can range from doing nothing, to a form letter ("we would like to help you out—which way did you come in?"), to a serious response, to the recognition given to complaints by Johnson & Johnson, which believes that anyone who takes the time to complain is a very special customer, and can become a valuable source of information over time.

Transforming processes (benchmarking and reengineering them) is hard work. It should be reserved for processes that are critical—that are selected by clinging firmly to the golden cord of reason. The work is especially hard when the processes cross functional and organizational boundaries. But because that is where the payoffs are greatest, we need to do it. To not only benchmark and reengineer, but also to implement processes, it is necessary to involve the process owners—those who perform the process activities—directly in the benchmarking activity. This speeds both implementation and the accompanying learning and change processes.

■ A company in the automotive components business decided that one vital core competence would be its ability to reduce costs and prices more quickly than its competitors—and its customers. That is, it wanted to generate a cost reduction rate greater than the productivity increases being achieved by its automotive company customers, in order to ensure its preferred vendor status. Several critical capabilities supported this competence, including joint new product development, information-sharing, schedule coordination, productivity improvement programs, and achievement of reduced costs by its vendors. In this last area, a major benchmarking effort concentrated on a process calling for a supplier to generate a cost-savings idea, to then be evaluated by the company and then by an automotive company customer in its products. To the surprise of many, this process took two years. The automotive components maker is now reengineering the parts of this process over which it has control (significantly reducing the number of hands that touch a cost reduction proposal). It has benchmarked its new approaches against sister plants, and is in the process of examining the practices of other companies outside the automotive industry. Only after it has done whatever it can do internally does the firm plan to work with its suppliers and its customers. The overall effort is large, and the process is taking a long time, but the benefits are also critical to the mission of the firm. If this process is significantly better than that of competitors, a distinctive competence in cost reduction can be achieved.

The Resources Facet

If the phrase, "you are what you eat," makes any sense, then an enterprise is what it has and consumes in the way of resources. The three fundamental resources in any enterprise are people, information, and technology. If a firm has useless people, it will get useless output. If it has an inadequate information resource, it cannot keep up with the leaders. If it works with second-rate technology, it is likely to be second-rate in efficiency. People, information, and technology (spirit, mind, body) are the triad of resources that differentiates one company's output from another's when all start with the same raw materials. Some would add money to the list, but money is what the firm uses to pay for people, information, and technology—money cannot add value on its own. Others would add materials to the list, but here too, it is the transformation of raw materials into finished goods by the application of people, information, and technology that is the real way a company adds value.

Making major changes in the people resource is a critical part of most transformation efforts, but it is not enough to focus on lean organizations, empowerment, reduced managerial levels, and the other popular buzzwords so often heard today. The golden thread of consistency, integration, desirability, and feasibility must provide the central focus to guide transformation in the people resource.

The same argument holds—and is even stronger—for information and technology transformation. We have all seen far too many misguided information systems. Moreover, the deployment of people in information systems departments is often mistakenly focused on maintaining obsolete computer programs that inhibit—not support—the desired transformation. And without the right technology, certain key objectives are simply impossible to meet. Total quality control (TQM) programs, for example, almost always require changes in technology in order for quality to be *manufactured* into the products—not inspected into the products.

Linking Resource Transformation to Process Transformation

Although there are resource connections to all the other seven facets of enterprise transformation, the most obvious linkage is to processes. Changes in processes will almost always require changes in the resources required for the processes. The hardest to achieve are often in the mindsets and behavior of the people. Paradigm shifting is just not an easy task—and it needs to be reinforced constantly through training, executive leadership, daily attention to details, and a host of other activities. Many total quality programs start off well, only to fail because some executive fails to follow through with the right action—or demonstrates to all a lack of commitment through a shortsighted decision that comes at the cost of TQM.

■ The CarnaudMetalbox example illustrates the problem well. A new factory manager comes into a plant that is in the process of transforming from a hierarchical and departmental focus to one based on a just-in-time philosophy: empowerment, cross-functional communication, fast throughput, little to no inventories—all driven by customer focus. But the new person did not have the same paradigm, and the result was a serious mismatch throughout the organization. This mismatch was particularly strong in the case of the perceived need for the people, information, and technology required to make the transformation work. JIT processes require people who understand the need for velocity in the material flow—instead of the traditional view that says processes work better if separated by large buffer inventories. Information needs are simple, and focus on the demand for the end item, based on "customer pull" rather than "manufacturing push." And the technology needs to be focused on the overall flow, not on optimizing each piece of equipment independently.

■ Alps invested significant efforts in redesigning equipment to facilitate "customer-oriented thinking" and the processes that support it. All machine changeovers followed the dictates of Shingo's famous rule: "Single-minute exchange of dies (SMED)—no changeover more than nine minutes." Some machines had to be specially designed to achieve this goal. Equally large changes were required in information to support customer-focused information systems. And people had to learn new paradigms, focusing on variety and speed rather than on traditional measures of productivity. In this case, the consistency between the deployment of resources and the transformation objectives was quite clear.

Transforming People

Resource transformation necessarily has to follow the dictates of consistency, integration, feasibility, and desirability. And resource changes are most closely linked with process changes. People transformation is the most complex. In true transformation, one often needs to change skills, actions, and behavior—and the fundamental paradigms for seeing the enterprise: what it needs to achieve transformation.

The people who most drive transformation have conceptual and independent thinking capabilities, are self-assertive, are willing to face conflicts and be decisive, have a nurturing relationship with people who work for them, and can motivate others. Several approaches to transforming people have been developed as part of our Manufacturing 2000 project. One developed by Morgan Gould is called "the change wheel," shown in Figure 2.4. The four quadrants of change shown indicate different phases of change. At the bottom left is transformation. It is here that fundamental shifts are made. After the fundamental transformation, there is a need for "building," as shown by the arrow moving from the bottom left-hand quadrant to the upper right-hand quadrant. Thereafter, fine-tuning often follows—until a new crisis arises. Crises usually lead back to the next transformation.

The arrows in Figure 2.4 show the permissible routes of change. The key for people to understand change is to identify what sort of change segment the enterprise is in: fine-tuning, crisis, transformation, or build-

Figure 2.4

The Change Wheel

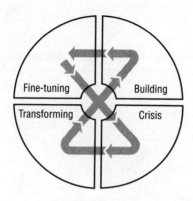

Source: R. Morgan Gould, "Managing the 'How' of Change," *M2000 Executive Report,* no. 16 (November, 1994): 3. Reprinted with permission.

---

ing. The important point is to understand that the changes required in transformation—both for the people in the enterprise and the drivers of the transformation—are fundamentally different from processes in the other kinds of change.

Transforming Information

Transforming information resources and rethinking the overriding information strategy is a key part of most enterprise transformation efforts. It is hard to think of a major improvement in an enterprise that does not require implementation of new information management approaches. New systems need to be implemented, new data need to be collected and processed.

Figure 2.5 shows a very useful framework for understanding information transformation. It depicts three distinct targets for information transformation. At the bottom is the application of information technology, where the emphasis is on development of infrastructure, operating systems, hardware, networks, and technical expertise. The top right information transformation targets come under the heading of information systems. Here, the emphasis is on applications software, data management, functionally oriented systems, and transaction-driven systems

Figure 2.5

Information Transformation Targets

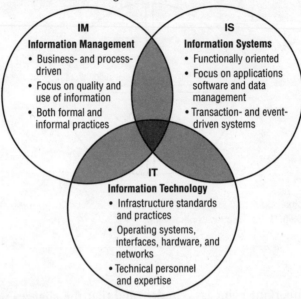

IM
Information Management
- Business- and process-driven
- Focus on quality and use of information
- Both formal and informal practices

IS
Information Systems
- Functionally oriented
- Focus on applications software and data management
- Transaction- and event-driven systems

IT
Information Technology
- Infrastructure standards and practices
- Operating systems, interfaces, hardware, and networks
- Technical personnel and expertise

Source: Donald A. Marchand, "Strategic Information Management," *M2000 Research Project Update,* IMD, Lausanne, Switzerland, Spring 1994, 3. Reprinted with permission.

development. Finally the upper left transformation targets are devoted to information management, with an emphasis on business applications, processes that link organizational units, the quality of information, and informal practices.

A key result of this classification is that we can differentiate between what Benjamin Porter calls "discretionary" and "nondiscretionary" spending for information services.[3] The former is for developing information management—with a focus on new uses and business applications. The latter is on the operation and maintenance of existing information technology and systems. The former needs to be invested in, while the latter needs to be managed for minimum cost at an acceptable service rate.

Donald Marchand has a closely related set of ideas that include a four-level model for thinking about how to improve information management and technology:

□ *Understanding and communicating performance.* Here, the key question is how well is the company doing, with a focus on reporting performance criteria, measurement, and generating reports.

□ *Continually achieving incremental improvement in quality and effectiveness.* This level addresses the quality improvement of information management and technology. One focus for efforts here is to apply the total quality management concepts to the transformation of information: implied are emphases on leadership, strategic quality planning, human resource development, and customer focus—all in the context of information management and technology.

□ *Seeking dramatic business improvements.* The third level of transforming information concerns how to use information management and technology to gain and sustain competitive advantage. The focus is now business-driven as opposed to information systems or technology-driven, with emphasis on the use of information as opposed to the handling of information or technical issues.

□ *Developing competencies to enable the transformation of the business.* Marchand's fourth level calls for applying information assets and technology to achieve distinctive enterprise competency. Here, the goal is clearly on doing new and better things—as opposed to doing the same things better.

Transforming Technology

The actual way technology gets transformed is again very complex, as well as specific to particular situations, but from our overall interest, technology needs to be seen as a major piece of the puzzle, which needs to fit with the others. Changes in technology have to be evaluated in conjunction with other resource changes, and their implementation has to be coordinated with the overall transformation set of objectives. But sometimes technology change is the *basis* for a complete redefinition of the business and its strategic intent. Examples include fiber optics for Corning, digital switching for Northern Telecom, or even the process for making feta cheese from cows' milk, which transformed MD Foods, the Danish farmers' cooperative, into one of the world's largest cheese exporters.

In some firms, the technology transformation is much more significant than in others. Nokia Mobile Phones, one of the Manufacturing 2000 Board companies, is a good example of a "dominate or die" strategy. From its base in Finland, without vertical integration, Nokia competes with firms like Motorola, Matsushita, and Ericsson. The transformation in Nokia has been profound. The growth in units has been phenomenal, while unit prices have fallen even faster. The fall in price per unit means that Nokia must continually add features at the same time that it has to transform other aspects of the business—including aggressively buying up competitors so that the base of operations can be continually expanded.

Nokia has been faced with a constant and rapid technology transformation, particularly in the product design technology. Mobile phones are constantly improved—they are smaller, lighter, more versatile. Nokia has had to build partnerships and alliances with key suppliers while maintaining its own distinctive design competencies. There have also been major technology changes in manufacturing—new processes, greater integration, and faster response through distribution channels. These technology changes have had profound impacts on the people and information resources as well.

The Outputs Facet

Our fifth facet is an enterprise's outputs, or the bundle of goods and services it produces. This is a very natural view, in that firms are almost always described as being in the "such-and-such" business, and industrial groupings are based on outputs. But industrial groupings tend to focus on the goods side of the business, with too little attention paid to the service component of every business. In many transformation projects, a key driver is to achievement of increased perceived value (and service content) of the outputs.

Adding more services to the outputs of a business is a natural evolution in business practice. The local merchants know their clients and what sorts of special features will make them more satisfied (and likely to return). But transformation of the services dimension of these businesses is better defined as "revolution" than "evolution." Where the game is paradigm shifting in terms of the bundle of goods and services provided, the result is also a fundamental need for transformation in most of the other facets or views of the enterprise.

■ SKF, in its transformation from selling bearings to providing trouble-free operations is a good example of a fundamental shift in paradigms as far as outputs is concerned. To provide kits that help end-users make repairs, the company had to provide all the parts for a particular job, along with lubricants, maintenance instructions, and even tools to ensure proper installation and subsequent use. The result was a massive increase in the number of part numbers handled internally and a great increase in the number of items provided to the customer. But there is more here than just an increase in part numbers. Trouble-free operations has meant a new attention to understanding and solving customer problems. This also requires a detailed knowledge of the business practices of the businesses that distribute SKF products. Their operations also need to be "trouble-free," and this in turn makes still more demands on the outputs required from SKF. Achieving these shifts in outputs requires major changes in resources, processes, and competencies as well as in the overall mission.

■ Alps, in implementing "customer-based thinking," went through a similar transformation in the outputs provided to its customers. In some cases, the number of batches going to customers in a given time period could increase by fifty times. Even though the products provided might be the same, the bundle of goods and services has been dramatically changed. Invoicing, payment practices, quality controls, and many other aspects of doing business with Alps have changed fundamentally. Achieving these changes has required paradigm shifting in many parts of the organization.

■ Consumer products companies such as Nestlé and Unilever have been under constant pressure from the hypermarkets to provide faster and more frequent deliveries. In some cases, the change has been more evolutionary than revolutionary, but in Procter & Gamble's (P&G) provision of goods to Wal-Mart, there has indeed been a fundamental change in the outputs provided. The underlying change has been to develop more "information content" in the bundle of goods and services jointly created by P&G and Wal-Mart. This has been achieved by "cross-docking"; exact sales figures for each P&G item at each Wal-Mart store are electronically transmitted from Wal-Mart to P&G at the close of each business day. This allows P&G to plan its outputs (shipments) so that when a delivery reaches a Wal-Mart warehouse, it never goes into stock. The warehouse becomes a break-bulk operation, and the goods simply go across the dock.

■ We have described the fundamental conflict between a London University's stated mission (to contribute financial institutions in the City of London and the rejuvenation of London's East End) and its actual mission (to balance the budget). Without resolution of this mismatch, there could be no meaningful transformation. Another way to look at this situation is in terms of the outputs. The present research output is simply not useful to the City of London and East End clients. One way to encourage transformation would be to identify what outputs would indeed be useful, and to establish measurement and reward systems accordingly. This could be a reasonable step toward achieving the desired transformation. Looking at the situation negatively, if this change in output orientation is not made, there is no hope at all for achieving the stated mission statement.

Service Outputs

A key transformation in outputs facing almost all firms is the rapid increase in the "services" portion of the "goods and services bundle" provided to their customers. This is easily seen in the SKF and Alps examples. Consumer products companies also are adding nonproduct attributes to their bundles in the form of speed, delivery improvements, and customer partnering concepts. In virtually every case of service enhancement, a critical ingredient is better use of information and computer-supported decision making. This is even more profound in the service industries such as banks and insurance companies, whose product is almost entirely information.

Figure 2.6 illustrates the relative proportion issue. The Y axis depicts the proportion of products relative to services in the overall bundle of

Figure 2.6

Relative Proportion of Products and Services

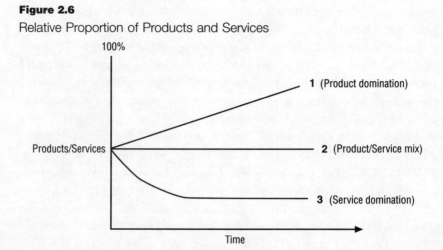

goods and services, and the X axis portrays the evolution in the mix over time. While both products and services are improving, which needs to improve at a faster rate in order for the enterprise to dominate (and what are the implications for transformation)?

The curve labeled (1) in Figure 2.6 denotes enterprises whose primary battle is being fought now with new and improved products. A clear example is in the automotive industry, where a quality struggle has taken place. A similar competitive game was once the case for television sets. But now the relative difference in quality among these products is perceived as not as great, and the game well may shift to improved services. Sony increasingly sees its game as what comes out of the television set (the entertainment).

Curve (2) in Figure 2.6 depicts an enterprise whose relative proportion of products to services is relatively stable. Examples might include suppliers of automotive components and consumer products firms for which just-in-time deliveries and customer partnering are the service orders of the day, yet better products are equally important.

Curve (3) is best illustrated by the computer companies. The need to improve the "boxes" has been decreasing rapidly relative to how the boxes are used, and the ways the customers are served. In fact, a major criticism of IBM and DEC is that they have not reacted soon enough or forcefully enough to this relative change in importance. If an enterprise perceives that it is on curve (1) or (2), when the real game is on curve (2) or (3), it will take a crisis to force the transformation. But all too often, the approach in some of these transformations seems to be: "ready—shoot—aim."

Focusing Outputs on Customers

A critical step in examining the outputs facet of enterprise transformation is better understanding of what the customers' inherent problems are—and what the enterprise might do to solve them. This requires a deliberate focus on the ways that customers use the products and services, as well as what "keeps them awake at night." That is, everyone talks of customer focus as a great idea—like motherhood—but making this overarching goal a reality requires hard work. One needs truly to understand the customers and their problems. One then needs to redesign the bundle of goods and services provided to them. Adopting a true customer focus is particularly difficult for companies that have been driven by an R&D or technology culture. This bias is a big part of the problem for IBM, Wang, and DEC, but seems to be absent at Dell.

The customer focus view also implies realizing that usually there is more than one customer to consider. The consumer products firms have the retailers and the final consumers. Automotive parts manufacturers have automobile assemblers and car purchasers. Nokia Mobile Phones has a distribution channel for mobile telephones that is based on specialty providers; this is becoming increasingly less necessary with digital technology. It is now possible to purchase a telephone and a "smart card," and to have the telephone become immediately operational. This implies a major shift in the distribution chain, new players, and new problems to identify and solve.

Focusing outputs on customers requires a dynamic view of customers and their problems. In fact, the customers need to be seen as needing themselves to go through enterprise transformation—with its attendant eight facets. Trying to understand how key customers or customer groups in fact need to change is critical to developing a true customer focus. If the company does not know how the customers are (and should be) facing transformation issues, then its knowledge of its customers is not sufficient. It is just too easy to focus on financial analysis of the customers, and not devote sufficient attention to their underlying problems and opportunities.

Finally, considering the transformation efforts of our customers can be important in deciding which customers we really want to do business with. Is their direction for transformation consistent with ours? Can we learn from them? Will they impede our learning?

The Strategic Response Facet

An enterprise can be viewed as the sum total of its responses and actions—the action programs it is undertaking to improve itself. If one wants to transform the organization, it is necessary to change its strategic responses. Every enterprise is doing something, and describing what the something is is one way to describe the enterprise. Similarly, making a fundamental change in these responses and actions is an entry point to enterprise transformation. The corollary is that if a true transformation is to occur, it will be necessary to fundamentally change the action programs. The definition of what is "better" will change (better things, not things better)—so the action programs must also change to focus on the new things.

This may sound obvious, but there are too many times when managers envision a transformation, but see completion of the current action programs as necessary preconditions before any new ones can be initiated. In many cases, the programs in place may in fact be counterproductive—based on the wrong paradigm. We have mentioned several examples in this chapter (CarnaudMetalbox, Alps, automotive parts manufacturers) where companies have implemented systems such as material requirements planing (MRP) to plan and control the flow of goods through manufacturing, and in some cases to the final consumers. But the new paradigms call for much more rapid responses, with material velocity the goal rather than material control. Totally new action programs are often required; sometimes it is necessary to admit right now to a mismatch, even if that implies scrapping a costly action program.

The actions view of enterprise transformation necessitates a critical review of all action programs and their match with the transformation objectives. If, for example, transformation is started as a top-down paradigm shift based on customer focus and with a newly defined strategic intent, one needs to examine current actions carefully to see which ones best match the new objectives, which are counterproductive, and how a revised set of action programs should be prioritized.

Conversely, sometimes a transformation is driven more by the action programs themselves, but the search for match among the other seven enterprise facets is no less important. Thus, if a firm embraces MRP, JIT, TQM, the European Foundation for Quality Management, business reengineering, or some other major action program, it needs to ask if its existing set of resources, processes, and competencies are consistent with the action program. We often find important mismatches. Managers might decide that one of the three-letter processes is a good idea, but not understand the real implications for the linkages with other dimensions of transformation—or in fact not recognize that they have started down a path of transformation. Without explicit recognition, there is little chance for success.

We can look at some of our example companies to see how responses and actions undergo a transformation.

■ At Alps, the elimination of mass production meant that many of the existing improvement efforts needed to be scrapped. Alps, like most Japanese companies, used the "small steps" or *Kaizen* approach to improve its operation constantly. But the focus of this approach is based on classical productivity measures, high utilization of machines and workers, departmental structures, job shop manufacturing, process layout, and judicious use of buffer inventories to allow the various organizational units to optimize their individual operations. The new paradigm, rapid flow to satisfy customer wants—with no inventories—made many of these improvement efforts counterproductive. Alps did not give up *Kaizen*, but now focused it on different targets evaluated with different metrics. Continuous improvement was needed in setup time reduction, in overall flow time from order receipt to customer delivery, in scrap reduction, and in the elimination of paper and other transactions.

■ SKF had always focused on being the lowest-cost bearings producer. This entailed action programs based on long runs, standard products, and high-volume contracts. Segmenting the market into original equipment manufacturers (OEM) and after-sales service required different manufacturing infrastructure choices. Improvements (action programs) needed to be similarly evaluated. The transformation to trouble-free operations called for major new competencies (and their consequent capabilities, processes, and resources). But it also required changes in the ways improvements were made in bearing manufacturing itself.

■ Nokia's purchasing organization once took a traditional view of its role in improving company performance. Since a high proportion of the costs are in purchased components, it was imperative to keep these supplier prices as low as possible. In the traditional view of manufacturing, this implies a great deal of comparative shopping, negotiations on prices, and measurement of purchasing effectiveness on price reductions. When the emphasis for success in this business shifted to rapid new product introduction, the primary emphasis in purchasing necessarily changed from price to delivery times and to flexibility on the part of suppliers.

Strategic response is the set of actions taken. The integration and consistency imperatives dictate that the responses specifically address the challenges. Because transformation means "doing better things—not doing the same things better," it implies a major change in strategic response or action programs. Thus Alps needed more than small-step continuous improvement focused on productivity improvement; the new paradigm calls for actions directed at highly individualized customer needs and speed. Similarly, SKF needed to change its improvement efforts, which were focused on long runs and high volumes, to understanding and solving customer problems in using its bearings. And Nokia's purchasing group needed to work with suppliers to achieve speed and flexibility, rather than the long-run low unit price.

The Challenges Facet

The seventh facet of enterprise transformation is the hardest for most people to grasp. An enterprise can be viewed in terms of the problems, opportunities, and challenges that it faces. Enterprise transformation, therefore, needs to be seen in terms of the changes in those problems, opportunities, and challenges (we call them all "challenges" from now on). In today's fast-paced world, it makes sense to continually evaluate the enterprise and its need for transformation in terms of the challenges it faces—and for the enterprise to understand clearly the major shifts in those challenges.

In chapter 3, enterprise transformation is seen as occurring in response to forces and constraints—both internal to the enterprise and external to it. But our basic model for enterprise transformation uses the terms "internal discontinuities," defined as those forces and constraints unique to a particular enterprise, and "external discontinuities," which impact all the players in a particular industry. The discontinuity idea comes closer to expressing the concept of major changes in forces and constraints. Challenges must also include the expectations that customers and stakeholders have of a company.

For most companies, transformation is made for particular reasons—which can be expressed as the set of challenges it wishes to tackle with the transformation. By continually catalogueing the set of challenges it faces, the enterprise has a better understanding of both the need for change and the direction it needs to take.

Almost all the transformation examples we have noted could be used to illustrate the changes in challenges faced. Here are some others.

■ Toshiba one day came to the conclusion that its ability to commercialize new technology—especially the technology it developed itself—was not sufficient. That is, the challenge to the company was how to better gain benefits from new technologies developed internally. The company needed first to identify the reasons why it was not able to achieve the benefits it felt were warranted by the development of basic technology. The focus on challenges was therefore (1) comparative with other firms; (2) complete in that it dealt with several dimensions of the problem; (3) determined to be profound enough to require transformation; and (4) led to a clearly articulated set of change imperatives for the company. The result was a paradigm shift in the commercialization of technology in the company, abandonment of several old practices and metrics, and some very good results in practice thereafter (the laptop computer being one).

■ A company manufacturing household cleaning products for the European market had several factories in various countries to establish local presence, and to minimize tariffs and transportation costs; challenges were expected to change with development of the common market. The firm also had excess capacity, increased pressures on price and frequency of deliveries, and rapidly increasing costs of introducing new products. The firm summed up its new challenges—and the paradigm shift required to meet these challenges—as developing pan-European marketing and manufacturing.

■ A company producing plastic items for use in the home wanted to transform its approach to the environment from one based on adversarial relationships with various environmental interest groups to one in which environmental performance was seen as a competitive advantage. This conclusion came from an analysis of the current set of challenges facing the company, including a growing obligation for companies like itself to prove that all environmental mandates were being met—throughout the entire supply chain; an increasing need to engage in dialogue with environmental activists; expanded need to reduce secondary packaging and to recycle whatever packaging was used; and a growing demand that companies create secondary products to use recycled materials rather than fill up landfills.

Identifying the present set of challenges is usually not an overwhelming task. A brainstorming session usually leads to some shared set of executive values on the key issues. What is more interesting, harder, and potentially more valuable is to speculate on the future sets of challenges that the enterprise might face. Even more difficult is to try to guess the future set of challenges that the customers will face—and what this implies for the bundle of goods and services we should produce for them.

Some firms, such as Shell, approach this problem with the generation of scenarios or potential stories about what might be the case. This is very different from forecasting or predicting the future. Rather, it is the process by which a "possible" or even "somewhat likely" possible state of nature might come about. The next question is: If this did come about, what could we ideally do about it? By thinking these scenarios through, total surprises are avoided, and responses to new sets of challenges are started earlier. Everything we know about the present state of affairs in business stresses that response speed can mean the difference between dominance and death.

A primary focus in facing the future has to be on opportunity-seeking. Waiting for challenges to occur and maintaining a bunker mentality are just not the routes to dominance. Instead, the dominating firms establish the changes. They increasingly will:

- ☐ See environmental concerns as opportunities to define the competitive game. Sultzer designs incinerators that establish new levels for pollution standards.

- ☐ Make their own products obsolescent. Unilever has developed a new technology for washing powder.

- ☐ Develop products that change the way people live—the Sony Walkman.

- ☐ Provide services before they are asked for—Bally's CAD/CAM device for computer-designed shoe fitting.

- ☐ Anticipate customer expectations. Siemens moves quickly into the electrical infrastructure market in Eastern Europe.

- ☐ Create product features that go beyond primary functional requirements. Casio produces calculators that play music and are solar-powered.

- ☐ Recognize the need for new approaches to employee relations. Heineken saw employee empowerment as fundamental to their future.

- ☐ Define the true distinctive competencies and make the hard choices on outsourcing others early. Hewlett-Packard is outsourcing its circuit board assemblies.

- ☐ Create supply chain partnerships allowing win–win for all the players—but at the same time capturing a commanding position (warehousing and distribution coordination between Wal-Mart and Procter & Gamble).

□ Add to the services proportion of their goods and services bundle. IBM and DEC are at least trying.

Making these proactive moves requires a company spirit that looks for challenges, that encourages experimentation, that is ready to unfreeze its current thinking, and that is not afraid to make mistakes. Achieving this kind of culture is a fundamental "challenge" for top managers.

The Learning Capacity Facet

The capacity to learn does not readily submit to inspection. It cannot be explicated like a mission statement; it cannot be flow-charted like a process; and it cannot be packaged like an output. Yet it exerts a powerful influence on whether an enterprise dominates or dies. Moreover, given the importance of learning capacity, it is essential to assess it, to improve it, and to transform it if at all possible.

Learning capacity permeates an organization. It is critically linked to—and shapes—the other seven enterprise facets, in that the strategic intent dictates the direction for learning, while the competencies and processes are the fundamental places where learning takes place. Learning typically requires redeployment of resources, focused around action programs, to produce new bundles of outputs (goods and services) and to respond to the challenges facing the enterprise. Learning reflects how well all this is occurring.

Many authors write about the importance of "the learning organization." Even more important issues are how to increase the speed of learning, how to be sure that the learning is focused on the right things, and how to enhance the capacity to learn. Learning is influenced by the skills, attitudes, behaviors, and underlying culture in an enterprise. Changing these is critical, and the change must be governed by the golden cord of reason.

All companies need to learn, but they also need to unlearn. The questions this poses are how to decide what to unlearn, and what direction is needed for the learning. Learning must be consistent with the other seven transformation facets—which themselves need to have an internal consistency. Changes in the other seven facets dictate what needs to be unlearned as well.

Learning must be related to strategic intent, and the golden cord is fundamental. Improvement and learning without integration may look and feel good to those doing it, but the result can be "pigeon flushing." Learning must be dictated by a clearly articulated strategy.

Best Practices

One popular way companies are increasing their speed of learning is through benchmarking and the sharing of best practices. Benchmarking is hard work, but, when it is done right it can lead to significant improvements. Well-designed benchmarking is almost always accompanied by business process redesign and reengineering, with the primary focus on transforming processes.[4] But best practices can include more than process-sharing. In Manufacturing 2000, we have created "learning networks" where firms share experiences around particular topical areas, such as information management, supply chain management, and human resource management. The sharing is at a fairly high level (such as overall objectives and improvement programs) as well as at the detail level (particular processes).

A key indicator of learning capacity is improvements in the "engines" or drivers for learning in place in an enterprise, such as the quality improvement program at KNP BT, the productivity teams used at Nestlé, the TOP program at Siemens, or the T50 program at ABB (to increase speed by 50 percent in many activities). The learning capacity question is: How good are these programs? How quickly are they improving?

Another example of practice-sharing is initiatives like the 1994 nationwide "Competitiveness Forum" run by the Confederation of British Industry (CBI) in the United Kingdom. In this case, twenty companies such as Sony, Kodak, ICI, and Coca-Cola opened their doors to up to twelve (screened) CEOs and directors, and discussed the key sources of their competitive advantage.

The underlying problem with any of these initiatives is whether the results do in fact lead to increased learning—both in terms of specific knowledge implementation and in the overall capacity to learn. Benchmarking of processes is more sure when done right (not "recreational" benchmarking, where casual visits are made to look over other processes without serious pre-study of the firm's own processes first). Visits of CEOs can indeed too easily lead to recreational results. This is particularly so because the practices usually need to be implemented by other members of the enterprise, and the golden cord is required to ensure consistency and integration.

Learning Examples

The acid test for learning capacity is the translating of new lessons into actions. Learning from other organizations is useful only when the lessons learned result in enterprise transformation.

■ John Brocke, a factory manager for Nestlé in the United States, attended an M2000 forum to describe his experiences when a corporate "Improvement Team" examined his plant operations. The outside influence was seen as producing both pluses and minuses, but the net results of the study were the implementation of some major improvements at his factory. Coming from a learning culture, John Brocke also benefited from comparing his experiences with those of other managers at the forum who discussed their approach to cellular manufacturing:

> I took copious notes. One of the issues was the importance of support from company headquarters. They also talked about the steps needed to get people involved and the fact that you need to be organized around a product and a process. At that time we were very functionally organized. Based on this, I knew that if I wanted to introduce cellular manufacturing into the plant, I needed to get support from my management. I presented the idea to my boss and other management at corporate headquarters. As a result, we got company approval and support, not only with investment but in involvement. Right now we have a third of our plant redesigned. In that third, we have broken down our functional organization. The people on the line monitor their own quality, set their operational goals, and track their daily performance. To date we have specific benefits—10 percent improvement in materials loss, and efficiency up by 8 percent.

■ BP Chemicals, U.K., believes that faster learning is critical to meeting the challenges of globalization; its management also believes that through careful study of others it can increase learning capacity. The objective is to improve business results faster than the competition. BP is not complacent about the size of the task it has before it, nor is it deluded into thinking it can just do it internally. Tony Priestly, performance measurement benchmarking manager, finds that exposure to other people's business processes and cultures has helped break down the barriers and inertia to change. Networking has helped promote breakthrough thinking and convey a clearer idea of how to respond to change and work with customers to create value.

■ Conversely, a health care provider in the U.K. achieved a new status as an independent entity providing health services to a district health authority. It now believed it was necessary to adopt market-driven practices from other industries. One effort was to commission extensive market research into satisfaction of the customers—both the district health authority and the patients. A key finding was that both classes of customers complained that they were not kept informed and had no details about the services offered and the associated costs. But these findings did not lead to improvements. The health care provider was not able to break out of the complacency that was associated with its former monopoly status. The culture just did not support real learning.

The Critical Role of Measurement

We have noted in several places the role of measurements. Figure 2.7 shows the relationships among strategic intent or mission, strategic responses or action programs, and measures.[5] The title of the figure,

---

Figure 2.7

Changing Performance Measures

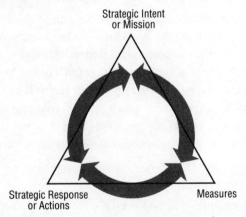

Source: Adapted from A.J. Nanni, J.R. Dixon, and T.E. Vollmann, *The New Performance Challenges: Measuring Operations for World Class Competitiveness* (Homewood, Ill.: Dow Jones-Irwin, 1990).

"changing performance measures," implies a continual need to reassess the ways in which enterprise activity is judged. If there is a shift in the fundamental mission or strategic intent of the enterprise, there will be a need for a corresponding shift in both action programs and in measurements. Similarly, if there is a change in actions (even with the same basic mission or strategy), there is always a need to see if there needs to be a change in the measures by which effectiveness is judged. Experience indicates that far too often changes in metrics result in the addition of new measures, when in fact there is also a need to eliminate some existing metrics. Unlearning necessitates elimination of measures.

Elimination of measures is important for several reasons. First, some established measures can be counterproductive to newly desired end objectives (such as productivity and capacity utilization measures when the objective is material velocity). Second, a measure that is important at one time may be less so later because a series of actions has taken place to solve the problem the measure was set to evaluate. Thus, if shipments are met 100 percent of the time, it may be less important to measure daily shipment performance than to adopt some new metric that focuses on a dimension of customer satisfaction that can be improved.

Finally, we come back to the role of financial measures. In some best-thinking firms, the measures now focus far more on nonfinancial measures than on the typically accepted financial metrics. There is more recognition of the difference between drivers and passengers and the importance of measuring the right things approximately (even those things for which directional correctness can only be determined), rather than measuring the wrong things with great accuracy and precision.

As interesting example of nonfinancial measures was seen at a Northern Telecom factory, where a new senior executive was presented with a detailed budgetary analysis. He very publicly threw it in the wastebasket and told his staff to forget those measures and that approach. From then on, he wanted them to work only on throughput time reduction, inventory reduction, and other metrics associated with a time-based competition strategy.

Corporate Performance and Learning Capacity

Measures and key performance indicators are basically how an organization describes itself (its performance) to itself. It "teaches" itself through these tools about success and failure, and it behaves accordingly.

A company's view of its corporate performance will, in turn, play an enormous role in shaping its responses, its resources, its competencies, and its outputs. This then calls for new measures, and the cycle keeps repeating.

Because of this powerful influence of corporate performance on strategy, it is clear that the enterprise will need to learn to assign it a proper role. For genuine transformation, there needs to be a change in the way the enterprise views corporate performance. The choice is between being ruled by the past or opening the mind to the future. It is a choice between remaining in the second industrial revolution mind-set or joining the third wave. It could make the difference between domination or death.

An excellent example of a company changing its metrics to infuse a transformation comes from the division of Bekaert that makes steel cords for tires. Managers became convinced that the company's transformation was critically dependent on teamwork; they completely changed the

---

Table 2.1

The AlliedSignal Braking System (Europe) Score Board

Company Values	Performance Measurement Matrix
Customers	1. Customer claims
	2. Customer scraps at 0 km
	3. Defects accepted by AlliedSignal (warranty returns)
	4. Delivery on time for after market
	5. Delivery on time for original equipment
Integrity	6. Number of hours without accident
People	7. Absenteeism
Teamwork	8. Total Quality Projects
Speed	9. Inventory turns
	10. Setup time
Innovation	11. Suggestions
	12. Prototype service rate
Performance	13. Line utilization rates (based on Total Preventive Maintenance concepts)
	14. Rejects on first acceptance
	15. Rejected parts (suppliers' quality)
	16. Sales per person
	17. Number of references
	18. Cost of product quality

Source: Georges Dissard, Vice-President Manufacturing, AlliedSignal Braking Systems Europe, Draney, France. Adapted from "Factory Management System," AlliedSignal Braking Systems Europe. Reprinted with permission.

evaluation and reward system for managers so that performance was measured in terms of team-working—with financial measures deliberately set aside on the assumption that these were the passengers.

Finally, the Automotive Division of AlliedSignal has adopted the set of performance measures shown as Table 2.1 to evaluate the performance of its factories. This new scoreboard was seen as absolutely essential to achieving division transformation objectives.

Summary

This chapter argues that the process of enterprise transformation can be embarked upon through any one of eight facets. Transformation is the sum of changes in each of these dimensions. The hallmarks of this approach are as follows:

□ Enterprise transformation, to be effective, must be consistent, integrated, feasible, and desirable across all eight facets.

□ The strategic intent view necessarily defines the overall objectives for the enterprise; transformation requires a redefined mission.

□ The competencies view of an enterprise sees it as having certain competencies and capabilities to undertake particular actions; again transformation requires new competencies.

□ The processes view focuses on infrastructure: the detailed processes and systems for accomplishing work—those that can be flow-charted, reengineered, and benchmarked.

□ The resources view is that an enterprise is made up of its people, information, and technology. Transformation requires changing and redeploying these resources.

□ The outputs view focuses on the bundle of goods and services that is produced to solve the customers' problems.

□ The strategic response view of an enterprise sees it in terms of the specific things it is doing to improve itself.

□ The challenges view is based on understanding the problems, opportunities, and challenges faced by the enterprise—at a particular time.

□ The learning capacity view is that transformation requires a firm to learn faster than its competitors—and to focus its learning with the golden cord of reason.

Enterprise transformation can be entered through any of the facets, but it necessarily includes them all. In any particular transformation effort, it is useful to attempt to identify explicit plans and progress made on each of them.

In the next chapter we develop a model that explicitly links the eight facets of enterprise transformation. It moves us from describing transformation to doing transformation.

3 The Model for Transformation

A model for transformation that provides insights into the process has been applied successfully in several of the Manufacturing 2000 companies. It is called a model for "Integrated Strategic Transformation." It is *integrated* because it provides the "golden cord" that runs right through from challenges and expectations to processes, skills, and resources, explicitly integrating each of the eight enterprise transformation facets. It is *strategic* because it allows a conscious proactive approach to transformation for dominance—achieving and sustaining market-based influence. If the approach to change is not strategic, then it is unlikely that the process will be consistent, feasible, or desirable.

Integrated strategic transformation needs to be seen as distinctly different from the many improvement programs that are now so widespread they have their own acronym: TLAs (three-letter acronyms). The journey is from second-wave to third-wave thinking—a journey that cannot be accomplished through just fine-tuning.

The model focuses explicitly on the four imperatives we have identified as prerequisites for enterprise transformation: integration, consistency, feasibility, and desirability. If the model is used to guide transformation, integration and consistency among the eight dimensions is ensured.

The feasibility of any proposed transformation can also be cross-checked with the integrated strategic transformation model. This is accomplished by assessing the detailed infrastructure and resource implications of the transformation: Do we have them? Can we get them? Can we afford them? How will the transformation impact corporate performance in the short and long run—can we take the hits? How about the implied rate of learning—is it a quantum leap that we can achieve? Is the golden cord well-understood?

Desirability of the transformation is also assessed using the model. Does the transformation allow the enterprise to achieve dominance?

Does it give the company the distinctive competencies that support a competitive advantage? What about the implications for those who are needed to implement the transformation—how hard will it be to get buy-in? What are the personal rewards for those who do it?

The model for integrated strategic transformation is depicted in Figure 3.1. The "golden cord" is represented by the set of two-headed arrows that runs from challenges at the top to outputs at the bottom. It links challenges to strategic intent, strategic response, competencies and capabilities, pro-

---

Figure 3.1

Model for Integrated Strategic Transformation

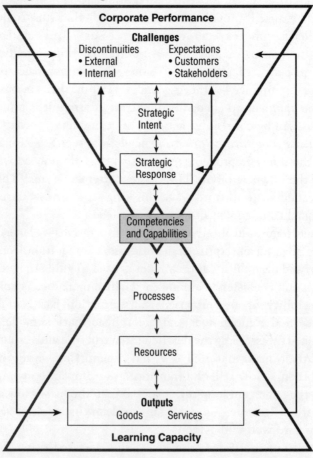

cesses, resources, and outputs. The top half is shown against the backdrop of corporate performance, and the bottom half is shown with learning capacity as its backdrop. In most cases, corporate performance has a powerful influence on the strategy-making activity, while the firm's learning ability shapes the things it does. Competencies and capabilities are shown as the integration or linchpin of the two model halves.

The top half or triangle is concerned with strategy and its linkages with challenges and appropriate actions. The net result of this assessment is the definition of new required competencies and capabilities. The bottom half of Figure 3.1 focuses on infrastructure—definition of the critical processes and deployment of the necessary resources to achieve the desired outputs. That is, what are the required detailed changes in underlying processes, systems and other supporting architecture to achieve the desired competencies/capabilities? Most fundamentally, the model shown in Figure 3.1 is devoted to achieving harmony between the two halves or triangles.

There are many models and approaches to formulating strategy, but the key question in all of them is how we in fact achieve the strategic intent. Similarly, there are many approaches to changing the infrastructure—such as business process reengineering, all the three-letter acronyms, *Kaizen*, quality initiatives, or empowerment. But in far too many cases, there is a disconnect between strategy formulation and infrastructure change imperatives.

The integrated strategic transformation model is first seen as producing a desired state (the objectives plus the golden cord). In fact, we will see that the journey is more important than the destination. It is not at all enough to produce a blueprint for where the enterprise needs to be: We need a process for getting there, and we will see how the model depicted in Figure 3.1 fosters this objective. It is much easier to identify a desired state than to prepare a feasible plan that can be followed to achieve it.

The integrated strategic transformation model can be used in several ways. In essence, it is a zoom lens that can be focused at several levels. The model can be applied to an overall firm, but the bottom half is necessarily at a high level of aggregation for large companies. It is easiest to apply in the context of a business or operation unit, but it has also been used very successfully to examine a particular segment of a business, such as its overall approach to the environment. We will see examples of these in the next chapters.

The Model—The Top Half

Because different people enter the process of change through different enterprise facets, theoretically one can enter the model from any point along the "golden cord." I think the most logical place to start is the top—the problem-solving environment. The top of the "golden cord" is tied to challenges. These are of two types: discontinuities and expectations.

The Challenges

Discontinuities. The top left-hand portion of the challenges block of Figure 3.1 lists two kinds of "discontinuities": internal and external. External discontinuities, such as a decrease in demand for mainframe computers, are seen as influencing all firms competing in the particular industry; internal discontinuities, such as managerial changes or financial pressures, are unique to each firm.

The term, "discontinuity," encompasses the forces and constraints that affect the enterprise. Thus external discontinuities include the economic, competitive, social, and political forces and constraints, as well as the technological thrusts that affect all the players in the industry. The most basic external discontinuities are those that have the potential to alter the ground rules in the industry (however "industry" is defined). Internal discontinuities similarly include these same forces and constraints as they play out uniquely in a particular enterprise, as well as current company strengths and weaknesses, resistance to change, morale, and managerial leadership.

But the idea of a discontinuity encompasses more than forces and constraints. The intention is to highlight the changes in the forces and constraints—those that are most current and critical, rather than just general trends and industry conditions. Addressing the overall forces and constraints is a necessary but not sufficient condition for true transformation. It is necessary to identify—and resolve—those key enterprise issues that keep the best minds in the company awake at night.

KEY QUESTIONS

• Are your present change programs adequate to meet the discontinuities and expectations?

- How far ahead are you looking when examining challenges? three years? five years? ten years?

- Are you looking deeply enough into challenges, or is corporate performance limiting the scope of inquiry?

■ Alps, the Japanese electronics manufacturer described in chapter 2, saw its general industry forces and constraints as including an overcrowded electronics industry, pressures on Japanese firms to restrict exports to the United States, major pressures on the yen, and eroding industry margins. Internally, the general forces and constraints included a lack of true customer focus and a tendency to focus improvement activities narrowly on doing the same things better. Carrying these ideas to the level of "discontinuities," Alps realized that it had an absolute need for growth, partially compensated for in the past few years by taking in work normally farmed out to subcontractors; it had reached the end of that solution. Another discontinuity was a dramatic change in the variety of products Alps was required to produce. Finally, there was a need to serve the new automotive electronics market that the company had established.

■ The manufacturing technology center (MTC) at a U.S. automotive components company is an internal consulting group that supports improvement projects in the manufacturing companies. The center had traditionally been an in-house consulting operation called in by a division to solve a particular problem. The customary forces and constraints in the group were directly related to the problems faced by the divisions: stiffer competition, shorter product life cycles, and other typical manufacturing problems of the 1990s. Most of the three-letter acronym solutions had been accomplished; traditional cost-cutting just was not going to be enough for the future. Additionally, MTC had its own general forces and constraints. The normal use of consulting studies was not as effective as leading-edge thin'ers felt it should be. MTC was not highly regarded in the divisions. There was a focus on hierarchy in MTC, as there was throughout the corporation. The "discontinuities" were largely associated with the speed with which some of these problems were increasing—and compounding. The fundamental discontinuity was perceived to be a lack of proactive consulting: Being called in after a problem had been articulated was just not sufficient (and all too often problems were articulated in cost reduction terms). MTC needed to be involved in cooperative problem identification and solution—focused on fundamental transformation. Internal discontinuities associated with this paradigm shift were the hierarchical and functional disciplinary approach of the MTC consultants. They needed to abandon this technique, and develop cross-disciplinary teams that could help articulate the overall problem and then identify the necessary depth required for a solution—and its implementation.

Expectations. The right-hand portion of the challenges panel in Figure 3.1 shows customer and other stakeholder expectations. Again, the focus is fundamentally on change: What are the changes in expectations of our customers? This almost always includes the major changes that are impacting the customers of the company, which usually means two or more sets of customers, such as automobile dealers and automobile owners for a firm making automobiles. Each of these sets of customers is facing its own discontinuities, from price to brand pressure to consolidation to environmental trends.

Also shown as important are changes in the expectations of other stakeholders. Included are the stockholders of the firm, the employees, the unions, the local communities in which a firm operates, the government, and pressure groups such as the "greens."

Changes in expectations necessarily impact the strategy of the company. Changes in customer expectations might include new product features, service enhancements, and new support linkages to help customers better succeed in their business endeavors. Trade customers traditionally expect high-quality products, timely delivery, help in keeping their stocks low, new product offerings, and cooperative advertising. But the best supplier companies understand that the set of goods and services constantly needs to be improved, and that by anticipating—and *exceeding* customer expectations, the firm can outperform its competitors.

■ The manufacturer of household cleaning products described in chapter 2 analyzed the problems facing its major retail customers (the hypermarkets); concluded that its interest was maximization of profit from each cubic meter of shelf space; and decided to offer a reduced product line (in terms of different stock-keeping units), lower prices, and more rapid deliveries, but asked to maintain its overall shelf space allocation. The result was a win-win for both the customers and the supplier.

■ Similarly, Mandelli, a manufacturer of machine tools and flexible manufacturing systems (FMS), provided total solutions to its customers such as Volvo, which included training engineers in how to design new engines so that they could be readily manufactured on Mandelli equipment. Customer expectations are no longer interpreted as looking for the least expensive piece of equipment to perform a well-defined task; instead, customers want equipment and supporting infrastructure to make new product generations—and do so rapidly.

■ Norsk Hydro, a large Norwegian producer of aluminum, fertilizers, and other products, has a policy of answering any question put to it by any interest group, if not immediately, then as soon as possible, and with absolute honesty. This requires a complex information system on environmental attributes designed to allow a wide-ranging set of queries. Norsk Hydro made this response by understanding—and even anticipating—a growing interest by customers and other stakeholders in environmental issues. By exceeding the present expectations, it is creating good will as well as setting a standard that competitors will have to meet.

The Golden Cord to Strategy

Figure 3.1 shows that discontinuities and expectations impact the strategic response of the company (i.e., the set of responses or actions that are taken in response to the discontinuities and changes in expectations). Strategic response is also linked to strategic intent. Strategic intent encompasses the way that a particular firm chooses to compete, where it sees itself going over the long run, and how it will measure performance—in the light of its industry context, external discontinuities, internal discontinuities, and the expectations of customers and other stakeholders.

The arrows from discontinuities and expectations to strategic intent are shown as two-headed because the well-run company is proactive; it not only exceeds expectations, but it also can cause changes in expectations and discontinuities. Some firms, by their strategic response (and strategic intent), will be able to influence these factors—to change the rules of the game—rather than being forced to respond to them. Firms such as Nokia Mobile Phones constantly make their own products obsolete with new designs; the incorporation of new technologies, moreover, is opening up a whole new way in which products are distributed, sold, and used. Proactive firms also see the environment not as a zero-sum game to be played against the greens, but as an opportunity to set the rules of the game—that the competitors will have to follow.

Strategic intent and *strategic response* (the actions taken to achieve the strategic intent) play the central role in Figure 3.1. Both strategic intent and strategic response need to be seen against a backdrop of corporate performance. That is, the strategic intent and the strategic response must reflect the overall corporate situation in terms of financial and other results. Thus, an IBM or a General Motors recently had to formulate its strategies and action plans in a much different way in the light of its more precarious financial situation.

The golden cord linkage to strategy is more profound than merely a passage from strategic intent to strategic responses. Strategy does not cascade down from on high so that everyone in the organization faces in the same direction. The integrated strategic transformation model adds some realism to this widely accepted fiction.

The discontinuities and changes in expectations lead to a set of explicit strategic responses: What are we going to do about each of these challenges? The summation or integration of these responses is in fact a statement of strategic intent. The key question is whether this inductive approach leads to a good match between this summary mission and the stated mission of the company. If not, either the mission or the set of actions (the strategic response) needs to be altered. The link between discontinuities and expectations and strategy thus becomes a cross check for consistency and integration, based on matching the top-down approach with the specifics derived from a bottom-up technique based on specific actions.

The Model—The Bottom Half

Figure 3.1 is usefully seen as two halves, with "competencies" as the overlap. The top half of the integrated strategic transformation model is concerned with consistency, integration, feasibility, and desirability—from a macro or strategic point of view. That is, the top half focuses on general direction-setting, where the enterprise assesses disturbances in the outside (and inside) world facing it, determines an overall strategy, and formulates a consistent set of action programs. The final issue is then to decide what new competencies are required to carry out the action programs.

The bottom half of the model is concerned with details and infrastructure—with the consistency and integration of the competency needs, the supporting processes, and the necessary learning and its associated skills, attitudes, and behavior. All of this in the end calls for resources—and their deployment to enable the new competencies.

The Competency Linkage

The middle of Figure 3.1 shows strategic response and strategic intent as influencing—and influenced by—the competencies and capabilities in the enterprise. If the firm has a core competency in some technology, this will influence its long-run strategy and its particular action programs. If a U.S. firm in the solar energy business has patent protection for a particular type of solar process, this influences its response to customers as well as its investments in capital equipment and marketing.

KEY QUESTIONS:

- Is the strategy feasible?

- What capabilities and detailed processes are required to support the competencies?

- What are the requirements for implementation and subsequent improvement?

- What are the new skills, attitudes, and behaviors?

- Is the existing capacity for learning sufficient to achieve these goals?

- Do we have the right people, information, and technology—and how does their current use compare to the transformation dictates?

The competencies box in Figure 3.1 needs to be seen in light of the golden cord concept. When the set of strategic responses has been determined (in light of the discontinuities, expectations, and strategic intent), the next question is: What are the new competencies required to achieve these responses? That is, what competencies—along with their capabilities and detailed processes and supporting resources—need to be in place in order to achieve the desired strategic response objectives? An enterprise's current competencies—and the new ones needed—need to support the set of strategic responses. Some competencies are longer-lasting than others, and most require continual upgrading.

"Distinctive" competencies are often based on expertise. Examples are patented designs (e.g., the Polaroid camera), unique manufacturing techniques (e.g., the Michelin radial tire), or branded products (e.g., Nescafe). Increasingly, the ability to achieve constant transformation is becoming a distinctive competency. Distinctive competencies allow the firm to achieve a definitive competitive advantage: produce superior outputs, exceed customer expectations, and distinguish itself from the competition. Distinctive or core competencies are those that are critical to a company's long-term success (e.g., design or manufacturing processes). Other competencies that are not critical, such as printing the paychecks, in many cases need to be viewed as candidates for outsourcing. Such a decision, however, is quite complex and needs to be based on a long-run perspective of how competitive advantage is to be achieved in a particular industry context.

There is a natural tendency for distinctive competencies to degrade to essential competencies, then to routine competencies, and finally to candidates for outsourcing. Thus the patent protection of Polaroid and the manufacturing processes of Michelin are no longer distinctive, although the Nescafe brand name still commands a price premium. Nestlé works hard to maintain this distinctive competence through its major product and process developments.

■ The Nestlé name is critical to the company. A source of continual problems for the company is the Finnish oil company, Neste. Neste's introduction of a brand of special biodegradable motor oil for snowmobiles, called Nes-Kat, was not well-received by Nestlé, because of its candy bar named Kit-Kat. This may all seem trivial to the noninitiated, but to those preserving the distinctive competence of the Nestlé brand names it is serious business.

Processes

Competencies can be seen as requiring underlying capabilities that in turn are supported by detailed processes (by definition these can be flow-charted, reengineered, and benchmarked). The golden cord of reason here is from the discontinuities and changes in expectations to the actions the firm wishes to take in response, to the improvements in current competencies and the new competencies required to make those responses, to the underlying capabilities and detailed processes necessary in order to enable the desired competencies.

While a core or distinctive competency is supported by processes and capabilities, it is more than a collection of processes and capabilities. A more accurate way of looking at the relationship is as a hierarchy or network. Although processes (and capabilities) support competencies, some competencies, such as engineering, allow new processes to be established; and in the absence of certain capabilities, such as supply chain management, some new processes could not be implemented.

Some processes, however, support multiple capabilities and competencies. Processes are the basic building blocks of capabilities and competencies. A process is a set of interconnected activities to fulfill a stated objective that is measurable in terms of efficiency against a predefined standard. In many cases it is useful to further divide processes into subprocesses for better understanding.

Processes also support capabilities. Some capabilities, such as employee attitudes, process adaptability, project management, and flexible operations, are usually not seen by the customers—except in terms of their effects, such as low prices, good deliveries, and fast customer response. But other capabilities, such as after-sales service, delivery flexibility, and product application know-how, are more visible and directly linked to customer expectations. Processes, linked with resources, create capabilities—both those seen by the customers of the firm and those that are not. Customers are impacted by the distinctive or core competencies of the firm, such as brand management for a Nestlé or a Unilever, and providing these competencies involves many capabilities that are not transparent from the outside. A distinctive competence of McDonald's—consistently high-quality food—is seen by the customers and is a key reason for the success of the company. Some of its capabilities and processes, such as fast service and food preparation, are somewhat visible, but others such as employee training, motivation, and scheduling are not.

The Resources

The resources (people, information, and technology) need to be consistent with the overall mission, the detailed action programs established, the new competencies required, and the other dictates of Figure 3.1.

The enterprise seriously pursuing transformation is well-advised to take this overall view, which includes first conducting a careful examination of the discontinuities that are impacting its industry, its customers, and its own internal situation. It also needs to analyze the expectations of its customers and other stakeholders—continually looking for ways in which it can proactively exceed or change expectations—or even perhaps *cause* discontinuities. All this thinking then must be reflected in the company's strategy. Logical questions are: What should the objectives be, and even more important, what are the action plans necessary to achieve those objectives? Finally, what new infrastructure do we need to put in place (and what old infrastructure needs to be removed) in order to achieve the action plans?

■ A European company in the automotive components business developed a list of external discontinuities that includes restructuring in the worldwide automotive industry and a growing trend toward outsourcing by automobile manufacturers. Internal discontinuities included cumbersome product design capability, too long a design period for new products, and not enough collaboration with major customers in the design stages. Customer expectation changes included what was referred to as the "Lopez factor," globalization and regionalization patterns that are quite different for different customers, and an interest on the part of end-users in more environmentally friendly automobiles. The strategic responses to these discontinuities included a new organizational structure that features regionalization, supply chain management, simultaneous engineering, and strategic alliances.

The match with strategic intent is not too bad, but the company needed to convert a fairly general mission statement into a much more concrete set of strategic priorities—that could be understood by the various divisions and would be consistent with their action programs. A set of new core competencies was determined as necessary to support the entire set of strategic responses. Included were product and process development, global and local business management and culture, and joint venture management. Each competence was in turn examined in terms of the necessary changes in infrastructures that were required. What needed to be learned, and what needed to be *unlearned?*

Learning Capacities

In the bottom half of the model, competencies, processes, resources, and outputs are shown against the background of the firm's learning capacity. Here one must be sure that the learning objectives are in line with overall corporate objectives and measures. The objective for any firm is best practice—in competencies, capabilities, and processes—as well as in learning, skills, attitudes, behavior, and resource deployment.

Gaining competencies and capabilities is not a one-time achievement. Learning needs to be continuous and rapid, if distinctive competencies are to be maintained. Learning is supported by the skills, attitudes, and behavior of the enterprise employees. Skills need to be constantly upgraded—but the directions for the upgrading need to come from the golden cord. Similarly, changes in attitudes and behavior also need to be directed by the golden cord of reason.

The golden cord is also critically connected to learning in that the strategy for the dominant firm requires rapid learning. Furthermore, top management needs to apply constant pressure for learning, to develop and maintain a widespread perceived need to learn, to identify the discontinuities that necessitate learning, and, most important, to provide the directions for learning—to identify the triggers that motivate learning and unlearning.

Unlearning is difficult to master. It implies reducing or dismantling an installed base of knowledge. It requires a deliberate focus on practices that need no longer be done, and, more important, on paradigms that are no longer valid. Thus, Northern Telecom found a key problem in purchasing was the evaluation of purchasing performance in terms of purchase price reductions—instead of in terms of supplier partnerships and joint new product development. Changing this process required deliberate abandonment of some traditional measures of purchasing performance, development of new ones, and (more critically) development of new communication channels with suppliers so as to nurture win-win solutions. Similarly, just-in-time manufacturing often requires unlearning the traditional focus on machine and labor force utilization, while team-working based on coaching needs both new metrics and the abandonment of mind-sets based on command and control.

A good example of "unlearning" took place in one of the M2000 companies that needed desperately to transform the infrastructure of its information systems group to support its other transformation efforts. The company outsourced its entire information systems efforts—including hardware, software, and people—for a three-year period to give it the time to develop the new resource base to operate a fundamentally different management information systems activity.

Practices are the way of doing things. There are practices for competencies, capabilities, processes, and even for learning—and each of them can be described and at least conceptually benchmarked. But benchmarking is much more straightforward for processes, because they can always be described with a process flow diagram and its associated measures of time, distance, and relationships. Competencies, capabilities, and learning are harder to describe (and emulate), but they are in fact what makes the difference between dominance and death. Thus, the processes for preparing accounts payable documents might be the same in two firms, while their supplier management capabilities could be markedly different. Moreover, one firm may well have a much greater rate of learning—its real capability is being enhanced at a faster rate.

The practices of competencies and capabilities can be described in written or diagrammatic forms, such as organization charts or physical layouts, but these descriptions almost never capture the real reasons for the success of a competency or capability. They are just too aggregated and do not focus on the key processes, resources, and accumulated skills, and the integration of all these elements. Those interested in benchmarking are usually better off trying first to identify the distinctive processes needed and focus attention on the process level.

For the practice of any competency, capability, process, or skill, it should be possible to identify critical success factors (CSFs), which measure effectiveness (in terms of strategic intent), as well as key performance indicators (KPIs), which measure efficiency against some predefined standard performance. Efficiency is also measured by comparative benchmarking. Benchmarking is based on KPIs—but also (and most important) practices. That is, the metrics are less important than the ways. Practice becomes the standard for evaluating performance—and it is essential to describe the practice, not just measure it.

Measuring learning is also possible, but it is critical to focus on measures that support the golden cord. Firms often measure productivity in great detail, when they should critically examine its relation to the stated strategic responses. Productivity, by definition, is output divided by input, but in far too many cases the approach to increasing the ratio is to squeeze the denominator.

Linked to the firm's learning capacity—its practices and measures—is the issue of corporate performance (shown as the backdrop to the top half of the model). Corporate performance exerts a powerful influence on shaping strategy—perhaps too powerful, because it tends to insulate a firm from reality. In the true picture, it needs to be seen as symmetrical to learning capacity if there is to be any consistency.

In fact, the two halves of Figure 3.1 need to be seen against each other. The top half sets direction; the bottom half determines how to achieve the direction. But the backdrop to the top half, corporate performance, needs to be seen more as a passenger to the driver of the bottom half backdrop, learning capacity. That is, too many firms are making short-term decisions to enhance financial measures of performance, when in fact they should be concentrating on outpacing their competitors in terms of customer service and other less concrete measures of effectiveness. The learning needs to be focused on those activities that will really make a difference.

Many firms, for example, are correctly engaged in business reengineering. While this is a knee-jerk reaction to faltering corporate performance, it will not be appreciated that there are three distinct levels of reengineering. The potential payoffs grow as the focus shifts, but the requirements for success also shift—the efforts have to be integrated with the overriding strategic objectives of the firm and driven by key executives:

□ *Streamlining* is concerned with taking the fat out of a particular process. The focal point for the activity is an audit of current processes to find ways to perform them more cost-effectively. Streamlining is usually associated only with improvements in processes, or at most one or two capabilities. This activity is largely accomplished using classical industrial engineering methods. An example is improving the accounts payable operations in a company. There the focus might be on the time required to process an account payable, the steps and approval processes, and the record keeping. Benchmarking probably would be to the time requirements and approaches for these issues in other companies.

□ *Value-driven reengineering*, a second level of business process reengineering, is still not typically driven by strategic intent and strategic response. Here the Figure 3.1 focus is on processes, capabilities, and the rate of learning achieved in them—but linked to one or two existing competencies. This effort is concerned with redesign of a series of linked processes that in total deal with some flow of materials, documents, or ideas, typically crossing organizational boundaries. For example, a firm might wish to redesign the flow of information between itself and its most important suppliers. The typical emphasis is on improved flows of material or faster exchange of information, such as for new product design.

□ *Business transformation*, the most complex form of business process reengineering, is that associated with implementing the overall view expressed in Figure 3.1. The objective is to implement a major redesign of the business infrastructure, based on major shifts in both the strategic intent and strategic response, in order to respond to the new market conditions that are faced. Perhaps now the scope includes a different technology base for the company, new make-or-buy decisions, outsourcing, and strategic alliances—driven by a major discontinuity in the marketplace such as that faced by an IBM. In this case, the business process reengineering (and unlearning) would be focused at all three areas—competencies, capabilities, and processes—but linked to the specific strategic responses the company is trying to make.

The key point here is understanding the inherent differences among the three levels of reengineering—as well as the appropriate managerial focus—and the different roles that benchmarking needs to play.

The Model and the Eight Facets of Enterprise Transformation

Chapter 2 describes eight views or facets of an enterprise and emphasizes that transformation needs to be seen in terms of the changes in each of the facets—as well as all the facets integrated. The integrated strategic transformation model is designed to support this summation. For each facet, a series of questions can guide discussion within the organization:

The Strategic Intent View. The strategic intent view of enterprise transformation results in several critical imperatives:

☐ Is the strategic intent focused on the right issues?

☐ Does it address the discontinuities and changes in expectations of customers and other stakeholders?

☐ Is it consistent with the actions and improvement programs being undertaken in the enterprise?

☐ Is it being used to determine the new competencies required in the enterprise?

☐ Is it understood by the people who work there?

☐ Does it guide day-to-day actions?

The Competencies View. The competency facet of enterprise transformation can similarly be linked to the integrated strategic transformation model:

- Are new competencies explicitly identified as necessary to achieve transformation?

- Are competencies consistently linked to strategic responses?

- Are the competencies supported by state-of-the-art capabilities and processes?

- Are distinctive competencies being renewed and strengthened?

- Are noncore competencies being reviewed for outsourcing?

- Are competencies that are no longer in line with marketplace dictates being unlearned?

The Processes View. The most critical issue surrounding transformation of processes is selection. One must focus reengineering efforts on the right processes:

- Are the processes that are being reengineered and benchmarked explicitly tied to necessary competencies?

- Do we have explicit measures of efficiency and effectiveness for them?

- Is attention primarily on practices—and the learning of new practices by process owners—or is it more on metrics, or experts "telling" process owners what needs to be changed?

- Are the enterprise's most critical processes as good as any in the world?

The Resources View. Resources are the underlying support of the entire enterprise transformation effort:

- Are the key resources—particularly people—deployed in ways that match the key strategic responses deemed as necessary?

- Are information resources used too much to support largely obsolete processes or competencies that are no longer distinctive or core?

□ Are the linkages from desired competencies to capabilities to processes to resources clear?

□ How are resource requirements being determined—are they linked to strategic responses?

□ Is downsizing being evaluated in terms of its impact on fulfilling strategic response mandates?

The Outputs View. The outputs view of enterprise transformation focuses on the necessary changes in the bundle of goods and services that needs to be provided to customers to exceed their expectations:

□ Have changes in customer expectations been examined explicitly?

□ Has this examination been done for the different types of customers such as immediate and end-user?

□ Have changes in customer expectations been expressed in outputs?

□ Have the expectations of other stakeholders been critically evaluated and factored into the necessary bundle of goods and services that must be provided?

□ Are customer expectations being exceeded?

□ Does the firm know how its customers evaluate it relative to others in the industry?

The Strategic Response View. The strategic response of enterprise transformation focuses on the specific set of "action programs":

□ Do the action programs match the stated strategic responses?

□ What current action programs are being undertaken that are not dictated by the strategic responses?

□ Are there actions mandated by the stated strategic responses that realistically are not going to happen?

□ How consistent are the actions with the enterprise's stated mission?

□ How consistent are the actions with the strategic intent and the set of challenges that the enterprise faces?

The Challenges View. In the last analysis, if the enterprise transformation does not adequately deal with the real challenges faced by the company, all will be for naught:

☐ To what extent does the statement of discontinuities reflect the true challenges facing the enterprise?

☐ How well are the changes in expectations of customers captured—all of them?

☐ Are the problems and expectations of other stakeholders articulated adequately?

☐ Are the strategic responses really going to take care of the discontinuities and changes in expectations?

☐ Are the strategic responses feasible and desirable?

The Learning Capacity View. The learning capacity facet of enterprise transformation explicitly recognizes the need for both implementation and evolution:

☐ What is required to implement the transformation? Are there the necessary resources, and can they be marshaled to achieve the required changes?

☐ What are the distinctive competencies and their underlying capabilities—and what ongoing improvements need to be achieved to keep them distinctive?

☐ What are the changes in skills, attitudes, and behaviors needed to support the transformation?

☐ Are the measurements of learning consistent with desired corporate performance and *its* measures?

A Complementary View of Enterprise Transformation

When the Manufacturing 2000 project first started looking at enterprise transformation (the research project was then called "restructuring"), a model for transformation was developed based on three dimensions of change and the redeployment of three critical resources. This model provides a useful cross check for the strategic intent transformation model.

The Three Cs Prism

Any transformation encompasses three distinct (but related) dimensions, which can be depicted as a three-sided prism or pyramid (see Figure 3.2).

- □ *Culture* includes the broadest, most enduring (and most difficult to change) aspects of business. Included are the values, beliefs, and strategy, and "the way we do things around here." Current culture directs and constrains transformation efforts.

- □ *Configuration* relates to both organizational designs and relationships, and to physical or geographical distributions of people, capital, and equipment. Changes in subunit missions, plant charters, and organizational forms all represent potential configuration changes.

- □ *Coordination* refers to management and control within the business system itself. Transformation normally requires new flows of information, cash, and materials, as well as new sets of managerial responsibilities.

Some transformations are focused primarily on culture, while others are on configuration or coordination. They are all related, but it is funda-

---

Figure 3.2
The Three Cs Prism

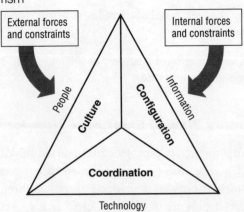

Technology

mentally easier to change coordination (e.g., put in an improved factory scheduling system) than configuration (e.g., reduce the number of factories and change their charters) or culture (e.g., the ways we do things around here).

The foundation for enterprise transformation rests on three fundamental resources: people, technology, and information. These three resources form the base of the pyramid in Figure 3.2. The model lets us define enterprise transformation as:

A proactive response to the competitive environment by significantly changing any one or more of the three dimensions of a company (culture, configuration, coordination), through deployment or redeployment of its resources (people, technology, information).

The Cross Check

The Three Cs (people, information, technology—PIT) pyramid model is a complementary way of viewing enterprise transformation. It is most useful as a reality check to the eight-facet approach of the integrated strategic transformation model. For each facet, the underlying question concerns the changes in culture, configuration, and coordination—as well as the necessary redeployment of resources.

- □ The strategic intent: What are the implications of the change in strategic intent for required changes in the culture of the company? How about the organization (configuration)? What new controls will be required—and which existing ones need to be discarded? What are the resource implications?

- □ The competencies: What do the new competency requirements imply for resources? What kind of a culture is necessary to best integrate the new competencies into the organization? Will there be new organizational forms and reporting mechanisms? Do we need to change performance measures?

- □ The processes: What are the resource requirements of the new processes? What will be required to implement them? What do we need to unlearn? Is the change a "paradigm shift"—i.e., a change in mind-set?

- □ The resources: If people are to be redeployed, what is the consequent necessary change in culture? What particular parts of people, information, and technology are no longer appropriate?

□ The outputs: What are the changes in culture required to produce the different set of goods and services? What kinds of configuration—and information systems (coordination)—are necessary to deliver and support the new bundle of goods and services? What resources are essential to exceed customer expectations?

□ The strategic response: Does the set of action programs require a different culture to achieve them? What are the requisite changes in configuration and coordination? What are the resource implications—do we have them?

□ The challenges: What kind of culture changes are required in the enterprise in order to meet the discontinuities and changes in expectations? How do the challenges impact our existing organization structure? Is the enterprise realistically able to meet the challenges?

□ The learning capacity: Does the required learning imply a fundamental shift in culture (as is the case if empowerment is part of the response)? Do fundamental shifts in organization call for different behaviors? What are the implications for learning if new forms of information systems are to be implemented?

The cross check against the strategic intent transformation model is essentially to conceive of an eight-by-six matrix, with the eight facets or views of transformation as rows, and the Three Cs PIT as columns (Table 3.1). In each matrix cell, the issue is the implications of a C or P, I, or T for the particular facet. Summing the rows leads to an understanding of the overall change in each facet. Summing the columns does the same for culture, configuration, coordination, and each of the three resources. The overall benefit is to provide a reality check for the managers who want to implement a true enterprise transformation.

Feasibility and Desirability

The four dictates for enterprise transformation are that it needs to be consistent, integrated, feasible, and desirable. So far our primary emphasis has been more on the first two of these. It is now time to turn briefly to the last two.

The cross check provided by the Three Cs PIT–eight facets matrix is one test of feasibility. When one looks at all the culture change imperatives, is it feasible? Similar questions need to be posed for the implied changes in configuration and coordination. And the resource ramifications are

Table 3.1

The Three Cs PIT Cross Check

	Culture	Configuration	Coordination	People	Information	Technology	Summation
Strategic Intent							
Competencies							
Processes							
Resources							
Outputs							
Strategic Response							
Challenges							
Learning Capacity							
Summation							

equally sobering for most firms. All too often there is a massive list of strategic responses, while at the same time there is downsizing with all its problems. Finally, when one realistically evaluates the here-to-there implications for each of the eight facets or views of enterprise transformation—is it feasible?

There is probably no enterprise in the world that has transformed a company and made optimal decisions on all these dimensions. What is needed is some prioritization, based on a realistic assessment of the transformation job, the resource requirements, and the availability of talent to make it a reality.

Using the Transformation Models

Defining the end state to be achieved by transformation is easier than determining how to achieve such a state quickly. Genuine use of the transformation models means results. If the transformation models are to be more than words, it is imperative that true implementation be the result. Implementation is the "how" of responding to the discontinuities, and the changes in customer expectations. It includes recognizing and dealing with constraints, articulating the desired paradigm shift, and following this up with a consistent, integrated set of actions and changes in competencies, with their underlying capabilities, processes, and resources.

In short, transformation models can provide direction and understanding of the path ahead, but in the last analysis implementation is based on management. People in the company have to face up to the imperatives for transformation implementation. Transformation needs to be seen as feasible, and it also needs to be seen as personally desirable from the point of those who are to implement it.

□ Top-down implementation is typically directed by senior management. The decision to undertake a paradigm shift is its responsibility, and managers need to be held accountable for success or failure. They need to form the overall objectives and approach for the transformation, to articulate the changes needed in strategic intent, to provide the personal leadership required to achieve the desired results and timing, and to remove blocks to implementation and unlearning.

□ Bottom-up implementation is typically required from a large number of people, especially the key managers who will lead the changes in key processes, and integrate processes, capabilities, and resources in ways that achieve the desired distinctive competencies. In general, it is axiomatic that the more people who buy into the new strategic intent, the resulting paradigm shift, and the implementation process, the better. The changes required in transformation are fundamental. In particular, recognizing and making explicit the necessary cultural changes are an essential part of the implementation process.

□ Project teams are key to transformation—which will almost always include changes to the formal and informal organization. Project teams themselves shatter existing organizational forms, and their increasing use is a recognition in an enterprise of the need for continual renewal. Those who lead the teams, as well as those who serve on them, need to see these efforts not as a secondary part of their jobs, but as the way that the enterprise is going to survive.

□ Education and open communication as to the fundamental discontinuities and expectation changes, as well as the responses and paradigm shifts (in clearly understandable language), are essential to create the necessary bandwagon effect. Too often the paradigm shift is stated as some lofty goal like "getting closer to the customer," but the organization sees only work force reductions in the offing. Clarifying "what's in it for me" is key to buy-in and successful implementation. Being clear about downsizing at the outset is critical. If unexpected cuts are made, a company can lose motivation (and capabilities) very quickly.

☐ Evaluation of the transformation efforts is a major challenge. Yet progress must be evaluated and communicated to those going through the transformation. It is often difficult to tell whether the results achieved are truly successful, or mediocre or poor—or if short-term results are being achieved at the expense of long-run health. Moreover, it is necessary constantly to manage the continuing impact of changing forces. It is inevitable that evaluation needs to be measured against a moving target— but the difficulty does not negate the necessity.

Summary

In this chapter we have developed a number of learning points:

☐ The enterprise transformation definition, based on eight views, facets, or dimensions, may be visualized as the strategic intent transformation model. The objective of the model is to provide a method for actually achieving enterprise transformation.

☐ Discontinuities and changes in expectations are the fundamental drivers for enterprise transformation.

☐ Strategic intent is the overall mission statement or set of strategic objectives, not a vague generality not tightly linked to specific actions. The model examines the top-down drive of strategic intent shaping strategic response, as well as the bottom-up summation of the desired responses with the stated strategic intent. The key objectives are consistency and integration.

☐ An enterprise's current competencies shape strategic response, but new competencies and their supporting infrastructure of capabilities, processes, systems, and resources enable the strategic responses.

☐ Making learning an explicit part of the model indicates the changes necessary to implement transformation as well as the ongoing requirements for improvement. Learning objectives and measures must be consistent with corporate objectives.

□ The Three Cs PIT model provides a cross check for the feasibility of a particular enterprise transformation.

□ For enterprise transformation to be a reality, it needs to be consistent, integrated, feasible, and desirable. The model ensures consistency and integration. Feasibility and desirability may be evaluated by looking at the match between the top half of the model and the bottom half. Is the desired infrastructure possible to achieve? What is in it for the people? Feasibility and desirability are also helped by the cross check with Three Cs PIT. In the final analysis, it is managerial leadership that will make the difference, and management needs to provide the atmosphere to support the myriad of individual initiatives required to implement true enterprise transformation.

As we examine the various parts of the model further, our fundamental focus is on using the model. That is, how can we make the model operational and integrate the various facets of the enterprise to achieve true transformation?

□ What are the drivers for transformation—the discontinuities and expectation changes—in actual practice, and how do we explicitly identify and prioritize them?

□ How does one get strategic intent and strategic response to be consistent and integrated, so that the details of enterprise transformation are mutually supportive?

□ How can the general concept of competency be devolved into explicit competency maps, with their attendant resource requirements?

□ How do we *use* the transformation model in actual practice—that is, what is the journey to reach the destination?

4 Enterprise Transformation Drivers

The most complex of the eight enterprise transformation facets concerns the challenges that the company faces. Chapter 3 describes this view as the "discontinuities" both internal and external to the company, as well as the changes in expectations of customers and other stakeholders. Although at first glance it would seem that the drivers for transformation are beyond the company's control, in fact leading-edge companies have considerable influence over these factors. Most important, however, is that any transformation needs to identify the underlying reasons for the necessary changes—particularly what is different for the firm, its industry, its customers, and other stakeholders.

Figure 4.1 is the top half of the model for integrated strategic transformation; it is our primary focus in this chapter. The chapter has two fundamental objectives: providing a better understanding of discontinuities and expectation changes (the drivers for transformation), and describing an explicit process that enterprises use to identify the particular drivers in their particular company situations.

Discontinuities

Discontinuities are the major changes, forces, and constraints that are influencing the future of an enterprise. But more important, discontinuities are the changes in these forces—they encompass not only what is, but also what is likely to occur, and *what might occur if we do the right things*. To look beyond the current set of industry and company conditions, it is necessary to stretch our minds, to focus on what is over the horizon, and to look at the discontinuities facing other enterprises with a focus on: Why not us? What keeps us from facing those kinds of problems? What opportunities do we wish we had?

Figure 4.1

Top Half of Model for Integrated Strategic Transformation

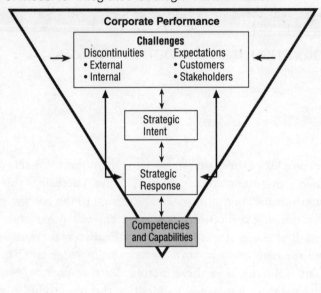

■ At a seminar run for technical managers from a large consumer products company, a senior executive suggested the group look carefully at IBM, Philips, Volkswagen, and any other company facing hard times. Even though conditions in their own company had been reasonably good over a long period, what was keeping them from facing the same hard times? What could they anticipate about competitive conditions? Who might be the real potential competitor?

If discontinuities are not properly understood—and subsequently reflected in the transformation process—there will be a high cost to pay. If your company can deal with them proactively in better ways than your competitors, it can achieve dominance.

Internal Discontinuities

Internal discontinuities are those that are unique to a specific business unit at a particular time. Included in internal discontinuities are things such as a new management team. Clearly, for example, Messrs. Iqnacio Lopez and Ferdinand Pietch represented major internal discontinuities when they took over Volkswagen, as did Robert Palmer at Digital, and Louis Gerstner at IBM. Top managers can make major changes, and it is important to understand the relative priority of those changes in transforming the company. A new management team frequently defines a new strategy (strategic intent) for the organization. It surely defines a new set of strategic responses. Thus the mere presence of a new management team needs to be considered an internal discontinuity—that needs to be integrated with the other discontinuities facing the firm. If the objective is transformation, it is critical that the new set of discontinuities—as perceived by the new team—be communicated throughout the organization in order to achieve consistency and integration. If this does not occur, expect to see yet another "flushing of the pigeons."

Mergers and acquisitions also represent internal discontinuities. The degree to which this is so is far too often not recognized. Their ramifications are important to analyze in terms of the enterprise transformation model. Mixing managers, cultures, processes, practices, and outputs is bound to lead to conflict. Each group is likely to think that its way is right, and the other is wrong. Many mergers that look beautiful on paper, from a financial point of view, just do not seem to come together, perhaps because one group feels that it is taking over the other, and makes that opinion quite obvious. The result is a letting go of the "golden cord." The real mission of the enterprise is guerrilla warfare, the core competencies become backbiting and deal making, and the processes are counterproductive.

■ A recent merger of two European service companies (direct competitors) made great sense on paper. Each was relatively small, and the combination provided a critical mass. But each firm employed highly talented entrepreneurs who believed that their company's approach to the marketplace was greatly superior to that of the other. In fact, as direct competitors, they were always finding ways to differentiate themselves from each other ("our outputs are greatly superior"). With the merger, all these independent managers were to become instant colleagues. But company outputs, processes, and practices were more different than anyone realized, and each group wanted to preserve its own—because they clearly believed them to be superior. The agenda focused on discrediting the opposing set of outputs, processes, and practices, and the organization was totally confused as to where it was going. After several years and three changes of management, things are beginning to settle down—but at a huge real cost to the organization.

Another typical internal discontinuity is a new venture, product line, or business activity. These all need to be recognized as potentially critical discontinuities. Many times the energy required to launch a new venture successfully is seriously underestimated, or the activity's impact on existing business is not properly understood. That new competencies are required is easily overlooked—or the assumption is that existing competencies will work, when this is just not so. Similar mismatches can occur in capabilities and processes.

■ A U.S. chemical company wanted to differentiate its products from commodities by moving into the "solutions" business. It had engineering talent it could apply to applications, and it saw several significant problems its customers faced for which it could provide help. But this new approach needed to be explicitly considered as an internal discontinuity. Responding to this challenge required factoring it into the strategic intent—as well as the strategic responses, necessary new competencies, and supporting infrastructure. It became clear, for example, that a change in measurements was required because the old metrics focused on tonnage, where this was now inappropriate. The sales organization also needed to be overhauled, new information systems for supporting customer partnerships were required, and new organizational configurations were necessary to direct customer-oriented teams instead of existing functions to specific customer problems.

The adoption of new technology can also be an internal discontinuity. General Motors and many other manufacturing companies originally seriously underestimated what was required to implement flexible machining systems (FMS) and other kinds of advanced technology. In many cases, the internal capital appropriation focused mainly on the purchase price of the equipment rather than on the other infrastructure requirements to integrate the new technology into the ongoing operations of the company.

Another internal discontinuity we have observed is potential erosion of a core competence. Nestlé early established a competitive advantage in terms of its ability to dry milk and to make other basic food products.

Now that the basic technology is fairly well understood, maintaining product leadership requires ongoing development of new extraction processes and other technical competencies. Coming to the end of patent protection represents another erosion of core competency. At one time, GKN Automotive had patent protection that essentially covered front-wheel drive. But those patents have run out, and the company has had to find new ways to compete in the automotive parts industry.

A far too prevalent internal discontinuity is downsizing. Hardly a day goes by that we do not read in the financial press that still another large company is swinging the downsizing ax.

A final example of an internal discontinuity is financial problems. The set of alternatives open to many companies today is fundamentally more restrictive than it was several years ago.

External Discontinuities

External discontinuities are the major changes, forces, and constraints—and particularly the changes in these—facing all the players in an industry. Included are overcapacity in the chemical industry, Russian "dumping" for companies in the aluminum business, growing power of major retail chains in consumer products companies, price wars in the airline industry, environmental mandates facing companies in the packaging business, and patterns of globalization that play out differently by industry, or even by customer in the same industry. Automotive parts suppliers need to contend with very different patterns of globalization for Nissan and for Fiat.

A focus on external "discontinuities" requires anticipating the changes in these factors—and their implications (i.e., the necessary strategic responses). In the global chemical industry, for example, overcapacity varies from product to product. Most firms have been moving into specialty chemicals and can be expected to continue. Prices and raw material supplies are also subject to change. The question of the hour is how this will all play out—and what are the resultant discontinuities? Shell generates "scenarios" of possible situations so that surprises can be minimized and opportunities seized faster than competitors.

Russian dumping of aluminum is a problem for all firms in the industry, and there is currently an industrywide attempt to cut capacity (this is also the case for some chemicals). But Norsk Hydro believes that its long-run survival in the aluminum business has to depend upon being the lowest-cost producer. The result is that at some times it will make more money than at other times, but it will always be better off than the other players.

Similar sets of issues arise for all external discontinuities. There are two fundamental issues for an enterprise: what are the discontinuities, and what are we going to do about them? Consumer products companies try to find ways to add more value for trade customers and final customers. In the face of increased competition in the airline industry, Swissair has made a major commitment to upgrade its fleet. In the face of increasing environmental pressures, packaging companies are forming joint ventures with recycling firms. An automotive components firm has committed to locating plants where its automotive customers choose to locate.

All these strategic responses need to match the discontinuities. There also needs to be an internal consistency with the strategic intent, and the set of responses has to be carried through to determine the new required competencies—the underlying capabilities and processes, and the necessary learning. In short, we must not lose sight of the golden cord as we respond to discontinuities.

Key Questions

The final set of ideas we need to consider in the area of discontinuities is how not to overlook what might be the most important discontinuities. This is a tall order, but worth trying nonetheless. We can pose some questions to challenge your thinking. How do these trends play out at your company? Are there resulting discontinuities that need to be considered important in your situation?

□ Marketing/manufacturing convergence, as well as other kinds of functional boundary reduction: Do you see a trend for functional boundaries to be reduced—and do you perceive a need for your firm to work in fundamentally different ways? If so, have you made these discontinuities explicit?

□ Different work patterns, such as flatter organizations, use of temporary employees, empowered workers, or the "virtual organization": Are these also trends that need to be on your radar screen?

□ Customer partnering, either as an industry trend, or as a specific issue in the enterprise: Do any of these apply to the future of your company?

□ Environmental pressures faced now or that can be expected to play a role in the future: Have you explicitly considered various environmental scenarios, and what they might mean for your firm?

□ Time to market, either in terms of the number of new products, or shorter product life cycles: What is happening here, and what are the detailed discontinuities that might impact your company?

□ Flexibility—as opposed to traditional approaches to productivity—in terms of customer responsiveness, deliveries, product mix, response times, and people capabilities: How do these issues play out in your company?

□ Totally new patterns of worker development and deployment: What are the expectations as to the kinds of people required in your organization, succession planning, and what one of my colleagues calls "psychological contracting"?

□ Information systems and information management: The rate of change in information management is one of the most dramatic engines for change in the world. How is your company comprehending the significance of this change and its implications for your company?

Changes in Expectations

Changes in expectations likely underlie our interest in transformation. We need to respond to what is changing, or what could be changed. The enterprise is probably already dealing with what has not changed (if this is not the case, the result would be an internal discontinuity). At least three constituencies must be considered immediate customers, customer end-users, and other stakeholders.

Immediate Customers

Immediate customers are those we sell our products to directly, who in turn sell to others or to the end-user consumers. The immediate customer for an automotive parts company such as GKN Automotive is the automobile assembler, say, Volkswagen. For Volkswagen itself, the immediate customer is the automobile dealer. For consumer products companies such as Nestlé, Johnson & Johnson, and Unilever, it is the retail trade customers, which increasingly are hypermarkets in many countries (but not in all). For consumer electronics companies such as Sony, the immediate customers are the retailers, including the large discount chains. For Nokia Mobile Phones, the immediate customer has traditionally been specialty stores, although this is changing as mobile telephone technology allows the product to be sold as a consumer electronics product. For consumer packaging companies such as CarnaudMetalbox, the customers are consumer products companies such as Heineken. For chemical companies such as Du Pont, Exxon, and British Petroleum, the immediate customers are industrial manufacturing companies. And for pharmaceuticals, the doctors are the immediate customer even though they do not "sell" the drugs to patients.

Our examination of the changes in expectations of the immediate customers needs to begin by asking what the problems of our customers are. What keeps them awake at night? What are they trying to do to improve profits or to achieve some other objectives? What are *their* transformation programs? What kinds of improvement programs are working in their industry? Who is at the cutting edge, and what are they doing? What are the different practices around the world, and what might we expect to be adopted by our customers? What could we do that would exceed their expectations? How can we help them better compete?

□ Changes in expectations for automobile assemblers include a need to reduce costs more rapidly, increasing competition in what have been somewhat protected markets, pressures for more frequent model changes, wage structures that are out of balance with worldwide levels, a need for fewer workers per automobile because of automation, and probably fewer automotive companies through mergers and acquisitions.

□ Changes in expectations for the hypermarkets include new forms of competition from the warehouse-type operators, maximization of each part of the store (contribution per cubic meter), better use of information resources (detailed sales knowledge of individual items in individual markets), increasing sales of house brands, joint product promotion with producers, and reduced distribution costs through multivendor partnerships.

□ Changes in expectations for doctors include a growing need to be informed about new treatment possibilities, (conflicting) pressure not to spend too much time with supplier salespeople, increasing worry about malpractice insurance costs in many parts of the world, the ramifications of new forms of medical insurance, and increases in the fixed costs of running a practice.

For insight into their own problems, companies are advised to ask what might be the analogue in another context. For example, the problems that consumer products companies face in dealing with their immediate customers are not unlike those that Nokia faces as mobile telephones are sold in discount stores. Observing the way concentration plays out in the automotive industry should be instructive to consumer products companies—and vice versa. Helping doctors gain skills, rather than trying to push products on them, might be achieved by observing customer partnership relationships in other industries.

Customer End-Users

End-users are the final consumers of a product. Sometimes there can be a difference between the person who buys the product and the one who uses it. The difference between the person buying pet food and the pet is one clear example (cats do not spend money, but owners know they can be very fussy). There are other products that are traditionally given as gifts, such as watches. This means that Omega needs to think about the changes in expectations for both parties. The gift should be perceived as special; the giver should be proud to give an Omega watch; the recipient should be delighted to receive it; and the watch needs to be technically excellent as well. Moreover, all the attendant expectations as to after-sales servicing of the watch need to be considered as well.

Both GKN and Volkswagen need to think about the changes in expectations of automobile drivers. Expectations of higher quality are clearly the case today. Automobile owners expect longer life, reduced noise, fewer problems, easier servicing, and that someone will take the car back when it is worn out. These expectations are what any average consumer would think of. For the top management team at Volkswagen, the analysis should be in much greater depth and probably differ by product line and type of user.

Similarly, Nestlé and other consumer products companies need to think about the changes in expectations of all the people who buy and consume their products. There are interesting demographic factors influencing these changes, such as greater numbers of old people, more people living alone, single parents, two-worker families, and the growing disposable income of teenagers. There are also changes in life-style, such as interest in microwave cooking for its speed, lower-calorie and other healthy foods, a growing interest in international cuisine, and shifts from canned or frozen foods to fresh. For the shoppers themselves, there is always some interest in making the shopping trip more enjoyable and easier. So companies selling detergent have been trying to put the same amount of product in smaller, lighter boxes, and there is increasing talk of home deliveries for some types of products.

For Sony and other television viewers, there are the expectations of television viewers and how they can be met or exceeded. In fact, "better" functioning television receivers present a problem for some customers. My eighty-two-year-old father-in-law just bought a Sony television and had to call the repair service two times, because he had pushed the wrong buttons on the remote control and could not get the set to work correctly after that. The repairman finally gave him a simpler remote control.

The end-users for CarnaudMetalbox's packages and cans are the same as those of Nestlé and Heineken. Beer drinkers may well have package preferences. One clear change in expectations for end-consumers in regard to packages is their interest in recycling and the meeting of other environmental concerns. In a similar vein, companies such as Du Pont need to think about changes in expectations of cooks who use Teflon-coated pans, and Johnson & Johnson constantly monitors information from customers through toll-free telephone lines and other means to do a better job of trying to understand end-user expectations and how the company might be able to better serve them.

One of my colleagues is studying an interesting issue related to changes in customer expectations with respect to quality. He notes that quality, in essence, is a surrogate for customer satisfaction. Customers are unhappy when the products they buy do not work properly. But now almost all products work reasonably well. Once, when Sony made televisions with one defect per one hundred sets, and the competitors made them with seventy-five defects per hundred sets, Sony had a definite advantage. But now if Sony makes televisions with one defect per one thousand sets, and the competitors have ten defects per thousand, almost no one notices that Sony is ten times better. This means that the game needs to shift to find new surrogates for customer satisfaction; quality has become a given, the ante to play in the game, but other things, such as new product features (or indeed simplicity) are required to win.

■ In the 1970s Texas Instruments was the preeminent player in the electronic calculator market. It believed in the Boston Consulting Group's famous "learning curve" model, which prices on the basis of volume that is achieved by continuous learning. This worked well, and when I bought my first four-function calculator for $125 in 1972, I was delighted with it. Two years later, I bought one with square roots and trigonometric functions for $65. When Texas Instruments cut the price again to $30, I was still happy, but when it was cut to $15 I really didn't care. Along came Casio, which offered solar-powered calculators and ones that play tunes as you use them.

Other Stakeholders

The expectations of other stakeholders also need to be understood and included if they might significantly influence enterprise transformation. If our employees are better educated and would be happier in an environment based less on command and control, this may need to be reflected in the detailed design of our transformation efforts. Unfortunately, in far too many companies the real operational set of assumptions about our employees is that they are idiots and thieves. If the labor union is more interested in job security than in other issues, this too might influence design of the transformation. Governmental organizations are constantly asking for information, and they expect compliance with all sorts of regulations. For many firms, anticipating these requirements—and in fact influencing them—may well provide a tougher competitive barrier to entry for others. Stockholders expect high and predictable rates of return, environmental pressure groups have expectations that will have to be considered, and local residents increasingly are concerned with any impacts our company operations might have on the environment, as well as on the local economy.

"Meeting" these expectations is the wrong approach. The dominant company sees these changes in stakeholder expectations not as an obligation, but as an opportunity. If your company can exceed these expectations, it can set the rules of the game. Better treatment of employees allows you to recruit and retain the best. Helping government organizations set the rules can result in rules that are easy for you to meet but tough for the competitors. Working with environmental pressure groups can be even more proactive: They have influence, they have facts (which often may be better than yours), and they are dedicated. Environmental groups can make great allies—and formidable enemies.

Key Questions

We can again pose a set of questions so as not to overlook what is really important in terms of expectations. How do these issues play out at your company? Are there other expectation changes that need to be included?

☐ Are our customers now interested in total system performance—as opposed to only performance in product features? That is, is the concern more than our piece of their life, and rather the overall performance where we might play a larger integrative role?

☐ Do our products and services have to fit better with those of other vendors? Is there now an expectation that ours will work well under a broader range of circumstances?

☐ Are our customers interested in "vendor partnerships" (or should they be?) as opposed to traditional buyer–seller relationships?

☐ What is the difference between "creating value with" our customers, as opposed to "creating products for" our customers?

☐ Is our technical expertise becoming a larger part of the bundle of goods and services that our customers expect?

☐ Do our customers expect us to help them serve their customers?

Identifying the Drivers

At the end of the day, it is all well and good to say we need to determine the discontinuities and changes in expectations in one world, but precisely how are we to do this? It is essential for the top management team in any business unit to identify explicitly the key drivers for transformation in their business. This is critical not just because the firm needs to have the drivers clearly perceived, but also because the top managers need to *go through the process* of driver identification. The journey is as important as the destination.

Brainstorming (with Post-it Notes)

The process we have developed for explicating the drivers is to convene a brainstorming session of the top management team, most usually for a business unit, but we have done it with an entire company. We devote about three hours of the session to drivers. Participants are each asked to write ideas on Post-it Notes, one idea per slip, each idea expressed as a sentence rather than a word or two, so that it is easier to understand.

The session begins with writing Post-it Notes for internal discontinuities, responding to the question: What are the major changes or forces for change and discontinuities that are unique to our company at this time?

Everyone sticks their notes on a flip chart as they are written, so that others can see them. The thoughts are written with dark pens so they are easily read from around the room. This continues until the group runs out of ideas. The process encourages everyone to contribute, in an informal environment.

When no one can think of any further ideas, a facilitator gathers all the Post-it Notes together. Each is then moved, one at a time, onto the middle of a flip chart and read. The facilitator then asks whether everyone understands the idea. The objective here is not to evaluate the importance of the idea, but only to ensure that its meaning is understood by all. The person who contributed the idea may be asked to explain its meaning, and the note is revised or rewritten as needed.[1]

After the meaning of each idea has been verified, the note is moved to the other side of the flip chart; this process is continued until all ideas have been read and their meanings clarified. At that point, each team member is asked if he or she can think of any things that are missing (requiring perhaps more notes).

Affinity Grouping and Titles

As the notes are moved from one side to the other of the flip chart, they should not be put in categories. This needs to be a separate step, although there is always someone who wants to do both steps at once. Resist the temptation! With all the ideas evaluated, the next step is accomplished by the entire team moving the notes into what they perceive as "affinity groupings"—this typically requires several arrangements. The number of notes in any one group should generally not be more than four or five.

The next step is to prepare titles for each grouping that summarize the meaning of the group of notes. The titles should be written on new Post-it Notes, in a different color so that the difference between individual ideas and titles is clear. Actually, the titles are quite important, and they often need to be revised several times. A good way to proceed is to divide the groups up among the team members, asking each person to propose a first title for a particular grouping. After the titles are put on each group, they need to be discussed to see if everyone agrees that each title expresses the essence of the note grouping.

The next step requires each team member to vote on the relative importance of the various groups. A simple method is for each team member to have three points, two points, and one point, which can be assigned to whichever three groupings he or she decides. The choices should be made silently, with all deciding before the choices are written by each team member next to the particular groupings. Thereafter the points are tallied, producing a rough Pareto analysis (the 80/20 law) of the relative importance of the various internal discontinuity categories.[2] A typical result at this stage is five to fifteen groupings, with one or two clearly seen as much more important than the others.

When the Pareto analysis has been completed, the final step is to compose a sentence for the entire flip chart, which summarizes the overall set of internal discontinuities that the enterprise faces and indicates the relative importance of particular groupings. An example might be something like:

□ The most critical internal discontinuities facing our company are associated with integration of the Ajax acquisition into our overall operations, and how to get the complete management group to function as a true team.

The concluding sentence is written at the bottom of the flip chart, and the final chart is taped on the wall for future reference.

External Discontinuities and Customer/Stakeholder Expectations

The process described to identify internal discontinuities is now repeated for external discontinuities. These are the major changes, forces, and constraints impacting all the players in the industry. The Post-it Note process is repeated, using a new sheet of flip chart paper. The result is another set of idea groups, the Pareto analysis, and a concluding message.

The process is then followed for changes in customer expectations, in two passes on two separate flip charts, corresponding to two different classes of customers. The usual division is for immediate customers and final customers. That is, a consumer products company has trade as well as final consumers, and pharmaceutical firms have doctors as immediate customers and patients as final customers.

The objective of identifying changes in customer expectations is to focus clearly on the needs of customers in determining how to achieve enterprise transformation. It is critical to anticipate the needs of the customers, with the objective not only of meeting expectations, but also in fact exceeding them. Many successful transformations are based on a very proactive approach to helping customers solve their problems—even if the customers are not fully aware of them.

Finally, the Post-it Note process is applied to other stakeholders such as employees, unions, stockholders, and pressure groups. The overall result is five flip charts, each with key messages, backed up by typically twenty to thirty prioritized groupings of notes. An equally important result is that the top management team has reached some consensus on the key challenges facing the enterprise—taking into account the myriad issues that occur to different people but that have never been made explicit. This is why the journey is at least as important as the destination.

An Environmental Example

The strategic intent transformation model can be applied to an entire company, or, better still, to individual business units. But it also can be applied to some kinds of individual issues. For example, a major thrust of IMD's Managing the Industrial and Business Environment (MIBE) project is to investigate how environmental issues can be pursued for competitive advantage—and the requirements in a company to achieve this advantage. The enterprise transformation model has been adapted for this objective. The brainstorming team is no longer concerned with all discontinuities and changes in expectations, but focuses now only on the *environmental* internal and external discontinuities, two levels of customer expectation changes in regard to the environment, and the environmental expectation changes of other stakeholders.[3]

We demonstrate the process of applying the model at one of the MIBE firms. This example shows how the model works on this single environmental use. In chapters 5 and 6 we show the linkages of discontinuities/ expectations to strategic response and strategic intent and to core competencies.

The company is a machinery manufacturer, which as a part of its operations sells equipment to improve the environment. The company has an excellent reputation both for the quality of its equipment and for its corporate values. Its corporate mission statement clearly states its environmental goals and policies. Environmental reporting is an accepted part of the annual report. The business unit in our example designs, manufactures, and sells industrial equipment that reduces pollution.

The company believes both (1) that environmental friendliness is a basic requirement it is willing to meet, and (2) that environmental friendliness should be good business. It actively pursues an environmental agenda and wanted to use our model to diagnose its operations: Does the company need a transformation of its environmental efforts and programs?

Internal Discontinuities

Table 4.1 shows groupings of the company's internal discontinuities that came out of the Post-it Note process. There are three groupings of the twelve ideas produced. "Constraints" received the most votes as the most important group of internal discontinuities. The overall summary of the

---

Table 4.1

Internal Discontinuities

"Organizational and financial constraints limit our ability to meet environmental mandates."

Awareness (13)	Constraints (24)	Stimuli (11)
▪ Environment is an integral part of TQM ▪ Visible commitment to environment signed by all senior executives ▪ Educational campaign to raise commitment of corporate staff to the environment ▪ Written corporate commitment to lead to sustainable development	▪ Culture/organizational constraints inhibit sales of totally integrated solutions ▪ We are asked to deliver on the environmental mandate without additional funding to do it (generate the funds yourself but not at the expense of the bottom line) ▪ Conflict between short-term financial results and long-term environmental solutions ▪ Sometimes our internal high quality standards in plant designing do not allow company to compete in local markets	▪ "Innovation award" for realized environmental projects ▪ Corporate stimulus for increased debate about the environment within the business; "pro-activity" ▪ Midrange planning must include environmental dimensions ▪ Company views the environment as a good business opportunity

internal discontinuities is that: "Organizational and financial constraints limit our ability to meet environmental mandates."

External Discontinuities

The external discontinuities are obtained in the same way. Table 4.2 provides the groupings. Of the four groupings "rules and regulations" are perceived as the most important. The overall summary message for the external discontinuities is: "Our external pressures stem from existing and changing rules and regulations."

Customer Expectations

The business unit considers industrial and municipal units its immediate and end-customers for pollution equipment. Table 4.3 is the result of the exercise for changing customer expectations. There are four groupings of ideas, with cost/performance pressures and meeting today's needs the most important. Meeting tomorrow's needs is close behind. The overall summary message for customer expectations is: "Cost-effective solutions, with tactical support, that meet and exceed today's requirements."

Many of today's customers are less interested in meeting tomorrow's requirements than one might think. Only the "concerned" customers hold this view. One group of customers wishes only to meet today's standards at the lowest cost, with no more pollution reduction than mandated by existing environmental regulations. Its reasoning is that once certain equipment is certified as meeting requirements, in most cases the requirements are not tightened for such a unit until the equipment has served its useful life. Another group of this firm's customers holds quite the opposite opinion. These customers want to anticipate regulations—and in fact perhaps hold themselves to higher standards that will make life difficult for their competitors in the future. They are also interested in equipment that is designed to permit subsequent upgrades. The primary difference between these two groups of customers appears to be that one sees the environment as a constraint—while the other sees it as an opportunity.

Other Stakeholders

Table 4.4 provides the result for the changes in expectations of other stakeholders. There are quite a lot of them when one deals with environ-

Table 4.2

External Discontinuities

"Our external pressures stem from existing and changing rules and regulations."

Rules and Regulations (24)	Costs (13)
■ Global and regional harmonization of rules	■ Trade-off between growth and environmental costs for countries in development
■ Nonuniform implementation/application of environmental mandates	
■ Environmental concern has shifted from water to air to soil (residues)	■ Shift from "cost thinking" toward "investment thinking"
■ "Watchdog" capabilities are improving— Increased growth of environmental Intelligence	■ Additional engineering costs for construction approval documentation
■ Growth in environmental liability of companies and managers	■ Fear of new technology coming along that will make a current investment obsolete
■ Regulatory approval processes are more difficult	■ The poor are getting poorer and cannot afford environmental protection
■ Shift from "end of pipe" to "in-process" treatment	■ Customers want help with financial issues
	■ Economic pressures cause "backing off" from environmental standards
	■ "Green solutions" are perceived to be more expensive

Environmental Reporting and Standards (6)	Change in Market Structure (3)
■ Pressure from media (FORTUNE) to be among the best "eco" performers	■ More information at every stage of projects to be given to customer/authorities
■ Growth of "green" funds following corporations with good environmental performance	■ Globalization and regionalization of customers
■ Environmental performance is an important criterion for lending institutions and investors	■ Gaps between what people say and what they do
■ National environmental management standards starting to "pick-up"; customers will expect companies to comply with them	■ In certain sectors, peer pressure is driving environmental initiatives/expectation of performance (e.g., VW and the recyclable car)
■ Increasing pressure for more detailed environmental reporting	■ "Responsible care" program of chemical industry (worldwide)
■ Increasing pressure to have an operating strategy document on the environment	■ Environmental pace-setters (e.g., Germany, California)
	■ Environmental change is constant

Table 4.3

Customer Expectations

"Cost-effective solutions, with tactical support, that meet and exceed today's requirements."

Cost/Perfomance Pressures (15)	Meeting Today's Needs (15)
■ They need to meet green legislation at lowest cost	■ Plants have to have a high degree of safety in normal operation *and* in emergency situations
■ Lower price levels	
■ Expect lower emissions at lower costs	
■ There is no perceived difference between environment and other business; they buy what they can afford	■ Better references, i.e., proven plant experience
■ Plants have to meet or exceed today's regulations at lowest possible price	■ A lot of customers do not want to be *pushed* toward lower limits of pollution
■ Performance of waste treatment according to new emission regulation but:	**Pressure Groups (7)**
—for the lowest price	■ Raise green profile to public and customers
—no more than required	
■ Customers, shareholders expect that "environmental problems" will not slow down their "development" rate	■ Help in eliminating opposition—technical and political support

Meeting Tomorrow's Needs (11)	
■ The need to be able to meet stiffer future requirements	■ Help to deal with activists
■ Applied processes should not create new problems in other areas (or future)	■ Attract "green" investment
	■ Ability to demonstrate benefits from extra performance
■ *Concerned* customers are thinking *now* about the higher environmental requirements that will exist in the *future*	
■ Desire for modular design that enables upgrades	
■ Some pioneer customers are willing to have lower pollution limits (investment of more money)	
■ Industrial customers expect more flexible plants, i.e., wider feed parameters, more versatile	
■ Consideration of *all* waste streams and anticipating future pollutants	
■ Customers want turnkey design, construction, and operation of plant	

mental issues. The table shows eight groups of ideas, with technical design excellence, costs versus user benefits, and reliable and high performance operations as the most important. The overall summary message for changes in the expectations of these other stakeholders is: "Solutions that are technically excellent, cost-effective, and reliable."

Table 4.4

Other Stakeholder Expectations

"Solutions that are technically excellent, cost-effective, and reliable."

Technical Design Excellence (14)

- Plant operators want protection against legal threats
- Proven solutions for operators (no R&D on-site with risks)
- Plant operators wish to have a showpiece "of latest" technology
- Consultants are:
  —looking for innovations
  —politically concerned
- Greens are interested in getting technical support/designs to meet their demands

Costs versus User Benefits (14)

- Taxpayers want assurance that their money is invested properly
- Plant operators expect minimum operating costs
- Community does not want to pay for it
- Consultants expect to play a major role in "business" definition

Reliable and High Performance Operations (10)

- Health and safety of future generations
- Greens and communities expect higher degree of residue recycling
- Clean and safe community
- Green guarantees for consumers
- Community demands highest level of safety
- Health and safety for employees

Company 5's Cost/Benefit (6)

- Shareholders: extra money, the "green" payback
- Safe investment, less risky projects, leading to assured profits for shareholders

Environmental Systems/Solutions (3)

- Plant operators want protection against "green" threats
- Solutions that do not create more problems for operators, i.e., landfills, special long-term storage
- Politicians expect integrated solutions for waste problems of a region
- Municipalities and politicians expect high credibility of our company (new technology implies high risk)

Expectations of Greens and Communities (3)

- Measurable improvement in lower emissions
- Creation of processes for full recycling of waste without emissions and residues
- Solutions other than incineration of waste
- Incineration plants with practically "zero" emissions
- "Zero"-level emissions
- Everything to be recycled—without waste to be landfilled

Green Aura (2)

- Employees like to work in a "clean" company—green pride
- Politicians supporting us want fundamental improvements, motivated by the green vote
- Green image and reputation for consultants
- Increasing employee awareness on green issues

Third Parties in Decision Making (2)

- Consultants expect us to do their work without paying us for this service
- Consultants do not want us to be their only alternative for a given project
- Consultants look for a reliable company, selling reliable technology

Additional Views of Transformation Drivers

The key objective in using the Post-it Note approach to identify and organize the underlying transformation drivers is to find out what is really important in the world the company operates in, so that these drivers become an integral part of the overall transformation process. But the exercise is not the only method for coming to grip with this set of issues.

The Customer Activity Cycle

Sandra Vandermerwe has developed an approach she calls the "customer activity cycle" (CAC) model, which helps firms better understand their customers' true problems so that they can respond with an improved bundle of goods and services.[4] The key point in the CAC model is a focus on how the customers use the products and services provided—and how a company can help in all phases of the CAC. The phases include activities associated with prepurchase, when the customer is trying to decide what needs to be done; the purchase phase, which encompasses the actual buying, but also delivery, installation, and gearing up for use; and finally, the postpurchase phase, which includes after-sales service and everything to ensure that the decision to buy was a good one.

Figure 4.2 illustrates the CAC in one of Vandermerwe's examples. In this case, SKF, the Swedish ball bearing manufacturer became convinced that it served four distinct market segments, automotive and nonautomotive, and OEM and the after market, although all its operations were based as if it served only the OEM automotive market. This necessitated an "enterprise" focused on long runs, cost reduction, large unit sales, and so on.

The CAC shown in Figure 4.2 clearly shows that SKF customers were being helped with only a small part of their needs. To change its strategic intent to trouble-free operations means that SKF needed to transform the company into one that provides this service. Implied are massive changes in the bundle of goods and services offered to satisfy all the needs identified in Figure 4.2.

As one example in the automotive after market, instead of selling bearings, the company now provides kits to do certain jobs like replacing a clutch on a 1987 Saab. The kit would include the bearing, the new clutch plate, springs, washers, gaskets, grease,—everything needed to do

Figure 4.2

The Customer Activity Cycle for SKF Bearings

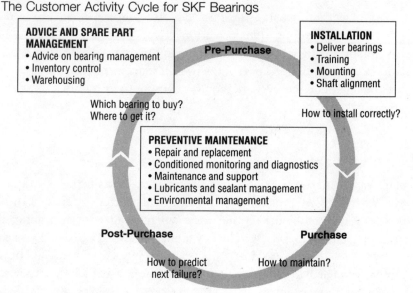

Source: Sandra Vandermerwe, *From Tin Soldiers to Russian Dolls* (Oxford: Butterworth-Heinemann, 1993), 67. Reprinted with permission.

the job—as well as special tools if they would help the user to do a better job and detailed instructions in various languages. Providing this expanded bundle of goods and services entails major changes in inventory control procedures, purchasing, partnerships with the customers, exchange of information to provide visibility into the customer inventories, and much more.

Vandermerwe provides many examples of application of CAC to business problems. They tend to seem somewhat obvious after the fact, but in each case, application provided a breakthrough in thinking. Take CAC application at Volvo Trucks. In this case, the model indicated that the key to understanding customer needs was thinking about minimizing the cost per kilometer, rather than the cost per truck. This meant that Volvo could indeed charge more for its trucks if they broke down less, and if it organized its service facilities so that trucks could be serviced at night when they would not be on the road making money.

A final example of the CAC application is at Nestlé, where the key institutional customers such as hotels care less about the cost of the coffee than they do about how to serve hundreds of cups of fresh coffee, all within a short period at breakfast time. The result has been cooperative efforts with suppliers of kitchen equipment to design equipment for use with Nestlé products and packaging to produce results that truly deal with the problems its customers face in using the products and services and their aim to serve their customers better.

Making Discontinuities and Expectation Changes

The ultimate goal with respect to discontinuities and expectation changes is not to react to them, but to cause them. That is, some firms so exceed customer expectations that they set the standard for the industry. Lexus is a good example.

In the last analysis, making discontinuities is changing the structure of the industry—to one's own advantage. It is about recognizing the inherent challenges in the particular industrial setting—and taking actions to alter the industry fundamentally. When Tyson Chicken said that it wanted to grow its business faster than the natural growth in the industry, it was clear it would have to change the nature of the industry and in the process drive some of the competitors out of business.

Another example of changing the industry is well illustrated by the division of Bekaert that manufactures steel cord for tires. It sells this product to tire manufacturers, who in many cases also manufacture their own steel tire cord, so this is what many would consider a "commodity" product. In 1989, the market for steel tire cord was very bad, with a large amount of industry overcapacity. Bekaert recognized this as an opportunity for dominance and was able to increase its worldwide market share significantly, allowing the firm to better utilize its capacity. The fundamental way this was accomplished was simply to ask its customers: "What do we need to do to sell you more?"

Others also redefine customer expectations to their advantage. The department store, Nordstrom, is a good example. Its employees actually compete to see who can do the most amazing acts of customer service. The story is told of a customer wishing to return an automobile tire. When asked if he had a sales slip, he said no. The salesperson then asked him how much he guessed he had paid for it and immediately gave him that amount. Nordstrom does not even sell tires.

Other firms that are causing discontinuities are Wal-Mart, with its revolutionary cost savings in distribution and logistics, and firms such as Du Pont and 3M, which are defining the agenda for environmental actions.

Under internal discontinuities we mentioned mergers and acquisitions. Frequently these are possible not only to predict—but also to foster. The firm that can make mergers, acquisitions, and joint ventures work faster and better will surely have an advantage. Far too many of these combinations are supposed to work because of proximity or some other law of nature.

External discontinuities are a bit harder, but not impossible, to influence. Clearly some companies view the environment as a place where they can define the rules by which all players in the industry will have to abide—rather than seeing the environment as some adversarial game that one should drag out for as long as possible, doing as little as possible. We know of a Scandinavian lumber company that is working hard to control the supply of lumber coming into Europe from Baltic suppliers. And what about Philip Morris discounting Marlboro? Was this not a preemptive move?

Summary

This chapter has more fully explored what we mean by discontinuities and expectation changes and described a process for making these issues real in your enterprise. The key learning points are:

- Internal discontinuities need to be seen not only as a current set of problems or issues faced by the firm, but also as potential opportunities that could be leveraged for dominance.

- External discontinuities similarly need to include those that could be or might happen, and perhaps we could *make* them happen.

- Changes in customer expectations are critical to redefining the rules of the game; we must approach this determination with an open mind.

- An explicit development of other stakeholder expectations can lead to exciting ways in which an enterprise can exceed expectations—and achieve dominance.

- The Post-it Note process for identifying the transformation drivers works! Use it.

□ The customer activity cycle model is another way to think about key transformation drivers. This is not an either/or issue; this additional viewpoint provides a useful adjunct to the strategic intent transformation facet.

The next step in the transformation model process is to link the transformation drivers to the strategic intent and strategic responses.

5 Strategic Intent and Strategic Response

In this chapter we make the first major linkage between the major elements of the enterprise transformation model. Having looked at the challenges (the enterprise transformation drivers), we must now connect them to the resulting actions in order to frame those actions to reflect both the overall strategic intent of the organization and its basic competencies. The result leads to clear identification of the golden cord through the top half of Figure 3.1, which we first saw in chapter 3.

The top half of the model depicts the relationships among the transformation drivers, the responses, and the strategic intent—all in the setting of overall corporate performance. Challenges drive responses, which are framed in the context of strategy, taking advantage of competencies, against a backdrop of enterprise performance. Enterprise performance influences the sense of urgency and the extent to which the short term can be forgone for long-term achievement. Competencies influence actions taken in that some actions are just more feasible than others.

Rather than merely formulate the overall mission and the actions derived from it, we find it most useful to iterate between the elements of Figure 4.1: What set of actions would be most effective in meeting the challenges posed by the discontinuities and changes in expectations? What is the implied strategic intent when these actions are summarized (such as in the Post-it Note process in chapter 4)? How does this strategic intent match the stated mission, and what modifications are necessary in either the mission or the actions, or both? What are the competence (and underlying infrastructure) implications of the desired set of actions? How feasible is it?

The classic relationship between strategic intent and strategic response is where the former dictates the overall mission and the latter the actions derived from the mission. But in the enterprise transformation approach, we find it more useful to move back and forth between strategic intent and strategic response—and also with other parts of Figure 4.1.

Strategic response is generated with a brainstorming session, where action possibilities are formed to deal with the prioritized challenges. When these ideas are grouped, titled, and prioritized, there is an implied summation which needs to be compared to the stated strategic intent. The result is usually a modification and further details being applied to the strategic intent. Also, in some cases, the actions (strategic response) need to be enhanced because they do not adequately respond to the overriding objectives or mission of the enterprise.

An example of the iterative approach of Figure 4.1 is our work with a firm in the packaging industry. The firm's stated mission statement was to be "number one" in a particular type of food product packaging. Working with the transformation model and reexamining their challenges, responses, and competency requirements caused managers to adopt a much clearer definition of what "number one" meant, including which sectors (and geographical locations) of this food product packaging were of first priority, what new technologies had to be mastered, what kind of time frame was reasonable, what the major action programs were, and what present activities were good candidates to outsource/eliminate in order to focus their limited resources.

Corporate Performance

Corporate performance provides the backdrop to enterprise transformation. More specifically, corporate performance necessarily establishes the context in which the overall strategy needs to be designed and revised—as well as the detailed action programs that are implemented to achieve the transformation. The set of initiatives that IBM, General Motors, or even Sony can undertake at this time is more limited now than when the companies were making excellent profits. When strategy is being formulated, past corporate performance and current economic health play a strong role in shaping these initiatives. Moreover, at some times past performance and current condition are the actors that drive the enterprise transformation design—and execution.

Short-Term Cost Reduction Dangers

When most people speak about their company's performance, they start reeling out numbers, "Profits down . . . return on investment up . . . etc." Unhappily, in far too many cases the resulting strategic response becomes exclusively focused on short-run cost reduction, and the implied strategic intent is parallel driven by financial objectives with little or no attention paid to the impact on other corporate objectives. Cutting costs *becomes* the action. Other actions are abandoned, customer expectations are ignored, and underlying discontinuities are not examined in depth. In short, the focus is entirely on the "passengers"—not the "drivers." Anyone can reduce costs in the short run—usually by doing something stupid. Unfortunately, this is reality. There just are times in the history of a business when there are no alternatives. But if this is always the situation, the future will be dim indeed.

■ A large Scandinavian metal factory had undergone one downsizing after another. When we visited, the workers absolutely cringed: Another guy with a tie; here come more layoffs. But in fact, there were many opportunities to reduce costs in intelligent ways. The firm had sixteen weeks of work-in-process inventory. Each reduction of one week would save the same amount of money as twelve workers' wages, and it should have been quite possible to reduce work-in-process inventory to four weeks. At the same time, the company would be much better able to respond to customer requests. Similarly, the company had computed its "cost of quality" to be 18 percent. Each percentage point reduction was equivalent to seventeen workers. Other cost reduction opportunities were very visible in just one visit. But without incentive to reduce costs on the part of either the workers—or their friends in industrial engineering (this would eliminate work and result in immediate firing of the associated workers)—the ax of downsizing was viewed as inevitable. When the ax fell, it hit indiscriminately. Costs were indeed reduced—but so were capabilities, morale, and hope for the future.

Costs need to be seen as passengers instead of as drivers. The real issue is the actions to take in order to improve operations so that costs will be reduced, not how to cut costs indiscriminately. The former approach is proactive, the latter reactive, and often the result of desperation. In fact, if the situation is desperate, then the meat ax approach might be the only feasible one. But in too many cases, we see thoughtless management reaction, which only leads to the need for doing it again.

Few firms have saved themselves into prosperity, and even those that have managed to make turnarounds, often re-emerge as much smaller— and less dominant—firms. Xerox, Ford, and General Motors have indeed turned themselves around, but they have not recaptured their market shares from Cannon, Toyota, and Honda. The downsizing ax is easy to swing, the results are predictable, there are lots of consultants to help swing it, and the financial community applauds the idea. We were visiting a large firm one day where a senior executive told us proudly how his company was better at downsizing than any other company in the industry. At that point, my colleague asked, "If you are so good at downsizing, why do you have to continue to do it?"

In chapter 1, we presented the double objective of reducing costs *and* increasing customer perceived value. This combination must be reflected in the measurement systems that are used to evaluate enterprise transformation. If not, the primary—if not exclusive—emphasis will be on head count reductions. The result will almost never be the dominance that is achieved by proactively responding to the challenges through providing a better bundle of goods and services—one that drives out those who can only play a cost reduction game.

The Inadequacy of Accounting Systems

Traditional accounting systems compound problems instead of addressing them. They often inhibit the task of genuine strategy making. Accounting systems were designed before the first industrial revolution, when the factors of production were totally different from those appropriate for the second industrial revolution, much less the third one.

Traditional accounting systems tend to:

☐ Report history to the external world rather than identify effective action programs for enterprise transformation.

☐ Focus on short-term financial results at the expense of long-term dominance, encouraging counterproductive decisions such as cutting research and development to "save money."

☐ Undervalue the company by accounting for only hard assets; the price paid for actually buying these companies is usually many times the stated book value of the firm.

☐ Focus almost exclusively on costs—especially direct labor costs—an increasingly minor element of value-added in today's manufacturing environment.

□ Ignore quality, timeliness, skill enhancement, and useful knowledge work—the real competitive dimensions and sources of value-added.

□ Retard implementation of modern manufacturing processes such as just-in-time (JIT) and total quality management (TQM).

□ Inhibit the emergence of appropriate new organizational structures.

□ Lack dynamism and flexibility—under the false assumption that time series comparisons are essential. Accounting measures are slow to respond to the changes in the competitive landscape—and the resulting need to change strategy and actions.

□ Focus on financial measures with an aura of exactness when nonfinancial measures are better. It is better to be approximately right than exactly wrong.

The strategy–actions–measures triangle (see Figure 2.7) represents the reality that change and adaptation are constant. Changes or actions are driven by an overriding strategy (where we are going), and the measurement system needs to be in synchronization. How else can we determine progress toward achieving the objectives of the action programs? Unfortunately, in far too many cases, new measures lag strategic initiatives and action programs, producing unclear results and confused employees.

In a competitive industry, everyone is watching costs. Winning, however, takes ongoing action programs to improve responsiveness, rapid development and introduction of new products or services, flexibility, quality, and constant enhancement of the bundle of goods and services provided. None of these is promoted by old-style performance measures.[1]

Many companies are significantly reducing the incongruities among strategies, actions, and performance measures. Few, however, have embraced change to the point where their performance measurement systems have evolved to keep step with (and drive) strategic imperatives. Our transformation model can play an important role by explicitly recognizing the need to determine the right measures to use in the corporate performance backdrop. That is, rather than meekly accepting financial measures as the only approach to assessing corporate performance, other goals need to be articulated. More importantly, once the golden cord between discontinuities, expectation changes, strategic intent, and strategic response has been determined, it is imperative to critically examine the measures of corporate performance for congruity.

Corporate Performance and Learning

The strategic transformation model shows corporate performance at the top and learning capacity at the bottom. The two should be seen as connected, as mirror images. The measures of corporate performance rely on continuous learning goals established for the enterprise infrastructure. That is, the change agenda for infrastructure systems and processes should not be thwarted by inappropriate measures of corporate performance. The capacity to learn is the driver for dominance; financial performance is the result.

Managers discussing internal discontinuities often mention poor financial performance. In a few rare cases, they also list their performance measurement systems themselves as an internal discontinuity. These companies have finally come to the recognition that a major challenge facing them is to overhaul the way that they evaluate progress.

■ Northern Telecom evaluated sales performance using traditional approaches based on classical geographic territories. When it implemented key account management for Fortune 100 companies in the United States and major governmental units, there was suddenly a need for a serious overhaul of performance measures; an even more fundamental change was required when a few firms such as Sheraton Hotels asked for a global contract. These changes in operations required new corporate initiatives (strategic responses), new supporting infrastructure, new measurements, and deliberate abandonment of older contradictive measures.

Executives must accept that the flow of ideas and causality in corporate performance is two-directional. Certainly, past corporate financial performance and present financial health shape enterprise transformation. But it is far too probable that a direct attack on these issues can be more harmful than beneficial. A mentality that says that financial performance drives strategy, and strategy drives actions, can easily dismiss actions that redefine strategy and strategy that supports learning (and associated financial benefits). Moreover, a focus on financial instead of nonfinancial measures is highly likely to result in results quite contrary to desires.

Integration, consistency, feasibility, and desirability of transformation requires integration, consistency, feasibility, and desirability of measures. If discontinuities, whether perceived explicitly or implicitly, are not addressed by the performance measurement system—or worse yet, are made worse by improving current performance measures—the firm has a major problem. Similarly, if present measures inhibit pleasing the customer, the firm is in trouble. If a set of strategic responses are widely agreed upon as the answers to the company's problems, but run counter to how success is evaluated, disillusionment in the ranks is guaranteed. If the measurement system runs counter to development of desired new competencies and supporting infrastructure, the firm is equally confused and hobbled.

The critical point is that the enterprise's learning capacity is intimately linked to performance measurements. Critical success factors (CSFs) and key performance indicators (KPIs) should have the objective of aligning competencies, capabilities, processes, learning, and culture with the major objectives of the enterprise and the developing of detailed measures to evaluate their effectiveness. Measures *must* foster learning—which is manifested in specific improvements in practices.

Strategic Intent

Strategic intent is the true mission, the operational corporate strategy, or whatever set of words one wishes to put on the driving force for the enterprise. The enterprise may be the entire company, a business unit, or some other grouping. If the strategic intent does not include dominance in some sense, proactive change is very unlikely. If properly defined, the strategic intent provides the beacon by which all employees in this enterprise can direct their actions toward dominance. If not properly defined, the strategic intent will be confusing and probably lead to cynicism.

The critical point is that we mean the real set of objectives that is driving the actions of the enterprise, not some public relations statement put together for the annual report or a commencement address. In too many instances, the real intent is not written down. There are hidden agendas, and the true guiding principles for the enterprise are not widely shared. The costs are enormous—paid for in confusion, inconsistent actions, little to no integration, lack of dedication, and poor morale.

The real issue is one of match or fit among the eight facets of transformation. Transformation is more than "tweaking." It is also more than "major change." A firm could change its competencies, its processes, its resources, or its action programs. It could face a new set of challenges, and it could even increase its capacity to learn. But fundamentally the

question becomes one of direction: Are we trying to do the same thing—
that is, accomplish the same objectives—or are we doing better things
(accomplishing new objectives)? *True* transformation encompasses a
change in direction: A new strategic intent that is well-formulated, consistent, and widely shared.

Stability

The imperatives for a useful strategic intent are that it be clearly understood, communicated, believed by the employees, seen as feasible integrated with the actions and measures; that it provide consistency to the
work done by the enterprise; and that it be *stable* for at least a few years
at a time. The strategic intent must not change at the drop of a hat,
although it will change periodically—as a change in paradigms. The strategic responses, on the other hand, can accommodate particular discontinuities and expectation changes as they arise or are perceived.

The stability of strategic intent depends on connection of discontinuities and expectation changes to strategic response and strategic intent.
For any particular enterprise, the issue is whether the discontinuities and
expectation changes are so large as to mandate a change in mission or if
new actions under the existing strategic intent are sufficient. This is not
a question of "success" or lack thereof. It is whether the current view of
reality and our approach to it need fundamentally to be revised.

Chapter 1 describes stages in an enterprise in terms of the "S curve"
in Figure 1.3. Indeed, a periodic shift in paradigms (on a proactive basis),
followed up with continuous improvement activities, is what leads to
dominance. The periodicity seems to be about three or four years in well-
run companies. In each case, the paradigm shift is accompanied by a new
strategic intent or true mission statement. The strategic intent must be
recognized by everyone and made a part of their day-to-day thinking.
This takes time and effort, so strategic intent changes need to be made
relatively infrequently. Moreover, the enterprise—and those who drive
enterprise transformation—must understand the gravity of changing the
strategic intent. Unlearning, new behaviors, culture changes, new competencies, supporting capabilities, and processes need to be put in place.
The enormousness of the effort must be comprehended if the real results
are to be achieved.

In far too many cases, aggressive mission statement changes are created,
but those who create them think that it is the creation that is the big

task. Development of a mission statement, compared to its overall implementation, is analogous to building a house: The architectural drawings are fun, interesting, and of course decisive in what will happen. But making them a reality requires a great deal of work by many people.

KEY QUESTIONS:

- When does a change program become transformation?
- Does it matter?
- What distinguishes one from the other—and what are the implications for managers?

Transforming Strategic Intent

The precise dividing line between a "major change" and a transformed strategic intent is hard to draw. A telling exercise may be for the management team to ask whether what it wants to see happen is revolutionary or evolutionary, and if their approach to seeing it through and their commitment is matched to the reality of their desires. Change that maintains the same strategic intent is fundamentally more straightforward than change that involves paradigm shifting and fundamental unlearning.

In transformation, all the imperatives for a true mission statement— and the dangers of not having one—need to be explicitly understood. The well-advised management team will go over each in some detail, to be doubly sure that the desired transformation requirements have not been seriously underestimated.

■ Alps, the Japanese electronics company we have examined in earlier chapters, provides a good example. Managers clearly understood the discontinuities and changes in customer expectations. The new markets in automotive electronics, much greater product diversity on the part of customers, just-in-time delivery requirements, growing restrictions on imports into the United States, and reduced sales growth (relative to natural productivity) implied a crisis in the near future if actions were not taken. The company was fundamentally committed to growth and wanted to avoid downsizing at all costs. The answer was to attempt to provide the ultimate in manufacturing: Anything, for anyone, any place, any time, with zero inventory.

The resulting paradigm shift was defined as "the end of mass production." Such a transformation required a massive effort to insure that all employees understood the new mission, its implications, and the actions that were required of everyone. The firm became a make-to-order company, with small lot sizes (requiring minimal setup times), and speed of material movement became critical—controls were minimized in favor of speed. Every employee was given a video depicting scenes from companies like Benetton, where the consumer desire for variety is emphasized; they were asked to view them and discuss them with family members to understand the implications for the fundamental changes needed and the current ideas they needed to unlearn.

■ An American machinery manufacturer provides the counterexample. It too felt the need to change and emphasized the need for solving customer problems, empowerment, teamwork, and a new spirit of cooperation. But its true mission had never really shifted. The top managers were under heavy pressure for immediate results, the shareholders were unhappy, and the need for a quick fix overrode any possibilities for genuine transformation. The program started with a bang. Many employees became enthusiastic, work began, improvements were coming, but in the end the management brought in a cost reduction team that dictated across-the-board head count reductions, irrespective of the relative needs and programs in progress. The stock market loved it, and the managers were heralded; but deep in the organization the sense of death is pervasive.

Key Questions

Let us now identify some of the key issues that one needs to be assessing as change programs are being designed and implemented. The most fundamental issue in strategic intent is the extent to which it is truly understood and believed in the enterprise. What seems obvious to managers can be all too obscure at lower levels of an organization. Managers need to use their antennae to check this out. Years of hard work to build trust and confidence can be destroyed in a single action. Fighting cynicism requires time, effort, honesty, and integrity. Keeping one's ear to the ground is probably the best way to find out whether the mission is understood. Surveys are another, but they are fraught with danger. If you ask people what is wrong—and they tell you—you had better be ready to do something about it. No follow-up is a sure way to feed the wrong fires. Moreover, surveys are myopic by definition. Breakthrough thinking requires much more than extrapolation and putting Band-Aids on gaping wounds.

Managers need to cross-scrutinize change programs to see whether transformation is or is not involved. Is there a paradigm shift here or not? Do we have to unlearn current practices, measurements, and ideas? How is this being done? How do we know it is being achieved? What are our means to tell?

If transformation is indeed to occur, in what stage is your company? What is the new paradigm? How well has it been articulated and communicated, and what is the series of plans and actions to deploy the concept? What are the new infrastructure requirements? Who is in charge of achieving them? How are the implications for work practices being evaluated—and how are the changes to be implemented?

The reverse problem is also one that needs to be examined. Does a planned series of changes constitute a transformation—without our realizing or naming it? This could be quite dangerous, because in this case the new true mission will come from below, rather than be established from the top. Moreover, it will take a long time for it to be communicated—and the results, both interim and final, may well not be to the liking of management. Not driving a transformation is simply an abdication of responsibility.

■ A U.K. consumer products company was made up of two independent operating units selling competing products and a corporate headquarters. A decision was made to consolidate all three units administratively, picking the accounting group from one, the purchasing group from another, and so on. The top managers thought they had done their job after deciding which groups had been chosen. But the results were a complete disaster. There was no real strategic intent, no operating culture, no decision making for what combined infrastructure was to be put in place (e.g., people attempted to continue with all varieties of payroll systems instead of standardizing one approach). The priorities for action were so unclear that one manager who was able to retain his sense of humor told his secretary each day as he left the office that if his boss called to please find out his or her name. There were many personal tragedies, including divorces and suicides; a second-level executive said that a takeover would have been far easier. The company spent so much energy on this change—groping without a clear vision or sense of direction—that it lost market share even faster and eventually was sold to a competitor for a fraction of its original value.

Strategic Response

Strategic response describes the set of action programs taken—either to implement a change effort or to implement a true transformation. It is the direct connection of the golden cord to discontinuities and changes in expectations that should provide the fundamental driver for the set of strategic responses. At the same time, the strategic response must be consistent with a clearly defined strategic intent. If not, implementation of the actions will be difficult, the belief in the strategic intent will erode, and the organization will become confused.

Deductive versus Inductive

A classic view of how the strategic response or set of actions is determined is that it would be driven by the overriding strategy. That is, strategic intent drives strategic response. But we see it a bit differently: The linkage of the challenges (discontinuities and expectation changes) is to the strategic response, as in Figure 4.1. The basic idea is to ask what needs to be done in the light of the challenges. What actions are indicated? That is, what would we do in the best of all possible worlds to respond to the challenges facing the firm?

The "deductive" approach implies top-down decision making with a cascade to lower levels. The "inductive" approach implies more emphasis on bottom-up, in that actions help define strategy.

It is the summation of these bottom-up responses that provides insight as to whether we need to change or improve the strategic intent statement of the company. That is, are we faced with transformation? Is an evolution required—within our present strategic intent—or is it a revolution—requiring a new mission with all the accompanying requirements? Finally, even if a revolution is called for, are we ready? Can we take one on, or should we wait for another day—and what are the implications of doing so?

Revolutions need to be recognized as such, and the resources need to be made available. Consistency and integration are required, as well as feasibility and desirability. The inductive approach to examining the golden cord that connects challenges, actions, and strategic intent forces explication of the issues and implications.

Focusing on the set of actions required allows one to consider the changes required in the other seven facets or dimensions of transformation. The connection to challenges has already been made, and the deductive–inductive links to strategic intent have been discussed. But what about the competency requirements? Will an adaptation of present approaches do—or will a whole new set be required? What about the processes and other infrastructure necessary—what are they and what are the change implications? What are the implications for learning and unlearning—will the basic culture of the firm need to be overhauled? What are the resource implications—do we need people with new skills? new technology? major changes in information systems? Will there necessarily be large redundancies? Finally, there is the connection with outputs: Is the set of actions directed at producing a fundamentally different collection of goods and services—fulfilling a different assortment of customer expectations?

Being fairly explicit about answers to these questions is helpful in resolving the fundamental issue—is this a transformation (or does it need to be one)?

Making Strategic Response Consistent with Transformation

Strategic response, or the set of action programs, needs to be consistent with an overriding mission or strategic intent. We all have a tendency to focus on action. Do it now, and worry about why tomorrow. As long as the result is not dysfunctional, this pragmatic impulse may be all right, but if the actions actually are leading to a transformation, it is important to step back and look at the implications. A transformation implies a change in strategic intent. The key question, then, is when does a set of actions (strategic response) necessitate a reformulation of the strategic intent or, put differently, does a set of actions fit with the existing strategic intent—or, even more important, with the underlying values of the company? What do we lose if this is not the case?

■ In one instance, a U.S. manufacturer had a long history of nurturing employees and of openness and fairness. An analysis of its distribution centers indicated that important savings could be gained by closing one. The question was how to do this. In spite of recommendations, a vice president in the firm flew a team into the town unannounced, arrived at the distribution center at nine in the morning, and had everyone out by noon. The results were (as predicted) a complete disaster for the rest of the firm. Trust was severely damaged, and confidence in the company has never returned to the previous levels.

■ A multinational firm was experiencing problems in its European operations. Sales plans were not being met, significant overcapacity existed in manufacturing, and financial results were poor. The company initiated a series of actions, including manufacturing standardization, business process re-engineering, reduced throughput times in manufacturing, narrowing of the product line, organizational delayering, and a redundancy program. The results were fairly good; profits improved, sales volumes were enhanced, and manufacturing costs were reduced. It seemed like a success. But yet. . . .

The focus was on actions (strategic response), and the set of actions was not thought of inside the company as a paradigm shift or transformation. They were seen as doing some smart things to solve a problem. The strategic intent of the company was not changed in any official way; it retained its emphasis on customer focus, outward-looking, growth, new markets, and enthusiasm. But in fact none of these was achieved. The customer base was being reduced, the primary focus was internal cost reduction, contraction was the name of the game, and morale was suffering.

The multinational's discontinuities and changes in expectations were not addressed in a thoroughgoing fashion. The responses of its competitors had not been seriously considered; competitors quickly matched the company's shorter delivery times and price reductions. The customers were initially delighted, but they quickly came back asking for more. A similar story relates to outputs. The bundle of goods and services offered to the customers was enhanced, but the enhancements were not of a sort to provide long-run advantage. On the contrary, they only fed the customers' desire for more of the same—which were not so easy to provide.

Providing even better deliveries, lower prices, faster responses, and more rapid evolution in product features requires new competencies, capabilities, processes, resources, skills, learning, and unlearning. But the multinational's emphasis on retrenching made achievement of them virtually impossible. By not viewing its actions as a part of an enterprise transformation, the firm never articulated these new infrastructure implications. Overall, what seemed like a good set of responses to some pressing problems were a Band-Aid on a serious wound. The intentions were good, the changes reflected right thinking, but the failure to see the problem in a transformative sense meant that the benefits were short-lived, and the company was not well-positioned to move on to the next competitive battle.

The moral to these stories is that action programs need to be viewed with a long-term consideration of their overall impact. In the case of the U.S. manufacturer, any short-term gains of the headquarters attack on the distribution center were trivial when compared to the effects on the remaining employees. For the multinational company, not seeing its actions in a long-run context caused it not to foresee the next set of challenges—and the necessary changes in infrastructure that would be required. When these challenges became apparent, the company was not well-positioned to respond to them.

Key Questions

Managers need to ask where a set of actions will lead to. That is, what is a reasonable scenario of future challenges and requirements, assuming the strategic responses are achieved? What is next? How does one follow on from the results? Do they stand on their own without further obligation, or will they create a need for future actions? Are future actions ones that can be achieved with the present resources, or will major new conditions arise?

To examine the strategic response in terms of the next set of challenges that might occur, one looks to what the reaction of competitors might be, what the next set of customer expectations will be, and what new discontinuities might arise. For each of these scenarios, there is a resulting set of infrastructure requirements—competencies, processes, and resources. Are these available—or can they be made available?

These questions looking ahead should not be taken as an excuse for not taking action. The point, rather, is to invest some energy in consistency and integration as twin goals; where is the set of actions headed, and can the changes be sustained—particularly in the light of subsequent responses to the actions?

A *Harvard Business Review* article raises the issue in terms of Japanese companies implementing time-based competition.[2] The authors note that in many cases, the advantages gained through these techniques are only momentary. Competitors can soon match the decreased throughput times, faster development cycles, and increased responsiveness to customer demands. The point is not to avoid implementing new competition techniques, but to recognize—at the outset—that actions will produce responses, raising a new set of challenges, and requiring a new set of responses. Those responses need to be guided by a clearly articulated strategic intent (existing or new), and they almost surely will dictate new competencies for their achievement. The real search is for *distinctive* competencies, those that are difficult to duplicate.

The Competency Connection

Chapter 6 is devoted to competencies, capabilities, processes, and resources. The goal is to pull the golden cord down through the infrastructure required to implement transformation. For now, we need to address the basic connections of competencies to strategic intent and strategic response.

Competency-Shaping Strategy

The arrow connecting competencies to strategic response in Figure 4.1 is double-ended. For the flow upward, we need to understand that both our overall strategy and our detailed actions are influenced by whatever it is that we do well. Competencies and their supporting capabilities, processes, and resources allow the enterprise to execute certain actions— and preclude it from others. Similarly, the set of competencies also makes it possible for some strategic objectives to be plausible and others not.

A company with great competencies in information systems design and implementation, for example, might find it more feasible to initiate a strategic response to form partnerships with customers or suppliers than would a firm that has more limited abilities to coordinate schedules and other information between the firms. Similarly, a competence in international management would seem essential for a company wishing to implement an overall strategy based on globalization.

Strategy-Shaping Competency

The flow down, from strategic response to competence, indicates that significant strategic responses very often require new competencies (and the resultant capabilities, processes, and resources) to accomplish them. A corresponding need for new competencies comes from changes in strategic intent. A new true mission will dictate responses and supporting infrastructure.

A basic issue of feasibility is raised by examining these connections: Are the new competencies achievable? What will be required to achieve them? How will these competencies fit with current competencies—and with our culture? Do we need a major unlearning experience? The key connection is that a major change in action programs (strategic response) or indeed a shift in strategy (strategic intent) will almost always entail new competency requirements.

■ An aluminum parts producer wanted to form value-added partnerships with one group of clients. A new competency in this case was new engineering talent in the particular field—coupled to the traditional technical base of the company.

■ An electrical components manufacturer came to the conclusion that its traditional European markets could not sustain it in the long run. It adopted a strategy (new strategic intent) of globalized sales (while retaining its existing manufacturing sites); it needed several major new competencies in sales and marketing—as well as new information systems to achieve this result.

The Systematic Customization Model

Andrew Boynton and his colleagues have developed a transformation model they call either "systematic customization" or "mass customization."[3] The model with its four distinct stages is particularly useful in deciding if, in fact, a series of changes are a paradigm shift or transformation. The ideas are valuable for understanding a natural pattern of evolution/revolution, and for charting the transformation steps necessary to achieve the desired new stage.

Figure 5.1 depicts the model and its four stages or quadrants. The firm is represented by its products and its processes, which can be either stable or dynamic. In the upper right quadrant, both the products and the processes are dynamic. This quadrant is labeled "invention." Here is the typical laboratory or craft shop, whose products are mostly prototype made with multipurpose equipment. Boston's Route 128, "Technology Highway," is an example. Many startup companies begin here, often springing from some bright idea developed at an area university. Silicon Valley in California is a similar place. These startup companies begin

Figure 5.1

Mass Customization Model

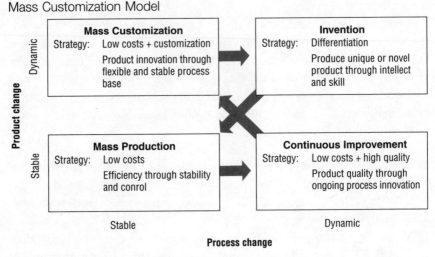

Source: Andrew Boynton, Visiting Professor, IMD. Presented at a Manufacturing 2000 meeting, IMD, Lausanne, Switzerland, October 1993. Reprinted with permission.

---

classically in the "invention" quadrant. After some time, many of them succeed and see their sales grow dramatically. At this point, they need to undergo a definitive transformation, which is from upper right to lower left, the "mass production" quadrant.

This essential transformation involves implementation of standard ways of doing things, the shift from a craft shop to factory mentality and culture, formal job definitions, the minimization of variability in all its aspects, adoption of formalized planning and scheduling, cost control, part numbering, and a host of other changes. There is an absolute transformation in all eight facets of the enterprise—as well as fundamental shifts in culture, configuration, and coordination. In short, this is a revolution, not an evolution—a transformation. The shift from invention to mass production clearly illustrates this. Many activities have to be unlearned, and some people who are extremely good in a laboratory/craft shop environment are a disaster in a factory culture.

The second transformation illustrated by the mass customization model is from the lower left to the lower right quadrant. This one is called "continuous improvement," epitomized by Toyota. Again there is a major change in the eight facets plus culture, configuration, and coordination. Rigid work rules are replaced by flexible work rules, tight job definitions by cross-trained workers, command/control by empowerment, bosses by coaches, stable nonvarying processes by ones that are continuously made better, specialized work centers by cellular manufacturing, material requirements planning (MRP) systems by just-in-time (JIT) approaches, which are both scheduling systems and a philosophy.

The next shift that often (but not necessarily) takes place is from the lower right to the upper left quadrant. This one is called "mass customization," and again requires a definitive transformation. Now, the cellular manufacturing needs to be able to make a much wider variety of products, essentially any product behind any other product. Planning and scheduling systems need to be able to deal with a much greater variety of parts; paper flows with customers need to be eliminated or significantly simplified; procurement needs to encompass a new type of vendor partnership based more on flexibility/responsiveness than on pure cost minimization; working rules need to reflect both simplicity in operations but at the same time predictability; and the company information systems need to capture learning in such a way that on new work only the new elements that have to be learned.

■ Many companies have the mass customization objective. Valmet, a Finnish company manufacturing paper-making equipment, can now take a much wider variety of orders, where each is unique, but at the same time process them in a highly predictable order. The design and manufacturing elements of each job are analyzed to find those that have been done before so that the new challenges of each order are well-known and highlighted. The firm has been able to reduce the time to make each order, resulting in a significant competitive advantage.

■ In a similar vein, Nokia Mobile Phones is working toward an environment where any configuration of mobile telephone can be made behind any other—and it will make no difference in planning, manufacturing, or logistics. Even more important, the company is incorporating the same approach into the design of new mobile telephones. Is is essential to continue to reduce the time to introduce new products, and one way to do so is to be very clear as to what is new versus what is simply a variation of what has already been done.

The movement described here is one that is both natural and necessary. That is, companies often need to transform from invention to mass production, and later from mass production to continuous improvement. In today's competitive environment, many enterprises are now transforming from continuous improvement to mass customization. In many cases, the driving forces for mass customization come from the marketplace. Customers such as Nestlé or Unilever are themselves transforming—to a more regional culture (as opposed to country cultures and approach). The result is a new ordering pattern—they become "Euro customers."

Other changes in customer ordering are also occurring, such as reducing the number of suppliers, or globalization. In all these cases, the net result is a new set of customer demands—that tend to be unique. Thus when Sheraton Hotels selected Northern Telecom as the supplier of telecommunication gear for all its hotels, this customer requirement—for one worldwide contract and order servicing—was a unique demand to be met. In the long run, this kind of request cannot be satisfied by exceptional approaches. It is necessary *routinely* to handle very different customer requests. The first demands fall in order servicing. Closely following are unique demands for logistics—and finally manufacturing.

Some companies are seeing the need to go back once again to invention, when it is time to start anew with totally untested ideas. In each of these movements, there is a true transformation, eight distinctively new enterprise facets, and a somewhat distinctive path to follow (as well as paths that do not make sense). For example, some firms that wish to go from invention to continuous improvement will ask why they cannot implement just-in-time directly, without first implementing material requirements planning (MRP). The answer is seen in the mass customization model. One first has to institute factory discipline and culture; thereafter, parts of the central control can be relaxed, but in each case a transformation is required. One needs to change paradigms—all eight facets of enterprise transformation plus the culture, configuration, and coordination.

The important point of this model for our purposes is that a company that examines its operations with the mass customization model may conclude that it is indeed in one of the quadrants and wishes to move to another. Fine. But the model clearly indicates that this is a transformation, not just a case of doing a few things differently. Moreover, the model provides a path, and an indication of the marketplace and other characteristics that are associated with each quadrant—as well as with the transformation requirements between quadrants.

Connecting Transformation Drivers and Responses

We explained in chapter 4 the Post-it Note process for identifying the enterprise drivers. We can use it here to focus on the linkage between the discontinuities/changes in expectations and the actions or strategic responses. The enterprise uses the process to identify the golden cord between them. The golden cord integrates the top half of the model shown in Figure 3.1

Again team members write sentences describing the best possible responses the enterprise might make in order to turn every significant challenge into a competitive advantage. They might first brainstorm without any constraints. That is, in forming their first set of responses, the team members should not feel limited by any current constraints in the company. Those can be added later—and may be found less critical than one might think.

Once the group has read all the ideas and clarified them, grouping and ranking of sentences follows. Some teams separately rank the groups according to (1) what the strategic responses would accomplish competitively, and (2) the inherent feasibility of achieving those responses. The overall goal is to determine the strategic responses, to prioritize them for subsequent action, and to establish the game plan for accomplishing the transformation.

The result of this process is again a sentence that summarizes the strategic responses and the game plan for transformation. In one case, a company manufactured (in several factories) a metal raw material used by a particular type of automotive components manufacturer. Its managers developed these linkages to strategic responses:

☐ The summary message for internal discontinuities: There is a present lack of leadership to integrate new technology, achieve synergy, and understand the inherent industry complexities.

☐ The summary message for external discontinuities: Significant changes are occurring in industry purchasing practices as well as in the purchasing structures of customer companies.

☐ The summary message for changes in end-user expectations (owners of automobiles): People want lower cost and higher performance.

☐ The summary message for changes in immediate customer expectations: We need to help them lower their costs through smarter cooperation (joint learning) in production and development.

□ The changes in expectations of other stakeholders are dominated by a shareholder expectation that the company will develop proactive world-class operations, spearheading into new areas.

□ The summary response for the set of prioritized strategic responses: A new market focus based on partnerships with customers, new ventures, understanding relevant needs, and making the necessary changes in manufacturing.

The Environmental Example

In chapter 4, we applied the transformation model to a business unit of a firm that manufactures industrial equipment. The particular business unit manufactures pollution control equipment for industrial and municipal customers. Its discontinuity and expectation change groupings, with their Pareto ranking scores (the total points assigned by the group based on three, two, and one points assigned to importance), and the overall summary statements appear in Table 5.1. The details come from Tables 4.1–4.4.

The Strategic Responses

When the executives for this pollution control equipment business unit considered what to do about the list of discontinuities/expectations summarized in Table 5.1, they generated more than fifty detailed strategic responses. They sorted these responses into eleven groupings. "Policy," "organization," and "product development" were the top three groupings.

The summary message in Table 5.2 is:
Strengthen the Organization, Its Approach to the Market, and Product Development to Foster Environmental Business Opportunities.

This summary message means that the company must even more directly target the environment and the solving of environmental problems as an important source of business. To do so, the organization needs to develop a better system of internal coordination and measures to reduce its own internal constraints (such as those that keep the firm from designing, manufacturing, and selling more totally integrated systems). The rules of the pollution game are fast changing—and the firm believes it can help set them. If its responses are good, the firm can

Table 5.1

Discontinuities and Expectation Changes

Internal Discontinuities

Constraints (24)

Awareness (13)

Stimuli (11)

Summary Message: "Organizational and financial constraints limit our ability to meet environmental mandates."

External Discontinuities

Rules and Regulations (24)

Costs (13)

Environmental Reporting and Standards (6)

Change in Market Structure (3)

Summary Message: "Our external pressures stem from existing and changing rules and regulations."

Industrial/Municipal Customer Expectations

Cost/Performance Pressures (15)

Meeting Today's Needs (15)

Meeting Tomorrow's Needs (11)

Pressure Groups (7)

Summary Message: "Cost-effective solutions with technical support that meet and exceed today's requirements."

Stakeholder Expectations

Technical Excellence (14)

Costs versus User Benefits (14)

Reliable and High-Performance Operations (10)

Cost/Benefit (6)

Expectations of Greens and Communities (3)

Environmental Systems/Solutions (3)

Green Aura (2)

Third Parties in Decision Making (2)

Summary Message: "Solutions that are excellent, cost-effective, and reliable."

---

shape the environmental agenda in ways that allow it to compete more effectively. All those responses must be based on a platform of equipment that operates in the real world with performance second to none.

The Mission Revisited

One final note about this example is informative. The group of senior managers working in the brainstorming session were initially skeptical

Table 5.2

Strategic Response

"Strengthen the organization, its approach to the market, and product development to foster environmental business opportunities."

Policy (11)

- Change traditional company approach to market; separate equipment manufacturing from engineering and contracting
- Establish a clear policy on how to do business in less-environmentally concerned markets
- Improve contracting and consulting capabilities (for integrated solutions)
- Take into account cost-effectiveness according to the operator's/customer's perspective to propose the best technical solution, including, if necessary, a financing solution
- Develop a clear policy, according to market requirements and profitability, for contracting, building, and operating

Organization (11)

- Exchange information globally within groups regarding different aspects of environmental technologies
- Open a consulting office/practice
- Act as a watchdog on trends in environmental legislation
- Push local activities even though it is a centralized corporation

Product Development (8)

- Ask customers what they want; find an environmental champion
- Modularize products to match changes in legislation
- Design/engineer products to set the regulations/rules
- Focus on new processes for residuals treatment
- Identify pioneer customers for new/improved products
- Make approval procedures a new business service, i.e., cash cow
- Push R&D activities because the company is losing leadership
- Be consistent; products that help the environment today should not damage it tomorrow

Measuring Performance (6)

- Emphasize environmental reporting (corporate and business unit)
- Establish environmental targets (emissions, waste, energy, etc.)
- Create a measurement tool to evaluate our environmental performance
- Create a company tool to measure return on investment for environmentally related projects

Working with Other Environmental Stakeholders (5)

- Create dialogue with communities and "green" groups
- Try to influence:
  —regulations
  —pressure groups
  through lobbying (Brussels) and supporting influence groups

Information Intelligence (4)

- Cooperate with authorities in different countries in order to anticipate new regulations
- Learn from green intelligence
- Establish updated legislation data base system comparing different rules and external discontinuities

- Improve communication with stakeholders (references, performance, cost-effectiveness)
- Invite pressure groups into the company; encourage employee membership to better understand pressure group concerns
- Lobby for global standards and energy taxes
- Become an environmental lobby group for the company

- Improve horizontal communications between and among company business units
- Pool internal resources from all company players to get
  —more references
  —better information base to support customers
- Develop marketing intelligence system to spot, interpret, and feed back future steps needed for environmentally sound solutions

Incentives (3)

- Offer financial rewards tied to environmental performance
- Strategic investments rather than immediate earnings
- Offer financial incentives for good environmental performance
- Provide procedures for reviewing environmental benefits of investments

Education

- Encourage people to think in terms of systems and relationships, not categories and processes
- Influence the mind-set of our end-customer
- Expose young creative engineers to the "business aspects" of environmental issues
- Promote cost internalization philosophy accept environmental cost for what it is
- "Educate Customer" on environmental programs as part of marketing

Public Relations and Communications

- Encourage green investors
- Make company's ability to create technical solutions to environmental problems more public to enhance corporate image on environment
- Have an environmental department/manager
- Be proactive in influencing policy makers to benefit from our technological distinctive competencies and raise standards
- Qualify for green funds and *Fortune* best ten performers
- Create a corporate policy to communicate environmental performance to the financial market
- Increase publicity of our systems and results
- Make greater use of political and financial levers

Costs

- Cover product engineering for entire life cycle of product
- Monitor conditions over time with regard to changing requirements
- Use proven technology to be adapted to local needs
- Create a lean production, therefore, a lean organization

Marketing

- From industrial alliances, e.g., with chemical industry
- Form partnership relationship with customers, i.e., look toward a responsible care program

about the potential of the approach—and perhaps about sticking pieces of paper on a wall. But as the session went on, it became increasingly clear that the group had never had the opportunity to come so directly to a consensus of opinion on what was clearly a tough subject. The group included engineering and research people, sales and marketing, manufacturing, and corporate headquarters representatives concerned with the environment—both as citizens and with the use of environmental concepts to foster competitive advantage.

About four hours into our brainstorming exercise, we came to an interesting breakthrough. Someone from manufacturing said: "Well, I know we have this mission statement, and I know it is important, but the reality of the situation is that in any quarter, if we have to make a choice between making our quarterly financial numbers and the mission statement, there is no question but we go for the quarterly numbers."

These managers started the exercises with a strong feeling that they were on the right track with their environmental business, and that at most the company needed to make some minor adjustments. As the manufacturing manager's comment indicates, however, it eventually became clear that a fundamental change was indeed called for.

Another Example

Company A manufactures machinery used in the packaging industry. Its manufacturing base consists of several plants in Europe, with additional facilities in the United States and Southeast Asia. Its customer base tends to be the larger multinational consumer products companies, with worldwide operations. Traditionally, each plant of Company A largely serviced its local market, except for some specialty items that were made in particular factories. In more recent times, however, the factories had become focused to specialize on particular product lines.

Company A managers began their inquiry into transformation by reading the literature on core competence, and concluded that its core competencies were design, precision machining of specialty parts, assembly, and field service. But having agreed on these, people found it somewhat difficult to see what they were to do thereafter. Strategically, it was clear that the set of precision parts they needed to fabricate internally was decreasing—which necessitated a better purchasing capability. The design capabilities were also shifting somewhat, in that the customers now were more interested in faster changeovers than in the usual productivity metrics. Assembly increasingly required the integration of electronics with mechanical features, and field service was becoming somewhat more complex for the same reason. But these changes were already well-recognized in the company, and the executives did not see where to go from here.

A group of Company A managers became interested in other transformation approaches. At a meeting of ten top managers, the transformation model shown in Figure 3.1 was explained. The group thereafter identified eighteen groupings of discontinuities and shifts in expectations, and gave each a title. Five of these were subsequently targeted as particularly important through Pareto analysis:

☐ Concentration and consolidation of factories by our customers in the consumer products industry—driven both by regionalization and severe cost pressures.

☐ Shifting of power from consumer products manufacturers to the manufacturers' (trade) customers.

☐ Environmental concerns—particularly about packaging materials.

☐ Structural overcapacity in the consumer products industry, and consolidation through mergers or acquisitions.

☐ Time compression, and a need to respond to unforeseen demands by our customers.

In responding to the various discontinuities, the executives then listed the strategic responses—what might be done about this discontinuity/expectation—to yield significant competitive advantage? Of the twenty-one resulting groupings, the five most highly rated were:

☐ Improve our overall supply chain management. Particularly, build better partnerships with suppliers and closer field service partnerships with major customers.

☐ Implement changes in organizational structure, with a focus on flexibility, reduced managerial levels, and diminished functional boundaries.

☐ "Globalize" sales/marketing activities to match the particular globalization patterns of our customers.

□ Increase our abilities in "mechatronics"—the integration of mechanical and electronic capabilities at all levels in the company.

□ Proactively help our customers solve their cost and increasing product diversity problems.

Each strategic response has a particular focus. The need to improve the overall supply chain management is not only for cost reduction. The company felt it needed to be more responsive—both to demand that was becoming less predictable, as well as to new product innovation. It was experiencing a major change in the product life cycle—not so much in the basic machines as in the add-ons and the customized features needed in particular situations.

The change in organizational structure is both a response to the marketplace and a response to an internal discontinuity. A good number of senior workers had recently left the company, and the younger ones have a somewhat different set of values and education. A few years ago, the company experimented with cellular manufacturing and self-directed work groups, and these were well-received by the work force. The new changes are a natural outgrowth of these efforts, but now they are seen as paradigm shifting—a fundamental change in culture, configuration, and coordination rather than the continuation of an experiment.

The globalization of sales and marketing to match the particular patterns of the customer globalization patterns is something many companies see as necessary. Many consumer products customers, such as Nestlé, are moving toward regionalization. Important decisions once made either by country management teams or by corporate groups are being replaced by regional decision making—with a somewhat different focus. But not all customers are changing in the same way, and it is critical for suppliers of these companies to adapt in whatever ways are dictated by the changes in organization of their major customers.

The increasing integration of electronics and mechanical features is largely dictated by the just-in-time movement. The customers are increasingly being pushed to deliver smaller batches of products to the trade at more frequent intervals. This in turn leads to more frequent batches and a need for packaging equipment to facilitate faster changeovers. The problems are exacerbated by environmental concerns. The producers of packages find it increasingly difficult to take scrap produced during changeovers to landfills. The net result is a need for integrated solutions

based on electronics and microprocessors to better control the changeovers of packaging machines.

Finally, the strategic response to help customers proactively solve their
cost and increasing product diversity problems is driven by an awareness
that the only alternative is ever more squeezed margins and reactive cost-
cutting that can too easily hurt in the long haul.

Cross Checks for Strategic Response

Everyone believes in action programs, but how often are they carried out
according to plan? A program always seems to take two to three times
as long as expected—even when the desired results have been achieved.
But that is also not the case for a great many well-formulated strategic
responses. We can identify some cross checks that might at least improve
the batting average for action programs (we consider this issue in more
depth in chapter 7, when we examine increasing the speed of learning).

Feasibility and Desirability

The four dictates we have identified for effective transformation are
consistency and integration (the golden cord) plus feasibility and desirability. Let us briefly address these last two issues.

A "reality check" needs to be applied to the desired set of goals and
the implied transformation. Are the strategic intent and the set of detailed
actions in fact reasonable to achieve? My strategic objective might be to
skate in the next Olympics, and I could even follow it up with a set of
actions that includes daily practice, the best coaches, and conditioning.
But because I have never been able even to stand up on a pair of ice
skates, and I am already about twice the average age of Olympic athletes,
the overall transformation does not seem too feasible.

At a lower level in the transformation model, the detailed new competency requirements and supporting processes also need a reality check.
Have we really identified the necessary competencies? What capabilities,
processes, and resources are necessary to achieve them? Are the resources
available? Where will they come from? Who precisely is to accomplish
which specific actions? What are they doing now that they do not need
to do?

Next, there is the issue of desirability. The formulation of strategic
intent and a consistent strategic response may have generated a creative

series of action programs—ones that will reverberate throughout the enterprise and be connected to the eight facets of enterprise transformation—but what about the people who have to carry them out? Is the transformation going to be seen as desirable by those who have to do it—or are they required to fall on their swords?

Too often managers may make plans that in the end have quite undesirable consequences for those who have to carry them out. This may not be avoidable, but one should at least not be naive about a lack of enthusiasm for the strategic intent when carried down the line.

A strategy is most desirable when there is widespread buy-in to the steps along the golden cord. Experience shows that strategists who descend from the Mount Sinai of their boardrooms clutching tablets of stone usually struggle to get their ideas into action: "We are going to become mass customizers." "We are going to be solution providers, not product vendors." "We are going to create customer prosperity." Managers need to remember that they are likely to be much more enamored with the slogans and the quick fixes than those who have to implement them. Those who have been around for a while know how to duck and let these new pronouncements just blow over their heads.

Good recipes for achieving buy-in are hard to come by, but lessons can be drawn from the transformation model—and the Post-it Note exercise for identifying the transformation route. Consistency is clearly an issue, as is a match between what is needed and what is measured (and not measured). Repeating the Post-it Note exercises at several levels of the organization is also a good idea; successful companies do not restrict identification of the transformation journey to a few individuals. Worker apathy, indifference, resistance, and hostility may be good items to include in the set of "other stakeholder expectations." Finally, setting the tone for what the form of work will be like after a transition, and acknowledging publicly that transformation is not a one-time event but an ongoing process, can be very useful.

■ Lars Kolind, Managing Director of Danish electronic hearing aid manufacturer, Oticon, sets this tone. Here is how he speaks about people:

> Our values are human values, a set of assumptions by management and staff. Only one category of people work at Oticon: responsible adults. They can manage their time, prospects, and careers. There is no personnel department and no absence reporting for white collar

staff. They are paid for results. We have reduced our time to market by 50%. We have a steady stream of inventions. At headquarters we have improved productivity by 50% in two years as measured by the ratio of sales to headcount. Between 1989 and 1990 alone, productivity increased by 20%.[4]

■ Lars Kolind expects to continue. Through creative thinking about human resources—by tearing up the second industrial revolution model of the pin factory—Kolind has managed to create an organization that thrives on challenge and problem solving. Organization charts and titles have been thrown out. Each employee needs to figure out how best he or she can contribute. The much-publicized people revolution in Sao Paulo manufacturing company Semco seems to be built on the same approach to workers as "responsible adults." Majority owner Ricardo Semler says of a company that managed to grow while Brazil experienced a devastating recession: We owe Semco's survival to workers who continually ask: "Why can't we do this better?"

The Mission–Corporate Performance Cross Check

Most firms have a corporate mission statement, which presumably summarizes the strategic intent and is consistent with the rest of the golden cord. In far too many cases, however, the mission statement is "fluff" that appears in official pronouncements but is of little operational significance. A key test of how operational the mission statement truly is can be seen by cross-checking the mission with the key measurements used to evaluate performance. In many cases, the mission statement talks of market focus, customer prosperity, partnerships, and similar nonfinancial issues; but the day-to-day running of the company is dictated by short-term financial measures and periodic operating performance reviews that are also dominated by financial metrics.

The learning organization will by necessity require new measures. It is much better to measure the right things, approximately, than the wrong ones with great accuracy and precision. In many cases, as long as the measures are directionally correct, that is as good as can be expected. For example, measures of true customer satisfaction are difficult to make, but surveys, complaints, focus group results, market trends, and sensing of various customer attributes will at least point in the right direction.

The problem of improper measures needs to be explicitly cross-checked against the viability of strategic intent. If the top management group does indeed come to what it sees as a transformed mission statement (with consistency and integration), it too may end up in the scrap heap of mission statement fluff if the managers do not choose the right measurements to support it—and, even more important, if the wrong measurements are not explicitly unlearned.

Cross-Checking Strategic Intent to the Rest of the Golden Cord

We have said that the journey is even more important than the destination. The journey also can be assessed in terms of the strategic intent—as a beacon that directs the journey. To the extent that the golden cord exists, and is well-understood, the journey is more readily comprehended. For the enterprise to truly believe in its set of actions—and to see where it is headed—as many people as possible need to understand the golden cord and each of the eight facets of enterprise transformation. It is only this understanding that allows the transformation on each of the facets to be coordinated, integrated, and focused on the facets that are most in need of attention at a particular time.

Some people question whether it is necessary even to have a strategic intent or mission in the first place. What use is it, apart from a marketing gimmick or public relations pronouncement from on high? Isn't it possible just to link strategic responses to discontinuities and expectation changes—and then get on with it? What is the point of tying all the responses, competencies, and other infrastructure to an overall mission statement?

In fact, in too many instances a mission statement is either absent or worthless, and in most of these cases the lack causes a great deal of tension in the organization. Quite simply, people do not see where they are going or why.

■ A consultant for a local authority discovered many contradictions between what were espoused as guiding principles or mission and the reality of the situation. On paper, there was an equal opportunity mission, but the rules were suspended to get a new director on board. A stated goal of excellent working conditions could not be met because there were severe pressures to attend evening meetings and meet unrealistic deadlines. An overt commitment to house the homeless was followed with their eviction from town buildings. The human consequences were high stress, workaholism, alcoholism, and lethargy.

Reports of these sorts of contradictions have become common in management literature. This raises an interesting paradox: If the strategic intent is obviously a gimmick, then why do actions that contradict it cause so much tension? And there is no clearly articulated mission, why do people have so much trouble identifying with the company? A well-thought out and clearly articulated strategic intent describes where the company wants to go: What are our true objectives, and how do we know if we are achieving them? Is it possible, as in the case of British Airways, to start with the powerful strategic intent of becoming "the world's favorite airline" and fundamentally transform the nature of the enterprise?

The true value of a single, clearly stated, simple, inspiring strategic intent is that it becomes the rudder for navigating toward the desired destiny. But it must be real, not puffery, and it must be cross-checked with specific actions to see if those actions support or negate the stated intent.

Many authors note the importance of managerial leadership and other such nostrums. But precisely what does this mean? How do managers know when they are leading well or not? It is probably obvious when leadership is a disaster, but how do we recognize mediocrity? Much more important, how do we help all managers perform their leadership roles better? The journey through the transformation model using the Post-it Note process may not be the ultimate answer, but experience indicates that it can be very helpful in most cases.

Summary

In this chapter we have further developed the strategic aspects of the transformation model, with two basic objectives. The first is to strengthen the golden cord concept, which integrates the strategic intent with strategic responses—which in turn are necessarily integrated with the drivers (discontinuities and expectation changes) and the resulting infrastructure (competencies, processes, and resources). The second objective has been to show how the Post-it Note process can be used to implement the basic concepts. The goal is to provide a tool kit for managers to link challenges with responses—and the overriding strategy.

Key points of the chapter include:

□ Strategic intent, or the true mission, needs to guide the development of strategic responses or actions, but the flow is not one-way. By focusing on the desired actions, a strategic intent transformation can be fostered, which can be much more compatible with the detailed action steps that follow.

□ Corporate performance provides a backdrop to both strategic intent and to strategic responses. A direct connection from poor financial performance to action steps, however, runs a significant risk of causing the enterprise to lose focus, and sever the golden cord that provides consistency and integration.

□ The match between the mission statement and the measurements that the enterprise uses is a key indicator of consistency and integration. It is also indicative of feasibility, in that a firm that desires one thing but measures another is unlikely to achieve what it desires.

□ The environmental and packaging machinery examples show how the model can be applied to a subset of enterprise activity, as well as how shifts in the marketplace result in responses other than reducing one's prices when things get tough.

□ The game plan for transformation has to be tempered by the overall set of company objectives, the firm's core competencies possessed by the firm, and its financial health. All these are cross checks of feasibility.

□ Desirability also needs to be cross-checked. Does a transformation plan include a realistic assessment of the impacts on people as individuals— and have the responses on their part been adequately understood?

□ The strategic intent itself, as well as the golden cord, need to be evaluated in terms of consistency, integration, and company buy-in. Transformation requires a clear beacon to prioritize actions and to judge performance.

6 The Infrastructure

The top half of the integrated strategic transformation model has as its primary objective the development of consistent and integrated linkages among discontinuities/expectation changes, strategic response, strategic intent, and the necessary backdrop of corporate performance. With that accomplished, the operative question becomes:

How do we *achieve* the desired strategic responses? What are the new competencies required, and what are the underlying capabilities, processes, and resources that enable those competencies? Finally, what do we need to unlearn? That is, what current competencies, capabilities, and processes (and their resource deployments) inhibit achievement of the strategic responses?

The bottom half of the model (Figure 6.1) is fundamentally devoted to infrastructure. It is here that the detailed change agenda is formulated. Processes have to preserve the golden cord of consistency and integration, but also need to be carefully assessed in terms of feasibility and desirability. They must be both doable and in the interests of those who are asked to implement it.

There are far too many strategic plans that simply are not properly supported with the necessary infrastructure changes to make them a reality. Suppose an automotive parts producer encounters a change in expectations from one of its major car manufacturing company customers, which wants cost reductions from its suppliers. The producer's response might well be to create customer partnerships where producer and manufacturer cooperate in the design stages of a new automobile. This response in turn would call for a new competence in shared design activities.

What are the infrastructure needs to support such response? Clearly the supplier would need to implement customer partnership thinking, new information linkages with the customer, new pricing approaches,

Figure 6.1

Bottom Half of Model for Integrated Strategic Transformation

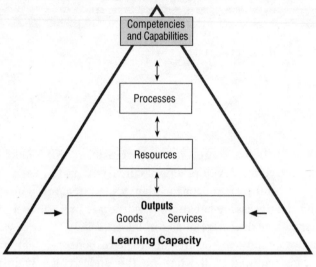

shared computer-aided design/computer-aided manufacturing (CAD/CAM) systems, and a host of other capabilities, processes, and systems. Moreover, serious "unlearning" would be needed. The customer can no longer be seen as an adversary; zero-sum thinking needs to be abandoned; the standard sales and marketing approaches need to be completely rethought; new linkages to the customer's purchasing group need to be established and old ones abandoned; old-style negotiation needs to be replaced with an emphasis on finding equitable win-win approaches.

But how feasible are these imperatives? Does the supplier have the resources to devote to these new ways of doing business? Is this manufacturer the right one to devote these resources to? Can the processes be changed for one customer—or does the firm need to do this for all customers? How will the demands of other customers play out differently? Should the producer be proactive on this, or wait a bit? Will this customer in fact play the game the way it needs to be played, or will it revert to old-style price squeezing after the supplier has made itself more vulnerable? Internally, can the required changes in culture, configuration, and coordination be achieved? Can the firm really unlearn what is needed? What are the implications for managerial leadership to make this a reality?

Then there are all the issues of desirability. Is this sort of arrangement in the producer's long-term interest? Is this the way to dominance, or is there another choice? Will the company make money in the long run at this? Can it be easily copied, or does this approach provide a new competitive advantage? Are the changes required in the interests of employees as they think about their own careers? Will they give them the necessary effort, or will changes just receive "lip service"?

The bottom line is that enterprise transformation requires more than a strategic point of view. Good strategy is necessary; it is not sufficient. At the end of the day, transformation is about change—change is about hard work—and it is hard work to design new systems and processes. That is, change is *about* infrastructure—this is what makes change happen. Far too many mergers, acquisitions, and other grand plans that looked great from a strategic point of view never achieve their intended results. A major reason is that the basic infrastructure changes required were not thought through, the required commitment was not made, and the immensity of the job was seriously underestimated.

Core Competence

Most of the literature on core competence focuses on the technical side. Thus it is said that Sony has a core competence in miniaturization, Honda in internal combustion, Cannon in optics, Corning in ceramics, and so on. Our experience in the Manufacturing 2000 project is that firms determine their core technical competence, and then say: Now what? Some answers to the question are usually fairly obvious. A well-defined core competence does often help in shaping overall investment policies, such as for a firm in integrated circuits: There are some new technologies that simply must be obtained, irrespective of standard financial considerations, as the cost of being in this business. Assessing core competency is also required when managers are determining whether a particular competency may no longer be core for the firm. For example, two companies we know in automotive components and packaging equipment have determined that soft metal machining is no longer an activity in which they have any advantage over subcontractors. Similarly, many electronics companies no longer consider it necessary to operate their own plants for making printed circuit boards. Finally, the core competence for many companies in the consumer products industry, such as Nestlé, is not only their unique technical competencies but more and more their competencies in brand management, logistics, and other "soft" areas.

The Hamel–Prahalad View of Core Competence

Gary Hamel and C.K. Prahalad define core competencies as the collective learning in an organization, especially understanding of how to coordinate diverse production skills and integrate multiple streams of technologies.[1] They further identify a core competency as having three critical elements. It provides potential access to a wide variety of markets; it makes a significant contribution to the values that customers appreciate in the bundle of goods and services provided; and it is difficult for competitors to imitate. These criteria apply to nontechnical competencies as well as to the more common view of technical competence. Nestlé's brand management surely satisfies these criteria.

A key concept that Hamel and Prahalad identify is that of exploiting "white space." White space represents the opportunities an enterprise has to combine core competencies in creative ways to find new bundles of goods and services that fall between current bundles (in the "white spaces"). Imagination is required to perceive these white spaces. White space exploitation requires determination, and leadership, and talent—as the authors illustrate. They show that Xerox missed opportunities developed at its Palo Alto Research Center, and compare this with more successful examples such as the Sony Walkman.

Exploiting white spaces requires first, identifying the opportunities, and next, determining what to do about them. An explicit identification of discontinuities and customer (and other stakeholder) expectations can be of help. That is, identifying challenges or opportunities is a first start to *exploiting* those opportunities. Doing so requires competencies—both existing and new.

Developing and exploiting core competence requires a strategic intent that focuses on competence *building:* identifying competence needs, and focusing measurement systems more on the competencies and less on the outputs. It also requires clear understanding of the resources that are essential to the enablement of competencies. Competence building allows the firm to create bundles of goods and services that exceed customer expectations. But it is important to focus on the competencies that create the bundles—not on the bundles themselves. It is easier for competitors to copy outputs than competencies; by the time they do so, core competencies should permit that bundle of goods and services to be yesterday's game.

An extension of Hamel's work is on the improper use of outsourcing.[2] Too many firms base outsourcing decisions on four questionable assumptions:

☐ Strategic intent must first and foremost be focused on the competitive position in the marketplace.

☐ Brand share is defensible without manufacturing share.

☐ Design and manufacturing can be separated.

☐ Market knowledge can be separated from manufacturing.

Articulating this set of questionable assumptions is very useful. It allows companies to understand more clearly what can and cannot be outsourced, as well as the critical processes, systems, and resources necessary to create the in-house infrastructure to support core competencies.

An Incremental View of Core Competence

An incremental view of core competence is that the required core competencies change over time, and that those appropriate for playing yesterday's game just might be a serious drawback for today's—and even more so for tomorrow's. For example, IBM has great competence in design, manufacture, marketing, and after-sales service for mainframe computers—which may be nothing more than an albatross in keeping it from responding to the latest discontinuities and expectation changes. Core competencies need to evolve—to meet the current discontinuities and changes in expectations, to develop the appropriate responses, and to enable whatever change in strategic intent is necessary.

For many companies, competencies in pushing products out the door (design, building, selling, servicing, financing) today hinder their ability to achieve a true customer focus. In some cases, there is just too much unlearning required. Might General Motors' long history of applying the latest technology, for example, have kept it from adopting the simplicity dictates of Japanese manufacturing?[2] An outsider's view suggests GM has seriously underestimated the paradigm shift required to move from Boynton's "mass production" stage to "continuous improvement."

The effect of downsizing on competencies is also profound. When a company downsizes, can it truly adopt the core competencies necessary to operate in the new environment, or is this just too tough—so the only way the company survives at all is to keep on with what well might be obsolete approaches and competencies? An interesting example is at Digital Equipment Corporation (DEC). The new CEO, Robert Palmer, saw the need for the company to break out of its "selling boxes" approach. This required a series of changes in organization, mentality, and competencies to focus the organization around particular markets and customer groupings. Unfortunately, in today's competitive climate, these changes could not be achieved soon enough to forestall further problems. Moreover, the necessary changes in infrastructure were just not understood very well—and not bought into. DEC then shifted back to its old tried and true approach of selling boxes. More recently the company has decided to abandon its classic matrix management structure. Whether any of this will create the fundamental competencies necessary to compete in today's computer marketplace remains to be seen.

Dynamic View of Competency

Figure 6.2 shows competence from a dynamic perspective. The basic idea is that competency needs to be seen in these four degrees of competitive strength. At the left-hand side of Figure 6.2, one finds "distinctive competence"; it allows the firm to achieve true competitive advantage over its competitors. Examples include patent protection (such as that enjoyed

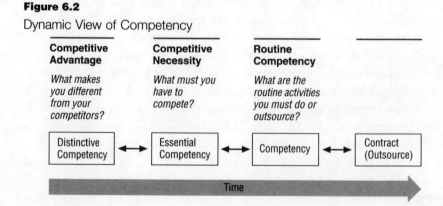

Figure 6.2

Dynamic View of Competency

Competitive Advantage	Competitive Necessity	Routine Competency	
What makes you different from your competitors?	*What must you have to compete?*	*What are the routine activities you must do or outsource?*	
Distinctive Competency	Essential Competency	Competency	Contract (Outsource)

Time

by Polaroid for many years), state-of-the-art designs (such as those produced by Nokia Mobile Phones), unique manufacturing competencies
(such as Toyota's just-in-time system), service provision (such as Federal
Express), after-sales service (such as Caterpillar's worldwide servicing),
branding (such as Smirnoff vodka), logistics systems (such as Wal-Mart's
cross docking), or even strategic assessment processes (such as General
Electric's business unit evaluation system).

The next level of competence shown in Figure 6.2 is "essential competence." This includes those competencies (and related capabilities, processes, resources, skills, attitudes, and behaviors) that the firm must have
in order to compete. Usually included are customer servicing systems,
some form of manufacturing or service creation, a design activity, and
other competencies that depend upon the particular business.

One more step to the right in Figure 6.2 is the set of routine competencies that must be done, such as preparing the payroll. Finally, the last
position in Figure 6.2 is "Contract (Outsource)."

In this view of core competency, competencies have a natural tendency
to move from the left to the right. What was at one point a distinctive
competency is copied by your competitors. Your core competence in
manufacturing is now well-known and available from several equipment
vendors. A distinctive design is made obsolete by a competitor's new
product. The Japanese car manufacturer's great advantage in product quality is less perceptible in the marketplace as American automobile companies have caught up with these quality levels. In the end, a particular
routine competence may not be worth the time or effort.

With the right efforts, competencies can move from right to left. A
routine competency such as delivering the goods might be improved, so
that significantly faster deliveries are made—allowing the company to
compete better. An essential competence such as short-run manufacturing might be enhanced, so that virtually any customer request can be
made to order and delivered within hours. An alliance with a customer
or supplier might be developed into a true partnership that significantly
improves overall value.

In each of the four categories of competence shown in Figure 6.2, there
is an underlying infrastructure of capabilities, processes, systems, and
resources that enable that competency. In order for a distinctive competency to remain so, that infrastructure requires constant renewal. If the
firm does indeed compete in the long run on its competencies, it needs
to see investments in them from a strategic point of view, not from a

narrow-minded capital budgeting approach. This vision requires the firm to understand the complex linkages between competencies and their supporting infrastructure.

Moreover, if a decision is made to outsource some competency, the entire infrastructure again needs to be considered. Some years ago, British Petroleum decided to outsource revenue accounting. It decided this was not an activity that it could do any better than a service bureau, and that the associated systems and resources were also not central to their business. Several of the Manufacturing 2000 companies are looking seriously at outsourcing portions of their information processing activities. Using the distinction that Benjamin Porter makes between information system infrastructure that is basically hardware and standard software and infrastructure that achieves some unique advantage, these firms are finding ways to outsource that portion of information systems that is not of strategic value.[3]

Outsourcing also requires divestment of the supporting resources for the competency. Some firms such as Electronic Data Systems (EDS) will not only take the routine systems processing off your hands, but will also take your people and your equipment. Similarly, Hewlett-Packard, in outsourcing its circuit board assembly operations for personal computers, turned its entire set of people, equipment, and factory over to a subcontractor. The key logic here is that these resources are not the ones that would lead to dominance in the long run. HP did not want to underestimate the required managerial thinking for the "care and feeding" of a large factory operation that no longer produced a set of goods and services central to competitive advantage. Circuit board assembly in-house was once an important advantage, and HP may still want to maintain some pilot operations for this. But with the growth of a fully competent supplier that can be integrated as a partner in Hewlett-Packard operations, there is no longer a need to maintain this manufacturing competency and all of its supporting infrastructure.

Dominance is largely associated with distinctive competency. A company that achieves (and maintains) dominance develops distinctive competencies and continually improves them. Continuous improvement of competencies that do not support the necessary strategic responses may feel good—but it will not provide dominance. Companies have finite resources and many competing needs. It is essential that resources be targeted to processes that support the distinctive competencies, rather than to those that are irrelevant to achieving dominance. An automotive parts manufacturer may be almost completely unwilling to make capital investments in soft machining because it does not see this competence as at all strategic.

To keep the right focus on dominance, it is essential to examine the golden cord periodically, to determine what challenges are really new, the ideal strategic responses to them, the competencies needed, and the relative priorities for learning and unlearning. Moreover, the examination needs to reach a conclusion as to whether a paradigm shift is required. All too often, the search for new initiatives turns out to be nothing more than old wine in new bottles.

Both Digital and IBM are examples of this problem. Other firms making money in the computer business are not trying to do so with a structure that made sense ten years ago. Making and selling computers was different when the price was eight times the direct cost, not 50 percent higher than the direct cost, as it is today. Today there is a fundamentally different set of core competencies and infrastructure; more important, there is a different strategic intent.

Competency Mapping

Once the firm determines the highest priority discontinuities, changes in expectations, and resultant strategic responses, it must determine the necessary competencies required to make those strategic responses: What has to be added in the way of competencies—and what needs to be unlearned? Then the enterprise needs to identify the underlying capabilities, processes, and resources that enable the competencies. The competencies typically need to be supported by new infrastructure.

In the bottom half of the enterprise transformation model in Figure 6.1, we need to develop the golden cord that links competencies to the underlying capabilities, processes, systems, and resources. The competency map provides this link by establishing a hierarchical relationship for the underlying infrastructure that enables a competency.

The Hierarchical Relationship

Figure 6.3 shows a competency map and the hierarchical relations that are imbedded in it. At the top, we have two core competencies, one of them shown as distinctive. Beneath this distinctive competence are shown two capabilities, with one again depicted as distinctive. The next

Figure 6.3
Competency Map

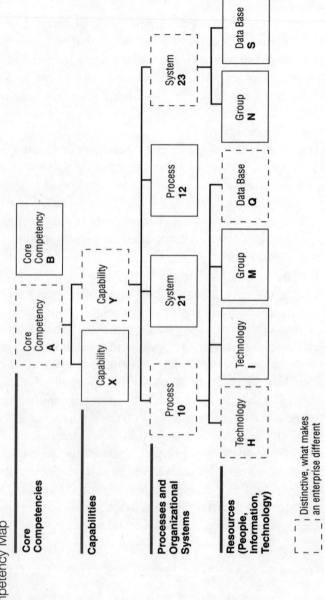

Core
Competencies

Capabilities

Processes and
Organizational
Systems

Resources
(People,
Information,
Technology)

Core
Competency
A

Core
Competency
B

Capability
X

Capability
Y

Process
10

System
21

Process
12

System
23

Technology
H

Technology
I

Group
M

Data Base
Q

Group
N

Data Base
S

Distinctive, what makes
an enterprise different

level shows processes and organizational systems. Finally, we see resources (people, information, and technology) as the last level in the hierarchy.

Processes in competence mapping must be capable of being described with a flowchart. If you cannot draw a flowchart for it, "it" is not a process. For example, people management might be extremely important, but it cannot be flow-charted. Neither can a training program that supports people management. But some supporting process, such as the series of steps in a particular training activity, can be flow-charted. This characteristic is of particular consequence in benchmarking. A detailed comparison of processes is at the heart of true benchmarking.

The number of levels in any particular competency map is essentially a question of detail and level of aggregation. It is not critical if more levels are labeled as subcompetencies or subcapabilities. In fact, the only significant reason for differentiating between competencies and capabilities is to have a distinct hierarchical level between competencies and processes.

Competencies, capabilities, and processes can be differentiated, although their hierarchical relationship is more important than exact definitions.

    □ A competency is the ability to integrate technical, managerial, and other expertise with capabilities, processes, and the knowledge base. The focus of competencies is more strategic than operational. The primary objective of a competency is to enable specific strategic responses—and the overall strategic intent. Examples include information management to support customer partnership development, joint venture management to better integrate a new business concept, and simultaneous engineering to speed commercialization of technology.

    □ A capability can be defined as the accumulated skill, know-how, learning, and culture associated with integrating and operating particular processes to achieve synergies. The focus of capabilities is more operational than strategic. Examples include managing partnerships with customers and vendors, operating manufacturing planning systems, and product/process innovation.

    □ A process is the basic building block or activity in an organization. A process, by definition, can be flow-charted and measured in terms of efficiency and effectiveness. It is the practice of processes that is most readily examined with benchmarking—and improved through business process reengineering. Examples include inventory control, training, product testing, the quote-to-cash cycle, and all the associated systems to support these processes.

Redefining the Hierarchy

The hierarchical relationship portrayed by competency mapping should be seen as more of a general construct than an absolute association. In practice, it is sometimes useful to take a process and redefine it as a competency (i.e., the achievement of excellence in that process). Thereafter, one can determine the underlying capabilities and subprocesses required. For example, if we take the achievement of excellent practice in inventory control as a desired competence, we might see education and training, personnel selection, implementation of consultants' recommendations, integration with customer (and supplier) information systems, and software selection as underlying capabilities. Each of these could in turn be broken down into subcapabilities and processes.

Determination of Competencies

To determine the new competencies required, we use the same process we followed for discontinuities, expectation changes, and strategic responses. After group members determine the strategic responses to the internal discontinuities, external discontinuities, changes in customer expectations (two levels of customers), and changes in expectations of other stakeholders, they group responses by affinity, title the groups, and prepare an overall strategic response summary statement. Now, the question is: What are the new or additional necessary competencies required in order to achieve these responses? A first cut at the answer is provided through the brainstorming approach, where a group of senior executives for the firm or particular business unit attempt to identify what competencies would be required.

Affinity Grouping and Titles

An interesting result of the Post-it Note exercise for determining competencies is that responses of the participants usually turn out to be "capabilities" rather than competencies. Although the intent is to determine competencies, it is the *grouping* of the responses, and the subsequent determination of a title for the group, that produces the overall necessary competency. For example, one group of executives produced a great number of separate items they found necessary to achieve their strategic responses, including five that were seen to have affinity:

☐ Cost-effective design.

☐ Design for manufacture.

☐ Effective sourcing.

☐ Low-cost manufacture.

☐ Inventory control.

After several iterations, the group settled on the title of "managed costing" for this affinity grouping. It is this title that is truly the necessary competence; the others are supportive of it (i.e., they are "capabilities"). It became apparent to the group that this needed to be a distinctive competence if the company were to be able to deal effectively with the set of challenges it was facing. Once the title for the basic competency is identified and understood, it usually becomes clear that other capabilities are also needed. In this case, the group determined the need for a capability in "measurement systems" that would allow management to assess its progress toward managed costing.

Business-Oriented Competencies

When a group applies the Post-it Note process to determine the necessary competencies, most applications end up focusing on nontechnical competencies. It may be that the technical competencies are assumed or taken as a given. To make many of the strategic responses necessary in today's business environment, it is clearly necessary to be faster, more responsive, less variable, more in tune with customer needs, more knowledgeable about marketplace changes, and more in tune with competitive issues. These responses require business-oriented competencies—distinctive competencies—in addition to technical competencies.

The Environmental Example

In the two previous chapters we examined an environmental example in terms of the internal/external discontinuities, changes in expectations of customers and other stakeholders, and strategic responses to these discontinuities and expectation changes. We use this same firm example here. The firm sells environmental pollution control equipment. Its overall strategic response message is: Strengthen the organization, its approach to the market, and product development to foster environmental business opportunities.

The Capabilities and Competencies

Table 6.1 shows the results of the Post-it Note process applied to competency determination. Of the five affinity groups, "marketing" and "organization" are the most important new competencies that summarize the underlying capabilities. The company was able to see that acquiring distinctive competencies in these two areas was critical to meeting the challenges it faced.

The marketing list reflects a need to be less in the machinery business than in the environmental business. This is directly connected with the company's perceived deficiency (internal discontinuities) in meeting environmental mandates as well as the executive group wanted. It is also consistent with the external discontinuities and customer expectation changes. For example, the capabilities included in the marketing competence detail a need for fast development of new products that can meet any changing environmental requirements. The implied match with stakeholder expectations is also clear. The achievement of technical excellence while being cost-effective mandates a marketing approach that focuses on these dimensions.

The new organization competency is similarly linked to the fundamental drivers and strategic responses. The organization needs to be structured as an environmental company, where functional boundaries between engineering and marketing disappear. The organization also needs to be designed to strengthen its interactions with outside third parties, including pressure groups and government bodies. One of the firm's internal discontinuities includes an organizational constraint that now keeps the company from delivering totally integrated solutions; the organizational changes are directly focused on rectifying this issue. Similarly, in the external discontinuity grouping of "rules and regulations" (chapter 4), there are a series of new and changing environmental influences and regulations. Responding requires competencies in dealing with pressure groups, anticipating (and influencing) regulations, and understanding the

Table 6.1

Environmental Products Company Competencies

Marketing (15)	Information Systems (8)
■ Strong and competent market approach ■ Fast development of new products according to future market trends ■ Specific market approach for the environment as a business activity (market-oriented contracting division) and for the environment as a general development opportunity (with measurable performance of product activity) ■ Compulsory feedback on marketing experience ■ Ability to identify what the customer/market really needs and to question/change our present structure to meet those needs	■ Gathering perceptions of market needs within three to five years (international marketing information system) ■ Corporate network to create data base on environmental trends and legislation ■ Global "info system" to capture facts and figures on present environment performance as base for targets (and later reporting) ■ Integrated strategic management of technology systems, a strategy of technology management ■ Early warning radar

Organization (13)	
■ New name for company ■ Integration of marketing and engineering capabilities ■ Network should extend to pressure groups, i.e., lawyers, politicians, ecologists, biologists, biochemists, public relations, marketing, geologists ■ Provide global service but act locally (central coordination, local action) ■ Competencies for: —Financing big environmental projects (work management facilities) —Operating these facilities ■ Build up a structure/competency for customer plant operations ■ Systems design philosophy ■ R&D department in Brussels ■ Engineering to be done at the source of the environmental problem	**Champion the Environment (8)** ■ A top executive politically active outside the home market ■ More influence on opinion leaders and decision makers in the environmental market ■ Interdisciplinary cross-functional forum on environmental issues **Measurement (4)** ■ Internal environmental performance benchmarks ■ Methodology to measure environmental performance ■ Reward systems for creative people

overall direction that environmental improvements will take. The overall impact of achieving this competency may well be a paradigm shift.

The match of the competencies with both the overall strategic response and the underlying details also shows the golden cord. Strengthening the approach to the market, establishing clear policies, focusing R&D to regain leadership in the field, and becoming "glocal" in character are clear mandates for new competencies in marketing and organization.

The less-weighted competencies are also consistent with the overall golden cord, and in some ways are almost subcompetencies. Information systems devoted to the new market and organizational requirements will be essential. So will measurement systems that clearly focus on environmental attributes and improvement in those attributes. And the "champion the environment" competence is completely consistent with the new organizational focus.

The Competency Map

Figure 6.4 presents a specific competency map developed for the marketing competency. It focuses on the new environmental needs as opposed to classic marketing capabilities. The capabilities arc market research (focused on the environmental aspects of the marketplace), customer-focused sales (focused on helping customers solve their environmental problems), environmental knowledge, marketing–engineering linkages (to speed new product/service development), and dialogue with pressure groups (to understand and perhaps influence legislation).

The environmental knowledge capability includes four subcapabilities: understanding legislation (including before it is passed), environmental performance measurement (new approaches and new areas, such as airborne versus waterborne), information systems, and education and training (inside the company, customers, and other stakeholders). The information systems subcapability requires five rather different processes: customer complaint system, university research assessment, legislative trend appraisal, industry association data assessment, and internal brainstorming. The intent here is to establish an information system that focuses on nontraditional sources of data, including a concrete way to integrate these critical indicators of the environmental marketplace.

The competency map illustrates the need for some quite different infrastructure to support the firm's desired new competency. Maps like this can help managers better understand the complexity of achieving even well-defined objectives.

Other Examples

Some other competency maps may clarify discussion and demonstrate how the ideas are applied in several different contexts.

Figure 6.4
Environmental Competency Map

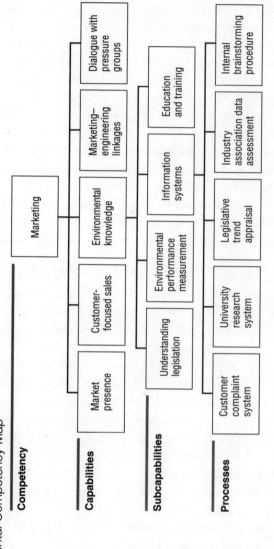

SKF Bearings used the "customer activity cycle (CAC)" model to focus on the detailed ways in which its customers use products and services. The results gave it an improved understanding of market segmentation and caused a refocusing of the product line (and added services). In essence, the company determined that it has two major product groupings, automotive and nonautomotive, and two major product markets, OEM and after-sales service. The after-sales market became redefined from "selling bearings" to "trouble-free operations," a move that implies providing training for installation and maintenance, and the packaging of kits to complete a service job.[4]

The move to trouble-free operations for SKF is a change in strategic intent, made in response to a better understanding of customer expectations, as well as a discontinuity identified as unnecessary bearing failures. The CAC analysis reveals the attendant set of strategic responses, including providing dealer training, end-user educational materials development, packaging kits instead of individual items, purchasing products from other vendors to make up the kits, and helping after-sales service parts dealers better market SKF products—a focus on the top half of the integrated strategic transformation model. The competency mapping addresses the bottom half and the new infrastructure requirements.

The key questions are: What are the necessary new competencies to make SKF's vision a reality? Which ones are distinctive? Logical candidates include supply chain management, information systems, new sales and marketing approaches, and an entirely different approach to customer service. What needs to be unlearned? That is, what current competencies and practices will impede achievement of the new competencies? Some likely suspects are traditional approaches to bearing manufacturing based on long runs and minimal product cost, with typical "mass production" approaches to defining costs and other measurements.

Figure 6.5 presents a sample competency map for SKF. The "supply chain management" competency is shown as requiring five subordinate capabilities: procurement, customer partnerships, vendor partnerships, manufacturing planning and control, and logistics. Figure 6.5 also shows that the manufacturing planning and control capability needs several processes to achieve it.

The first process shown in Figure 6.5 is inventory control. Full implementation of the new SKF vision will require something in the range of a hundred times more part numbers. Instead of selling bearings, SKF now needs to purchase many other items, and combine them into kits for

Figure 6.5
SKF Sample Competency Map

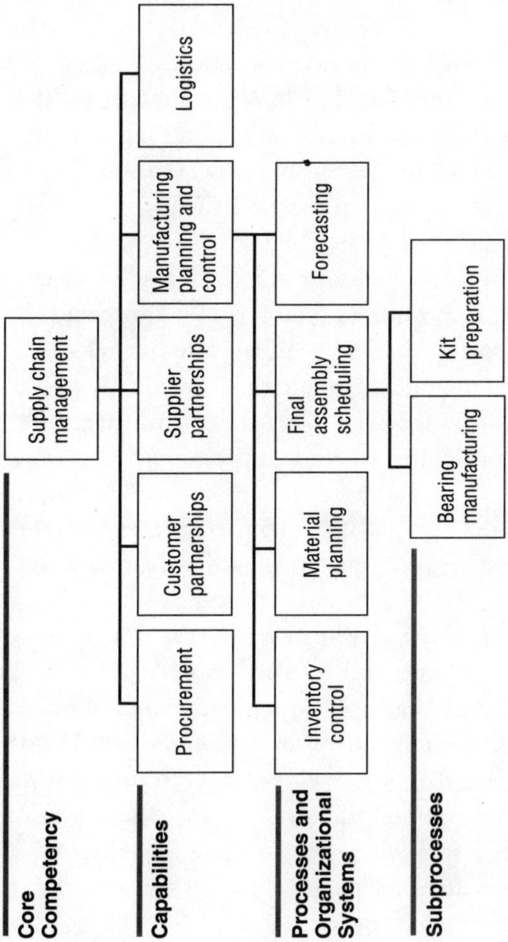

specific end-user needs. If the inventory control systems are not absolutely state-of-the-art, the result could literally bankrupt the company. The other processes are similarly critical.

Final assembly scheduling is shown as having two subprocesses, kit preparation and bearing manufacturing. Implicit is the need for some unlearning. In the past, bearings manufacturing at SKF focused on the automotive OEM business. That meant long runs and intense concentration on unit cost reduction. But now, there will by necessity be shorter runs, a need to be more responsive to customer needs, and a consequent need to unlearn the old paradigm.

Final assembly scheduling is in fact absolutely critical. If one has 100 kits of type A, no kits of type B, and a part that is common to the two kits, there is a big problem. In fact, the final assembly scheduling needs to be second to none. It should function ideally on a make-to-order basis, where kit orders received today are assembled and shipped the same day. This implies significant work (business process reengineering) as well as benchmarking of worldwide best practices. The golden cord leads down to this process as a critical distinctive competence. Here is where significant business process reengineering and benchmarking talent needs to be invested.

When we talk about infrastructure, the SKF example provides considerable insight into feasibility. The basic idea of selling trouble-free operations instead of bearings has a great deal of appeal. But increasing part numbers by a factor of ten or a hundred would give anyone pause for thought. Instead of buying bars of steel to cut up, it will now be necessary to buy castings, finished parts, gaskets, and a host of other items. Does SKF in fact know where to purchase these items? Which are the good and poor suppliers? What are the right prices? This represents a massive overhaul of purchasing practices.

Similarly, if we explode the "customer partnership" capability in Figure 6.5 for the automotive after market, we see we need to know the exact inventory positions of dealers, requiring point of sale terminals hooked to SKF. With 37,000 dealers, this is a formidable undertaking; so is limiting linkages to even the top 10 percent or 20 percent of them. Supporting all these terminals and the information systems that are required to drive them also makes one wonder about feasibility.

Figures 6.6, 6.7, and 6.8 are three competence maps developed by groups we have worked with as part of the Manufacturing 2000 research. They illustrate quite different competencies and their underlying capabilities

Figure 6.6

Customer Needs Competency Map

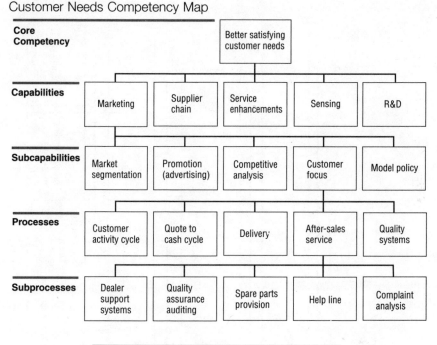

and processes. Figure 6.6 deals with a high-level competence of better satisfying customer needs. It eventually focuses on the after-sales process, along with five subprocesses that could be benchmarked.

Figure 6.7 is a competence map for product innovation, prepared for a company in the integrated circuits business. In this case, the competence map is carried to the level of resources that support two processes: evaluation methods for supporting an FMEA (failure mode and effects analysis) process, and review for supporting a cooperative evaluation process of the products with the customers.

Figure 6.8 addresses competence in people management. In this case, the group preparing the competence map saw the need for a change in corporate culture and capabilities as critical. The processes to support this change are indicated, along with subprocesses and resources for selected processes.

These examples should indicate the richness of the competency mapping idea. The procedure can be applied to virtually any competence

Figure 6.7
Integrated Circuits Competency Map

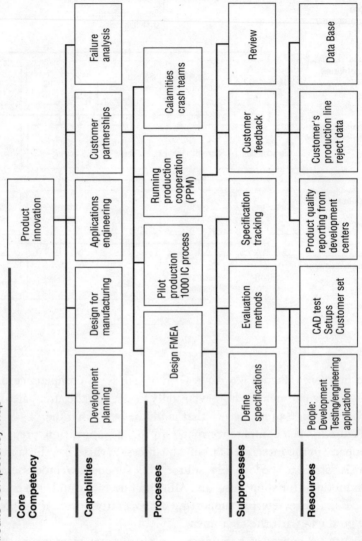

Figure 6.8

People Management Competency Map

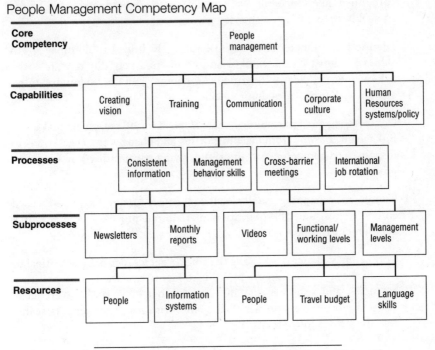

that a firm wishes to create, and applications are limited only by the imagination of the team working on it. The result is consolidation of many divergent opinions and consensus on the key competencies, their underlying capabilities and processes, and the golden cord that needs to be maintained to link them.

Summary

This chapter focuses on the detailed infrastructure required to accomplish the strategic response. The key points to take away are:

◻ Enterprise transformation requires much more than a set of good strategic ideas. The strategic response must be linked to the required competencies and to the entire infrastructure that enables these competencies.

☐ The meaning of core competence goes beyond the typical focus on technical competence. Our emphasis is on the net or new competencies required to enable the strategic responses.

☐ Distinctive competence needs to be directly linked to dominance—to achieve competitive advantage and be distinctively different. It is the achievement of clearly identified competence and the underlying infrastructure that provides dominance.

☐ Competency mapping allows the golden cord of reason to make the linkage all the way from discontinuities and changes in expectations to responses to competencies, their underlying capabilities, and finally to processes.

☐ Competency mapping usually leads to the need for new business-focused competencies, and the definition of required processes and resource deployment implications.

☐ Competency mapping—linking the competencies identified as critical to enable the strategic responses—leads to identifying the key capabilities, processes, and resources that are essential to achieve the competencies. These are the targets on which the enterprise needs to focus its scarce resources for improvement.

☐ Competency mapping provides a detailed look at the overall infrastructure requirements. These need to be carefully examined for feasibility; it is far too easy to underestimate the requirements for learning and unlearning.

7 Learning Capacity

The eighth and last facet of enterprise transformation is the enterprise's capacity to learn. As the base of the lower triangle of the transformation model, learning capacity is the foundation on which the infrastructure half of the model is based. It is the overall organizational learning that is the key determinant of enterprise survival—and this learning necessarily must encompass the entire organization: its competencies, capabilities, processes, resources, and outputs.

Rather than "Dominate or die," we can say "learn or die." In the final analysis, it is both *speed* and *direction* of learning that determine dominance or death. The firm that learns the right things faster than its competitors will dominate. Those that learn more slowly—or that restrict their learning to past challenges—will inevitably fade.

"Learn or die" connotes an approach to improvement, a method that is more important than a given state. That is, transformation needs to be seen less as the need to fix some problem or arrive at some solution than as an ongoing evolutionary process that needs nurturing. Learning companies will therefore explicitly recognize the need for a method, develop this method or transformation engine, benchmark it to that of other companies, and continuously improve it.

Learn or Die

Learning is the determinant of dominance or death, assuming it focuses on the right things—and ignores those that do not matter. Continuing to get better at yesterday's game is an exercise in futility, whether that game is buggy whips, mainframe computers, or any competency that does not line up with well-formulated strategic responses. In short, the golden cord applies to learning as much as to any of the other seven facets of enterprise transformation.

The Learning Organization

There are several definitions of the learning organization. A useful one for our purposes is provided by David Garvin: "A learning organization is skilled at creating, acquiring, and transferring knowledge and at modifying behavior to reflect new knowledge and insights."[1]

To develop this definition to meet the enterprise transformation point of view, we must add an absolutely critical caveat: The goal has to be *dominance.* Learning for itself is fine in an educational institution, but for a company the message is "learn or die," and the learning *must* focus on the achievement of dominance. Following the enterprise transformation model, the definition needs to reflect the strategic intent and the set of strategic responses, and focus on competencies. In fact, the learning organization continually "bundles and unbundles" competencies (and their supporting infrastructure) to respond to the ever-changing sets of challenges it faces. Bundling and unbundling reflect learning and unlearning; the firm must not only acquire new competencies and integrate them with existing ones, but also identify and eliminate those that impede its progress toward dominance.

Two quotations from Tom Peters about the learning organization are enlightening:[2]

□ "3M is trying to sell more and more intellect and less and less materials."

□ "Microsoft's only factory asset is the human imagination."

The "currency" for measuring the learning organization is its competencies. At 3M, the strategic intent requires distinctive competencies based on significant learning. The Microsoft example is a bit less focused; imagination as a strategic intent may not be well enough tied to the needs of the marketplace.

Digital Equipment Corporation (DEC) is another company example that illustrates the need for the learning organization to focus on dominance. DEC once created through its computer network an organization second to none in communicating—unfettered by organizational boundaries. It created, acquired, and transferred knowledge around the organization at a furious pace. It may also have been better than others at "modifying behavior to reflect new knowledge and insights," but these traditional aspects of the learning organization have not been enough to help it today. In fact they might even be a hindrance. Too much knowledge-sharing may keep an enterprise from a shared sense of purpose, from recognizing and agreeing upon a common definition of the challenges and strategic responses, and from rejecting complacency to embrace true urgency. A learning organization—but one not focused on the right issues for dominance—is just another example of flushing the pigeons. At some point an enterprise needs leadership, which cannot be based on brainstorming by 20,000 people.

Learning must reflect a changing of the rules of the game, in response to the discontinuities and expectations identified. In fact, the learning organization does more than this. The dominating firm *sets* the discontinuities and establishes the expectations, and its learning needs to focus on establishing the competencies to do so. Sony believes its long-run future is much less in the business of building entertainment "boxes" than in building what comes out of the boxes. This means that its learning must focus on the entertainment business, and it has to find the ways to develop distinctive competencies in this field. Sony's losses in the entertainment field may not really be losses, but rather a necessary investment in learning. In the long run, Sony needs to have more artists under exclusive contract; it needs to attract the best screenwriters; and it needs to improve its batting average for new motion picture releases. If it can achieve the competencies for these, it will be unbeatable.

All this is much easier said than done. How do firms become better learners? What do they learn from? How do they rid themselves of bad habits? How do they truly learn from experiences that even with perfect hindsight look like just so many anecdotes? How do we learn how to learn?

One way to learn is to clearly identify and study different forms of learning. That is, the learning (and unlearning) required for a transformation or major turnaround is fundamentally different from that associated with continuously doing the same things better. The implication is that managers must understand when certain types of learning are most appropriate.

Learning and Morgan Gould's Change Wheel

Morgan Gould's change wheel in Figure 7.1 distinguishes between two types of change. In the top half of the model, change is conservative and incremental, and the underlying approach to change is either fine-tuning

Figure 7.1

Gould Change Wheel

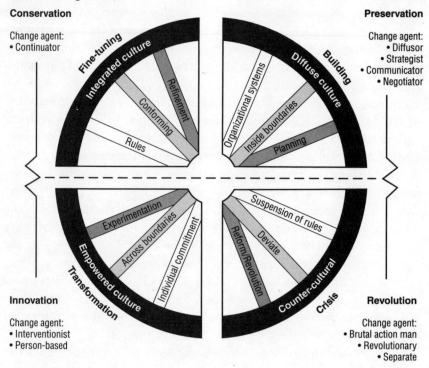

Source: R. Morgan Gould, "Managing the 'How' of Change," *M2000 Executive Report*, no. 16 (November, 1994): 3. Reprinted with permission.

or "building." The bottom half, on the other hand, focuses on change that is revolutionary (crisis) or transformational.

The important point is that while learning takes place in both halves the learning is also fundamentally different. The lucky firm can stay in the top half of the model for a long time. Its basic set of challenges, responses, and competency requirements is relatively constant, or is evolving in some predictable and consistent way. That means the learning, or at least the necessary learning approach, does not require a fundamental change in methodology.

This is different in the bottom half of the model—and it is certainly different when a firm moves from the top half into the bottom half. In fact, two key issues in transformation involve this difference. First, how does a company recognize that the discontinuities and other challenges make it necessary to move from the top half to the bottom half; and second, how does it actually achieve the movement to the bottom half? To make this transition implies an inversion of existing values, questioning of basic assumptions about the marketplace, rejection of present policies and practices, and recognition that alignment of the eight facets of the enterprise is just not correct. This means we must start anew—first with the challenges, then the responses, then the competencies, and then the infrastructure. But we must also find out how to learn—faster, better, and differently—and how we refocus learning on doing better things, not on doing the same things better.

The culture that supports learning is fundamentally different in the top and bottom halves of the change wheel. Fine-tuning assumes rules, conformity, and refinement. Quite the opposite is the case in the revolution/crisis quadrant. Here rules are suspended; conformity to many past ideas has to be formally rejected; and it is much more important to adopt new thinking than to refine existing thinking. Because making this kind of shift in culture is indeed revolutionary, one might well ask if it is even possible with an existing management team, or without an outside change agent such as a consultant to effect the necessary shift in culture.

A less dramatic, but still fundamental, cultural shift is required to move from the building quadrant to the transformation quadrant. In the former, the culture needs to support planning, improvement within existing organizational units, and adherence to an ongoing process for learning. In transformation, these are again set aside. Planning needs to be replaced or at least significantly augmented by experimentation. Cross-functional and other "outside-the-box" improvements are required. Individual commitments are needed to break existing organizational learning notions.

There is no way to underestimate the effort required to move from the top half of Morgan Gould's change wheel to the bottom half. Learning very well in one culture can be a significant detriment to learning in the other. Executives might look at the characteristics of each quadrant and recognize that they are doing bits of them. They will say they are committed to refinement (say, through TQM), or planning, or organizational systems change such as empowering the work force. All these efforts are fine, but they produce what Gould calls first-order change in an integrated culture where corporate values are shared throughout the organization.

When many companies find themselves with serious difficulties, however, they do not hesitate to abandon fine tuning or building, and adopt top-down command and control methods to force major cultural change, based on a newly articulated strategic intent.

Fine-tuning or building may be adequate for companies operating in relatively stable and growing markets, offering stable products or services that assume stable processes for their delivery. Given these conditions, it is possible to fine-tune your way to dominance—the Japanese have been successful at this for a long time. The real crunch comes when competitors have caught up, the market is fragmenting, new products threaten to make yours obsolete. Then you need to employ experimentation for real. Now learning becomes critical. Changing business processes is one thing—changing management culture is quite another. To abandon an integrated culture, by far the most common, and replace it by an empowered culture is a huge learning challenge. You are being asked not to change things, but to change the very ways of changing.

Learning for Radical Change

If Microsoft's asset is people's imagination, and this belief is tied explicitly to strategic intent, perhaps Microsoft is indeed that "lucky" firm where consistency and integration remain strong for long time periods, and its learning can proceed along the same direction. That is, Microsoft can basically fine-tune and build to maintain its dominance—without a major shift in culture. But at DEC, fine-tuning and building were antithetic. It needed to move to the crisis/revolution quadrant, and thereafter achieve the right transformation strategy. Its underlying culture and learning approach had to change to reflect this fundamental shift in direction. We can speculate that a culture that ingrains learning according to the top half of the model will have difficulty making the necessary shift.

Peter Drucker says, "Every organization needs to prepare for the abandonment of everything it does."[3] "Preparing" means *learning*, but of a different variety from fine-tuning and building. The latter approach to learning must instead be "unlearned." The new learning needs to focus at least as much on the "journey" as on the destination; that is, on the *how* as much as on the *what*. The point here is that the learning needs to shift from a first-order interest in the *manifestations* of the learning, to a second-order concern with the capacity of the learning, and the ways in which the learning needs to take place. This is where the comparison of practices—call it a form of benchmarking—needs to be focused.

Transforming the Learning Capacity

At many points we have identified learning capacity as one of the eight facets that essentially define the organization. True transformation inevitably involves a transformation in learning capacity. An enterprise might be a great learning organization in terms of the top half of the change wheel model, but there can come a day when no matter how good this learning is, it is basically misdirected. The game has changed. The vital discontinuities and expectations are just not the same; the strategic intent or mission is out of tune with reality; the set of action programs is no longer appropriate. The distinctive competencies and infrastructure requirements are fundamentally different. Learning that does not take these shifts into account is woefully inadequate.

The goal for the learning organization is not just to refocus objectives with the same approach. It is necessary instead to unlearn the old approaches to excellence *and* the old approaches to learning. Figure 7.2 shows this with a simplified and slightly changed version of the strategic intent model. The usual top label of "corporate performance" is replaced with "past performance." The key point is that corporate performance is in fact largely historical. It is based on reporting after-the-fact results.

The bottom label is the same as before, "learning capacity." For transformation, it needs to be the "antidote" to past performance, because we need

---

Figure 7.2

Past Performance versus Learning Capacity

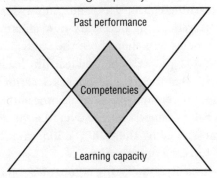

to avoid basing our learning on the past. The distinctive competencies (the currency for learning) need to be driven by new ideas, by rejection of old concepts, and by a realignment of the challenges, the strategic intent, and the strategic responses.

But the past should not be seen as something that has no value, or as something that can be easily overcome. Roger Martin discusses this issue very well. He points out that even if one develops new ideas with impeccable logic behind them, they often will be overruled in practice as decision makers fall back on strategic ideas and measures of effectiveness that once made sense, but no longer do.[4] The key point in making real change in this kind of world is to examine the past *candidly*, making the strategy and underlying assumptions explicit, then deliberately set aside the old ideas, institute the new ones—and establish measurements that enforce the adoption of these new concepts, so that progress toward the new objectives can be evaluated and rewarded and so that reversions to old strategic thinking will result in poor evaluations of actual results.

This approach clearly shows the absolutely critical role that measurement plays in learning. The right measures will support rapid learning— and learning in the right direction—while the wrong ones will clearly impede it. A fundamental premise is that whenever learning needs to change direction it will be necessary to change the way it is measured. Idea generation and individual initiative may be appropriate achievements to measure in Andrew Boynton's invention stage, but they are less so in mass production (where conformance to quality and schedule achievement are more appropriate). When one implements continuous improvement, the measures again need to change; now teamwork, suggestions implemented, quality improvement, and customer satisfaction are more appropriate. Finally, under mass customization, product variety, speed of delivery, and new features may be critical.

Finally, as the learning capacity expands, and is focused on adoption of new directions to reflect the necessary new alignment, the resulting distinctive competencies will shape both the strategic responses and the strategic intent. That is, properly focused learning leads to competencies that are so distinctive that the set of responses or actions taken is strongly influenced by these competencies. In fact, at some point the competencies are such a force for dominance that the overall strategic intent or enterprise mission is influenced by them. In the long run, *this* state needs to be the goal of the learning organization.

Perhaps the most basic issue facing companies today is whether they are learning at a faster rate (and more appropriately) than the speed of change in the challenges they face. That is, is the eighth facet of the enterprise transformation model (learning capacity) more robust—i.e., transforming faster—than the first (challenges)? The dominant firm is learning (and transforming) fast enough to set the pace—to sometimes create discontinuities and to always be a marketplace innovator—to exceed customer expectations and create new values for customers.

Learning can also be thought of in terms of the way that new competencies are achieved and existing ones strengthened, particularly in terms of distinctive competency development. If, for example, a distinctive competency in supply chain management is seen as crucial to dominance, then learning needs to be focused on the best ways to achieve it; the focus for the learning also should lead to competency that is not easily duplicated.

Learning Capacity and the Other Seven Facets

We can examine the direction and core of learning by looking through the other transformation facets or lenses. Is the learning in line with the strategic intent? Boynton's model with its four stages (invention, mass production, continuous improvement, and mass customization), for example, indicates that the fundamental style and focus of the learning is different when the firm is transforming from invention to mass production. The emphasis is deliberately away from science or craft approaches that involve tacit knowledge toward development of rules, practices, and standard ways of working with codified knowledge as an explicit goal. Clearly the type of learning is vastly different—at the individual level, at the department level, and at the firm level.

There is an equally definitive shift in learning approach when the company moves from mass production to continuous improvement. Individual learning is much more encouraged, sharing of ideas is accomplished in fundamentally different ways, and the knowledge repository for learning is much less well-structured. A similar dramatic change in learning approaches is required for firms that move from continuous improvement to mass customization.

The fundamental issue is that the learning approach, as well as its goals, usually needs to be changed when there is a fundamental shift in strategy, i.e., a paradigm shift. Parallel arguments can be made for changes in each of the other enterprise transformation facets; a major change in strategic responses can easily necessitate a shift in the approach and direction for learning.

■ A European chemicals manufacturer decided to support a "natural" cosmetics firm in its development of new products. For the chemicals firm, this means that its learning in its laboratory and in its manufacturing sites had to shift in ways to support this customer-based initiative. New processes (and abandonment of old ones) require that learning be directed to how to achieve the desired results. The overriding objectives for this learning came from the fundamental change in supporting the new market initiative.

■ Heineken has made fundamental decisions as to outsourcing of certain computer operations that have revolutionized the way learning is taking place in computer-based systems at the company. In essence, all traditional transaction-based processing has been outsourced, as have the computers to do it and the personnel who support these systems. This now allows the new management information systems group to focus their learning on implementing standard software packages and developing new uses of computing to more creatively link themselves with major customers.

Deployment and redeployment of resources equally influence learning direction and specific objectives. For example, focusing on processes that cross organizational boundaries implies learning with a similar focus, not learning with an outdated functional view of the world. Finally, the outputs themselves play a strong role in focusing the desired learning for the organization. If McDonald's wants to sell pizza, its learning (and unlearning) required to provide that output must be tailored to this end.

Learning and Information Management

Learning is largely about infrastructure, and supporting competencies, capabilities, and processes, the key building blocks for enterprise transformation. In our competency mapping descriptions, we include systems with processes. They are also capable of being flow-charted, and systems essentially are used to regulate processes.

A complex question in information management is the changes that need to be made to information systems to support enterprise transformation. The design of new processes that integrate once-separate areas and decisions almost always requires new information systems. One also needs to stop the information-processing that supported the old style of decision making. This is often difficult because that information-processing is integrated with still other areas not included in the new process conception.

This problem is compounded by the need to maintain two systems at once (likely producing conflicting information). A related issue is the installation of new information technology as firms migrate off mainframe computers to distributed processing, networks, and client-server architecture forms of computing. It is like the chicken and the egg: Should the transformation in information lead or follow enterprise transformation?

Our position on this is clear: Information transformation needs to follow enterprise transformation and be directed by it, but it needs to follow *closely*. We see several companies that have essentially ignored the information issues associated with their transformation, perhaps believing that the problems will disappear or at least become more tractable through simplification. This is a dangerous belief. In fact, surveys indicate that anywhere from 50 percent to 85 percent of executives who have reengineered their operations are "dissatisfied with the results."[5] The reasons are undoubtedly many, including indiscriminant downsizing under the rubric of reengineering, and pigeon flushing versus true transformation. But at least one set of problems derives from the mismatch between information systems and reengineered operations. Many firms have not adequately assessed the requirements in information management for enterprise transformation.

The issues associated with *learning* in information systems are more complex than how or when to implement new information systems. More fundamental is whether the learning and competency development in information management are in fact headed in the right direction. Are our efforts limited by existing constraints? Are we achieving the cost reductions for the firm that new hardware or software products should provide? Are we using information management to support fundamental strategic responses, or more to process routine transactions?

A way to represent this problem is to see enterprise transformation as like a sailboat, not a motorboat. The destination may be relatively clear, but we do not get there in a straight line. The winds and currents need to be continually assessed; we must tack periodically. The journey is even more complex than that, because learning is taking place at the same time; it is as if the boat were being redesigned during the voyage. One of the main sails for the boat is the information systems, but they too are being overhauled en route.

The fundamental issues are how to direct the learning in information management, *and* how to keep it in tune with the overall enterprise transformation efforts. Essentially, there is a need for senior management direction and coordinated planning for the various new infrastructure requirements, information systems included. It is critical that a visionary approach be taken so that overly complex information systems are not designed (based on today's view of the situation), but it is also important not to underestimate the information requirements associated with closer coordination of activities.

Practice Sharing

In many companies, there is little or no organized approach to sharing the best practices. Sister companies treat each other as if they were competitors—and in some ways they are. Managers are often in competition for better jobs; units face conflicts as to which product lines will be produced in which locations; there is competition for capital and corporate resources such as information systems support; and common suppliers or customers can also lead to competitive behavior.

The imperative of learning is that all units in a company need to share experiences, both good and bad, across business units. If at all possible, the enterprise needs to be on *one* learning curve, not on as many learning curves as it has business units. We do not argue for centralization or for conformity; each business unit has a unique set of eight enterprise transformation facets, which need to be reflected in its particular transformation agenda. But wherever possible, the overall enterprise needs to encourage joint learning based on practice sharing. One executive at IMD recently said: "I start with the fundamental assumption that for *any* problem we might encounter in any business unit, somewhere in our company we have expertise and experience that can be used as a launch pad."

Practice sharing needs to be seen as a win-win proposition. When it is done right, the unit sharing the practice and experience should be able to learn itself through the experience. Having another business unit critically examine one's practice should lead to better internal understanding of the practice and of how it might be improved. Moreover, practice sharing needs to be seen in a longer-run context. If business unit A shares a practice with business unit B, there is an implied reciprocity that over time should work itself out.

Transformation Engines

Successful enterprises, especially large enterprises, need to approach the development of learning capacity by building, and improving, what we can call transformation engines: ways to support transformation, business unit by business unit. The intent is also to learn how to do this better, so that the process of "doing better things" is not a unique experience every time. During each transformation the emphasis needs to be not only on the *results* of the change, but also on the methodology itself and how it can be improved.

Typically these transformations, by definition, are concerned with the bottom half of the Gould change wheel. This implies a fundamental change in culture and the approach to learning. One should not expect the enterprise unit itself to know how to make the necessary changes or how to learn effectively in this manner. Indeed the traditional patterns of learning have to be deliberately put aside. The issue is, first, how to support the particular business units as they go through revolution/crisis and transformation, and second, how to learn from each of these experiences so that the help provided is constantly improving. The more successful firms recognize the benefits in a unit-by-unit approach.

Learning at the enterprise level as a whole is more difficult, but in the end this is where dominance will be achieved in most firms. Business unit transformation may be the means. The *end* requires synergy among these units and *overall* learning. Achieving one global learning curve is not an easy task. Knowledge needs to be shared, overall learning needs to be fostered, and this requires appropriate technology to make it happen.

■ Nissan has three automotive design centers, one in Japan, one in California, and one in England. Each has the job of designing automobiles for the three major market areas of the world (Asia, the U.S., Europe). The company's belief is that these three market areas are different enough that any centralized approach to automobile design will not reflect local conditions and tastes. But in fact much of the automobile design work is similar, and even where differences do occur, the approaches to finding the solutions have common elements. The solution has been to implement one global computer-aided design, computer-aided manufacturing (CAD/CAM) system, where designs are shared and design problems solved with a common approach.

Learning Transformation Examples

The Manufacturing 2000 project focuses on both the development of new transformation frameworks and the observation of best practices. Among the latter are the ways that enterprise transformation has been implemented and the learning that has taken place in companies that are successfully transforming their enterprises. That is, what are the most successful "engines" that have driven learning (and transformation)? What are some common elements and necessary conditions? How can "benchmarking" (practice sharing) in transformation engines be facilitated?

Finally, there is the issue of direction or leadership for transformation. In most transformation programs in small- to medium-size companies, or in business units of larger corporations, there has been a charismatic leader who drives the change. In larger companies, more often there is some overriding defined approach, or engine, which also comes from the top of the company. An example is the T50 program of ABB, which directs every business unit to take on efforts to reduce many measures by 50 percent: new product design time, inventories, lead times, response times to customer inquiries, defects, and rejected materials. Experience is shared among business units—in terms of concrete results, the explicit changes in practice that permitted major improvements, and the implications for learning how to better support the "engine."

The Oticon Journey: Charismatic Leadership

Oticon, the Danish manufacturer of hearing aids, embodies the learning organization. The company has implemented innovative organizational structures, but more than that, it has created a new work environment where employees are challenged to learn quickly in order to continually transform the enterprise.

The Oticon journey has been inspired by Lars Kolind, the company's chief executive. He took over a company that had not kept up with the latest technology (particularly the move from behind-the-ear to in-the-ear hearing aids). Oticon's market share had been cut in half; it fell from first to third place in the industry; and significant losses had been incurred in the two years before Lars Kolind took over.

Kolind immediately instituted crisis management, slashing costs, refocusing business segments, and building partnerships with professional hearing aid providers. This was successful, and Oticon returned to profitability. But Kolind felt that nothing fundamental had changed: the company was just doing the same things better, and competitors could catch up fairly soon.

To improve the fundamental position of the firm, Kolind wanted the company to:

☐ Do something people are good at and like.

☐ Organize so that all workers better understand what they are doing.

☐ Establish as few limits as possible that stop people from doing a good and effective job.

☐ Offer many possible opportunities to develop in the long term, to change working tasks, to try bigger challenges.

Lars Kolind established several new goals for the company. Included were a 30 percent reduction in all costs in three years; more time spent on real engineering, real sales work, and real marketing, and less time on writing memos, finding fault, and putting out fires; solving problems in far less time; and spending much more time talking through issues with those involved, and less time running through formal channels.

Oticon created an office without walls, with no permanent desks or offices, where employees have only a small caddy to carry their work around so that paper is largely absent, and work stations supported by computers where teams form and work through problems as they come up. The organization overall has very few control mechanisms. Many people visiting Oticon's offices believe that what they see physically is what there is to see and understand. But beneath the unusual physical structures is an ironclad commitment to transformation, a culture and learning that supports transformation, and some fundamental foundations to support learning that is both rapid and directionally correct.

The new office arrangements were a break with the past, in that no one had a permanent job any more. This was clearly a shock for many people, and not everyone could adapt. But for those who did, life became more interesting. Everyone had to find ways to use their time wisely, working with others as it made sense. No one at Oticon has a title, even for a business card. People are encouraged to learn at least three different jobs, but to own none of them. In fact, employees have to define their own jobs. This encourages a maximum of learning, and it also clearly identified the need for a new type of information repository. Knowledge could not be hoarded or kept in particular places. A new computer system allowing everyone access to virtually any piece of information, and information *not* kept in other places, is a necessary supporting element in the enterprise transformation infrastructure.[6]

The Oticon story is one of success. All the goals set by Lars Kolind have been exceeded. Oticon employees are generally happy and excited (but some people could not adapt and left). There is a constant ferment of new learning, and the company is making excellent profits. Oticon is now applying these concepts to its factory operations as well, and is looking for new challenges.

Oticon is an interesting example of transformation—largely inspired by one individual—but in a relatively small firm. Many other firms have been studying Oticon's approach, trying to find ways they can incorporate the key ideas into their own approaches to enterprise transformation. At larger firms, there is a need to define and manage the overall approach.

Company ABC: Fostering Practice Sharing

Company ABC is a European multinational that operates in four major business sectors, all largely decentralized. In one sector, more than 100 independent operating companies serve particular geographic areas with a product line. There are six basic product groupings in this sector that use different materials and production processes.

Practice sharing was virtually nonexistent in this sector. In fact, one country manager explicitly ordered plant managers not to let anyone from one of the other countries into their factories. At a seminar, the lack of practice sharing emerged. The catalyst was a discussion of customer service and the need to understand customer problems. Several units expressed interest in performing customer surveys, and it developed that there were two or three that had considerable experience in this area.

This was the starting point for practice sharing. It was thereafter formalized, in that each operating company included a search for practice or prior experience in other operating units as a formal step before undertaking any major improvement project. The corporate unit in charge of fostering total quality management added practice sharing to its domain, in order to know where particular experience existed, to support interactions among the units, and to promote joint learning.

One part of the corporate efforts involved a short indoctrination course for any units involved in practice sharing. It is important for any unit sharing its prior experiences and practices to express them clearly, accurately, efficiently and without the bias of 20/20 hindsight. For the unit coming to learn, it is important to adopt an attitude of learning, not one of finding excuses why such practices could not be implemented because it is different, and the like. It was also necessary to develop methods for learning and transplantation, as well as for reporting back to the unit visited. The practice became that the visiting operating unit later reported its own experiences to the operating unit visited, as well as offered an invitation for a reciprocal visit.

These procedures were found to be both necessary and useful. By adopting a flexible protocol for practice sharing, the company has been able to tap a vast wealth of information and experience that had been largely hidden before. Although Company ABC has not attempted to quantify its returns from practice sharing, it believes they are significant.

The Siemens Journey: Developing Transformation Engines

Siemens is also undergoing enterprise transformation through its TOP program. TOP is a top-down directed program, originally established as a productivity improvement effort. It has evolved significantly from that rather narrow focus and now is the major catalyst for enterprise transformation at Siemens.[7] Frans Holzwarth describes the evolution of the project.

In 1990, the Siemens board became concerned that operational profits were not high enough and charged me with setting up a productivity center with three objectives:

□ To initiate and implement a productivity program with internal and external consultants.

□ To develop a strategy for productivity increases and train internal consultants to facilitate this process.

□ To launch and support a major productivity improvement initiative at Siemens.

My first team consisted of five people, and we quickly came to the conclusion that we would have to gain widespread employee support if we were to succeed. Our first action was to look at ideas from other companies such as Motorola and Hewlett-Packard to learn what had worked and what had not. We then set up some small pilot projects that allowed us to analyze parts of our own business and draw a number of conclusions. For example, many Siemens products were overspecified, and analysis of "best-in-class" suggested that we could save up to 50 percent off the cost of some products, primarily through improved management techniques like product and process design rather than reduced cost of labor. With the company needing to concentrate on products and processes, I quickly realized that if we were to succeed in our objectives we were talking about major transformation.

We met with the Board every three months to report on progress. Two key issues quickly arose. I became convinced that transformation would be a ten-year process, but the board had expectations of significant results within two years, and these had to be managed. Another issue was the use of outside consultants; there were different philosophies within the company as to the efficacy of such help. We had to decide if it was appropriate to use them to launch TOP.

TOP originally stood for "time-optimized process," but it has been personalized by different divisions over time (Turn On Power, Trust Our People). It took one and one-half years to develop a "standard" TOP approach, but we finally came down to four key steps. This is now the normal route we use when moving into one of the businesses.

□ Step 1, Analysis: Assessment of the potential for productivity improvement and the tools required. This is carried out by a team of four to six people, two internal consultants, and two to four people from the business over two months. Methods used for analysis include benchmarking, target costing, and reverse engineering.

□ Step 2, Restructuring: Restructuring is sometimes necessary, if a business is overresourced. It is driven from the top down with strong support from the management team. One lesson we quickly learned is that restructuring must come *first* and not be mixed up with the transformation following. Methods used include vertical integration, segmentation, and make-or-buy considerations.

☐ Step 3, Product and Process Design: This is a bottom-up activity using cross-functional teams that are strongly empowered. The number of hierarchical layers is reduced using a range of methods including time-based management, TQM, JIT, and design to cost.

☐ Step 4, Continuous Improvement: This involves wholesale transformation and culture change using methods such as *Kaizen* and policy deployment.

To use TOP, it became apparent that we could not raise productivity without removing certain cultural barriers. The company has traditionally been functionally and hierarchically organized. Information flowed up each functional hierarchy and incentives flowed down, but there remained gaps between and among the functions, necessitating a large number of managers simply to solve the problem of interfaces. We needed to change this functional orientation to a process orientation. At first there was opposition to the idea, but now it is openly discussed, and we have workshops for divisional managers to examine the issues.

The change means that we need only one-third of the managers we needed before. The process approach uses overlapping teams and networks, with members from different functional backgrounds. There is no separation of activities throughout the value chain, and feedback on problems is immediate, significantly reducing cycle times. Each process is run by the process owners, and the only truly important thing is to focus on customer benefit. Incentives are collective and based on outputs. We are looking at ways to track the customer more effectively. One experiment is to hold sessions for management and invite customers to present how they see Siemens, what they want from the company, and what needs improving.

Training is key. Much of it is developed in-house by internal consultants, and we are now influencing the official training program. The old two-week functional courses are being replaced by groups of managers from one business working on their own problems. The advantage is immediate. People from the same unit learn the same things and put them into practice as a team.

We currently have three types of projects under way—A, B, and C projects. "A" projects involve the entire business unit, with innovation in all products, processes, and structures—a full transformation. They are carried out only with experienced consultants and with a management team that is fully aware of the implications. They take a minimum of one and a half years. "B" projects deal with part of the business, a single product or an aspect, such as development of shorter manufacturing cycles. "C" projects are small, taking a matter of months and working within a single subject or function. We now have 45 "A" and 140 "B" projects, in addition to 250 smaller "C" projects. Overall we estimate that there are potential savings of DM 8 billion.

My own consulting team has grown to 25, and we have an additional group of 120 people all trained to run "A" projects. They work individually or in teams, and although they form part of the corporate staff, they work out in the divisions like external consultants. The projects themselves are financed by the divisions.

To date we are very satisfied with performance. Presented with our concrete results, managers realize they can no longer dismiss TOP. After three years, for example, the telephone business in Germany now has costs as low as Taiwan's. In the future, the program will move globally. This will bring its own set of challenges—conflicts between countries and product lines, the need to improve cooperation between units, and the best way to integrate different cultures and attitudes. We do not know where we will be in five years, but when you start initiatives like TOP, you have to accept that it is a journey into the unknown.

Other Transformation Journeys

Most of the Manufacturing 2000 companies are engaged in true enterprise transformation. The Siemens approach (development of transformation engines) has been adopted by most of the others. Some central purpose for transformation is established, but the major efforts are carried out in individual business units, each responding to its own perceived discontinuities and changes in customer expectations. A fairly common theme has been adoption of the best manufacturing practices such as JIT, time-based competition, and total quality management (TQM).

The TQM engine has been important for most companies. When done right, TQM puts a natural focus on interfunctional processes, links with suppliers/customers, and an overarching goal ("quality") that can be redefined continually outside the negative context of concepts such as "productivity," which is always seen as head count reduction. In all these "engines," there is a high interest in learning—on a corporate basis—from each of the specific applications.

In most companies, there is a vast untapped reservoir of knowledge that is not being exploited on a corporate basis. It is not easy to develop corporatewide learning, which requires true practice sharing among business units. Changing internal competitive behavior requires more than executive fiat. It is necessary to understand the reasons for the mistrust, and systematically eliminate them.

A similar issue concerns development of joint competencies across business units. Many firms could offer an entirely unique bundle of goods and services by combining the capabilities of their separate business units in creative ways. The challenge is how to do this without heavy-handed top management intervention or recentralization, with its attendant side effects.

Many excellent companies are now acutely interested in what comes after TQM, as well as what comes after world-class manufacturing. The interest is on two fronts. First, what is the destination? Second, what are the learning transformation implications? These questions are what makes study of innovative approaches such as Oticon so interesting. One needs to look "over the horizon" to see where the next major set of improvements is coming from, and what kinds of learning will be required to achieve them.

Definitive answers are not available, but there certainly are some candidates. Among the most popular destination candidates now pursued by M2000 companies are supply chain management, the "virtual factory" concept, early supplier involvement in design activities, totally new psychological contracting and human resource practices, a new focus on customer satisfaction that incorporates a more proactive approach than simply offering better quality and delivery, the much greater enhancement of products with services, and fundamentally different approaches to information management.

Summary

Chapter 7 brings us to the end of the eight facets of enterprise transformation. The dictate of "learn or die" requires constant efforts to identify breakthrough concepts, redefine the infrastructure to achieve them, and define the change agenda in order truly to create and maintain distinctive competencies. In the last analysis, those firms that dominate will have more than good ideas: They will have the ability to make them a reality.

☐ Dominate or die is really "learn or die." The firm that learns faster than its competitors—and learns in the right directions—will dominate; those that do not will not survive.

☐ The learning organization must be focused on dominance. A manufacturing enterprise is not a university.

☐ The "currency" for learning needs to be competencies. Distinctive competence development is the overriding objective. Achieving, and maintaining, distinctive competence requires learning that is clearly focused on distinctive competence—and all its supporting infrastructure.

☐ Learning for fine-tuning and building is fundamentally different from learning required for revolution/crisis and transformation.

☐ Learning needs to be focused on the right things. Transformation of learning itself is often the major issue. We need to unlearn the ways in which we have been learning and refocus on the new requirements of the market.

☐ Transformation of learning is as important as transformation of any of the other seven facets of enterprise transformation

☐ New information systems will be required to support enterprise transformation and learning. The *enabling* aspects of information systems need to be understood, with information system design driven by transformation design.

☐ Transformation engines are critical to large organizations seeking to renew themselves through enterprise transformation. Learning must take place from business unit to business unit—not only in terms of the end results achieved—but also in terms of the learning gained as a result.

8 People Transformation

In chapter 7 we discussed the concept of organizational learning: the fundamental determinant of the enterprise's ability to do better things continually and to do them faster. The imperative for this to happen is that the culture of the organization must support the right kinds of behavior in the people who in fact make the changes. Transformation often requires changing both the organization and the culture. *People* need to do different—better—things. Whether this in fact happens can be the difference between dominance and death. The "people issues" have been implicit in all our discussions, but it is useful to address people transformation directly. We can see it as a unifying issue against the background of the transformation model.

A major issue in people transformation concerns the ability of the company both to implement change and to achieve sustainability in the new ways people work.

■ The Sutton plant of CarnaudMetalbox made a major change in manufacturing, which included a culture change on the shop floor. Hierarchical levels were reduced, empowerment was implemented, just-in-time manufacturing was established, and excellent results were being achieved. The arrival of a new general manager with a different approach to factory management quickly reversed these achievements. The new culture and new behaviors of the workers could not be sustained. A great deal of frustration was generated as the shop floor was forced to resume the old ways of doing things.

Implementing transformation, sustaining it, and increasing the speed at which transformation takes place requires development and nurture of a culture that focuses explicitly on the transformation process—as opposed to only particular transformation objectives. Such a culture:

☐ Seeks opportunities.

☐ Refuses complacency.

☐ Has an ongoing sense of urgency.

☐ Accords with the objectives of key people.

☐ Understands the critical necessity for trust.

☐ Adopts new human resource practices.

☐ Fosters development of new psychological contracts.

Achieving this culture needs to be seen as an integral part of enterprise transformation, where specific actions are guided by the golden cord with its dictates of integration, consistency, feasibility, and desirability. These dictates can provide a definitive advantage in obtaining the right degree of employee commitment, reducing the cynicism that accompanies all too many change programs, and focusing activities so that we again achieve several critical "and" imperatives:

☐ Productivity *and* value enhancement.

☐ Cost reduction *and* personnel development.

☐ Long-run results *and* short-term results.

☐ Top-down direction *and* bottom-up implementation.

☐ Value to the enterprise *and* value to its employees.

Manufacturing 2000 People Research

The Manufacturing 2000 project has devoted several research efforts to "people transformation." The Gould change wheel shows that the mandates for change are quite different depending upon which part of the sequence the enterprise is in—and where it needs to go next. The change imperatives for people in fine-tuning are profoundly different from those associated with transformation. The kinds of skills required, the prevailing culture, and the leadership requirements are very different. An enterprise that moves from one stage to another requires a different leadership approach, a fundamental change in organizational culture, development of new people skills, a new agenda of improvement efforts, and in essence an entire new golden cord. In far too many cases, the new golden cord is not only not implemented—the need for it is not recognized.

■ A highly successful flooring materials company had experienced steady (but not spectacular) growth in sales and profits over the years. The management was paternalistic; the workers were cohesive and largely satisfied; the goals in manufacturing were mainly to reduce absenteeism, improve yields, and increase productivity; the action programs included training programs in machine maintenance, cross-training, and ISO 9000. When a major new competitor entered the market, the company hired a consulting firm that reduced head counts and cut costs to the bone. But preceding this action there was never any explicit change in strategic intent, nor clear recognition of the new challenges, nor formulation of the new competencies required to operate in the new environment. More fundamentally, the management maintained its old—and now outdated culture. The work force cynicism that ensued partially led in the end to this firm selling out.

Social Navigation

Some of the early work in Manufacturing 2000 by Chris Parker is called "social navigation." The metaphor of navigation implies that even with a clear objective for transformation, achieving it looks more like a sailboat crossing a lake and tacking as the wind requires than like a motorboat, which proceeds in more or less a straight line to its destination.

The social navigation concept implies that people and organizations are different, that these differences need first to be understood, and then to be reflected in the particular change initiatives developed in each organizational unit. One aspect of the social navigation research focuses on better recognizing these inherent differences, and reflecting them in the approach taken to particular transformation efforts. The process uses various kinds of behavioral indicators for individuals and their abilities to work together in groups, such as the Myers-Briggs and Belbin tests. Many managers make assumptions about the abilities of particular people to work together that are shown to be unjustified according to these metrics.

The contingency point of view reflected in social navigation is complementary to the "change engine" concept in that it recognizes that transformation is unique for particular business units. This uniqueness needs to be reflected in the choice of objectives, approach, tool kit, and implementation strategy. Corporatewide top-down mandates to adopt a particular tool kit in every business unit rarely work as well in practice as they do on paper.

■ Some years ago, we performed an audit of the manufacturing planning and control systems for a large U.S. equipment manufacturing company. Although the firm was successful in the marketplace, its internal operations were a complete mess. There was inventory everywhere; records were not accurate; informal expediting and crisis conditions prevailed; lead times were long; and customer promises were often not met. About 30 percent of units were "finished" with missing parts (requiring subsequent work). The obvious solution was a well-integrated manufacturing planning and control system and its accompanying discipline.

But, in fact, the vice president of manufacturing was a completely informal person as far as systems were concerned. He moved products out the door in spite of systems, not with them. He was also an autocrat; the prevailing culture was "command and control," and any decision of consequence was sent "up the line." There was no way his behavior could be changed, and his behavior dominated the culture; removing him was not feasible. He had been instrumental in building the company and had two years to go until retirement.

Recognizing this constraint, we recommended some peripheral actions that were in line with the overall objective that would not be a direct threat to the vice president and the prevailing culture, and then privately told senior managers that they would have to wait until he retired before moving the implementation beyond the planning stage.

The actual work of transformation is best achieved in business units rather than in one companywide effort. This allows unique constraints to be reflected, and detailed plans for transformation to be developed and integrated with the culture, structures, perceived problems, key players, and strengths and weaknesses of the organizational unit. The overall strategic intent for the company might be shared, but the unique challenges, particular competencies, people resources available, and situation of the moment determine the best choice of strategic response. This in turn dictates the exact changes required to the underlying infrastructure to achieve the responses. Some things just cannot be changed.

Systematic Customization

The work of Andrew Boynton and his colleagues also has some key people management implications. The transformation from "invention" to "mass production" implies fundamental changes in the culture and the ways that work is done. Behaviors, attitudes, skills, and knowledge that are highly useful in the invention quadrant of the Boynton model are dysfunctional in mass production. They have to be unlearned and new ones learned. The same mandate is true for a transformation to "continuous improvement," and again to "mass customization." In each case, there is an imperative for totally new culture and people management.

A laudable feature of the systematic customization model is that each transformation stage clearly indicates general directions for the kinds of behavioral, attitudinal, skill, and knowledge change requirements. But as the discussion of social navigation indicates, the specifics will be unique in every case.

Table 8.1 depicts the differences in work that are implied for the managers and the workers under each of the four stages of the systematic customization model. Achieving these paradigm shifts, changing the underlying culture, and overcoming the natural resistance to change requires particular leadership skills for each transformation stage.

New Psychological Contracting

Two contributions of Jean-Marie Hiltrop are particularly relevant for this chapter. The first is in what Argyris first called "psychological contracting" in 1960.[1] Fundamentally, the psychological contract between an individual and an employer relates to the expectations on both sides: job expectations, terms and conditions, how performance is to be judged, skill enhancements and other training, how promotions and higher status are to be achieved, and a general sense of where an employee's career is headed.

But in today's world of ongoing transformation, stability in a psychological contract is not a reasonable assumption. Expectations such as lifetime employment, career ladders, predictable career progression, and employer-directed professional development are things of the past: Instead we have ongoing needs to redefine the core competencies of the enterprise, and translate these into a people change agenda. This has profound implications for both the company and its employees.

Table 8.1

Work Requirements and Systematic Customization Stages

	Invention	**Mass Production**	**Continuous Improvement**	**Mass Customization**
Managers:	■ There is no explicit distinction between managers and workers	■ Thinkers ■ Directive ■ Well-educated ■ Planners ■ Command and control	■ Act as coaches ■ Encourage ideas ■ Build lasting teams	■ Managers as traffic cop, coordinate complex demands with flexible work force
Workers:		■ Doers ■ Obedient ■ Not educated ■ Task-oriented	■ Players—doer and thinkers ■ Share ideas ■ Long-term team players	■ Specialized ■ Work in instant teams
Both:	■ Craftspeople ■ Dual roles, worker and doer, are pronounced ■ Well-educated ■ Professional (external affiliation, cosmopolitan) ■ Intrinsic motivation ■ Individual-focused	■ Specialized ■ Trained on the job ■ Trained for company-specific solutions ■ Internal focus (internal, local to firm) ■ Extrinsic motivation ■ Individual-focused: motivation, rewards, work	■ Creative ■ Team players ■ Integrative (versus cosmopolitan and local) ■ Better educated (compared to mass production) ■ Collective motivation: targeted toward rewards, work ■ Broad versus narrow skill base ■ Good in transition game, flexible among different types of work	■ Independent, but can work in teams ■ Focus on skill development ■ Flexible ■ People are transaction-motivated ■ Responsive to change

Source: Andrew Boynton, Visiting Professor, IMD. Presented at a Manufacturing 2000 meeting, IMD, Lausanne, Switzerland, October 1993. Reprinted with permission.

There is a need for a new kind of psychological contract between the employee and the employer. The employee's need becomes ongoing skill enhancement, mobility based on professional excellence, acceptance of personal responsibility for career development, and a knowledge of the employment marketplace. The employer in turn has to assess its people requirements constantly (according to the kinds of issues incorporated in the enterprise transformation model), and thereafter transform its people resource in the best ways possible. Jointly, employer and employee need to recognize that security is less something that is given by an employer than something developed by each employee.

The impact of new psychological contracting on classic human resource management practices is profound. Many current practices have to be abandoned and new ones developed.

■ The Royal Bank of Scotland, in responding to the challenges it faced, dramatically reengineered its organization. The overriding change in culture was from "job-for-life" to an achievement-based culture where the people are expected to be more proactive within specialist roles, a new psychological contract. In the Glasgow offices, twenty pay grades were reduced to five, existing staff have had to reapply for redesigned jobs, and the new jobs have been advertised in terms of competencies without reference to pay or grade. One result has been that lower-ranking staff members have climbed in the new structure.[2]

A related contribution of Jean-Marie Hiltrop comes from a survey instrument he developed to measure employee attitudes on a number of factors. This work extends the classic personnel profile work such as Myers-Briggs and Belbin, but its focus is more organizational than personal.[3] The objective is to understand certain characteristics of a company, including its corporate culture, human resource policies and practices, and the criteria used to attract and retain workers. Hiltrop's survey is like the others in that it has no right or wrong answers. Rather, it allows one to see how employees feel about some cultural issues in their company, such as:

□ Openness

□ Formality

□ Proactivity

□ Centralization

□ Teamwork

□ Proficiency

□ Flexibility

      □ Creativity

      □ Loyalty and commitment

      □ Achievement and performance

It is hard to overestimate the importance of this kind of diagnostic to enterprise transformation. The first issue, openness, is especially useful in assessing the extent to which the people in a business unit are resistant to change. It also provides an excellent indicator of compatibility between different organizations, particularly important in the case of a merger or acquisition. The basic question of fit—between the people—is not asked in far too many cases.

■ At the time of this writing, two major European airline companies are merging parts of their operations. Hiltrop's survey indicates that the two companies are polar extremes on the openness measure. All the typical external indicators of compatibility, such as route structure and aircraft maintenance, may well turn out to be illusory. Achieving synergy between these two companies will be a very difficult undertaking.

Many transformations are based on achieving some perceived synergies between two companies, often by merger or takeover. But what if the two organizations are not compatible? What if the key people do not feel happy in the new organization? How dependent on (and vulnerable to) the people dimension is the whole proposition?

■ IBM has gone on the acquisition trail, trying to buy up software companies such as Lotus through hostile takeovers. The synergy between the two companies looks good on paper, and IBM needs these kinds of competencies and products to compete with Microsoft, but will it work? What if the software designers in the acquired companies decide to leave? Does the IBM mentality and culture support this kind of integration? What does it take to make it a reality?

Enhancing People Capabilities

The overall interest in Manufacturing 2000 in transformation leads to a definite focus on competencies and their underlying capabilities. In fact, investments in people capabilities need to be seen as central to transformation, in that the most critical resource available for transformation is the time of the people who will do it. Companies *must* find ways to free up time for transformation. It is not sufficient only to solve today's set of problems appropriately.

This is easier said than done. A culture that truly incorporates a sense of urgency cannot be satisfied only with meeting the day-to-day demands of the business—regardless of how well it does this. There must be time and resources devoted to the future, to long-term development, and to ongoing transformation. Every employee needs to work on the future, in a culture that is never satisfied with the present. When this imperative is pushed beyond the "nice to have" stage, it becomes crystal clear that time is the key; time must be made available, which implies getting today's work done in less time.

As we worked with one group of senior managers in the automotive parts industry, we constantly came back to the absolute necessity that each manager find a way to free up one day per week to work on transformation (better things) instead of being consumed with the day-to-day. The only way this can happen is to redefine the work at lower levels so that work done by those on the shop floor, or other firing line, is more encompassing, requiring far less supervision and coordination. The approach to work (and prevailing culture) in this firm needed to shift to one of empowerment and focus on integrated processes rather than one based on functional hierarchies.

The focus had to be on processes that are self-managed by teams with minimal functional oversight. The group did become convinced of the need to develop their junior colleagues and "not do their work." Whenever they were called in to assist, resolve a conflict, pass judgment, or otherwise intervene with classic command and control approaches, they became committed to *not* doing so—if they felt the people involved should have the necessary authority, information, and intelligence to solve this problem themselves. This was seen as an essential part of achieving the necessary cultural change. For each particular situation the group of managers acknowledged that:

☐ It would in fact be easier to do it themselves.

☐ The probability of mistakes would increase, and when mistakes occurred it was imperative not to assign blame and kill the new approach.

☐ It was the managers' own past behaviors that had set up the previous decision-making process.

□ The unlearning on both sides would not be easy.

□ Without this change in company culture, the managers would never be able to implement the dictates associated with their overall transformation.

Achieving these changes has not been easy, and the company has not completed the change. In every way, the managers' efforts are "people transformation." The company is doing better things with its people—not doing the same things better. The implications here are quite profound. Fundamentally, this approach to transformation begins with the recognition that the main constraint on learning and continuous transformation is time—the time of the people in the organization. Perhaps one or more new steps in transformation can be achieved with existing organization and structures and job definitions, but in the long run it is necessary to make a basic change in these elements.

Linkages to the Transformation Model

People transformation is obviously linked to the overall enterprise transformation. Indeed in most cases, it is a people change that facilitates the other infrastructure changes in processes and systems. But focusing on people transformation using some of the ideas we have developed can be of significant help in the detailed change agenda requirements.

Explicit Strategic Intent For People Management

We have noted that many mission statements are only vague wish lists. They do not adequately reflect what is to be done. Many companies have mission statements describing their employees as well, and these also are almost always vague wish lists. In one recent use of the transformation model, for example, the group made its mission statement "becoming the number one producer of packages for liquid products." This became revised to a strategic intent that includes a precise definition of "number one" (profits, not sales or units), the particular sectors to enter and not enter in the liquid products business (plastics, not glass), a timetable for achieving the number one position, and an explicit statement of what is to be done for particularly important customers in the liquid products business.

This precise focus of strategic intent on what is to be uniquely different for the customers is critical to focusing all the resources and energy of the company. It includes a detailed understanding of how the customers use the goods and services provided, over a life cycle including purchasing, installation, maintenance, refurbishment, and replacement. It is not some vague statement like "supplier of choice."

This group also had prepared a "mission statement" relating to personnel, which stated a grandiose objective that the company be the best place to work in the industry and be a fair employer. This too is so vague as to be meaningless. When the group applied the transformation model all the way down to competency mapping and the other detailed infrastructure issues, it became possible to be much more explicit about the detailed new processes and systems required to achieve the strategic intent—and the associated cultural and people transformation objectives (and imperatives). When these issues were aggregated, it was clear that a major shift in direction was called for in terms of people development. To frame the "people change agenda," a much more profound sense of customer problem sensing, practice sharing, marketing talent (as opposed to technical capability enhancement), and the ability to apply people resources across wider geographic boundaries were needed. The group also explicitly recognized the need to change the culture so that these people attributes were valued.

This explication process—top-down, then bottom-up, then top-down again—is extremely useful in many applications of the transformation model. Rather than allowing either no explicit strategic intent statement as to people transformation or one that is basically meaningless, the model requires companies to become quite unambiguous as to both the detailed change requirements and the overriding strategy for people development and deployment required to implement and operate the new infrastructure. The resultant uncertainties associated with psychological contracting can be significantly reduced.

The Desirability and Feasibility Dictates

The four dictates for implementing the golden cord through enterprise transformation are integration, consistency, feasibility, and desirability. Desirability implies that there is a win-win match between the goals of the enterprise and those of the individual employees who will be transformed in terms of their work requirements. Feasibility relates to whether the transformation can in fact be achieved—for whatever reason, human or technological. If implementation requires the implementors to fall on their swords, the chances for success are dim. Implementing the infrastructure requirements always has personnel implications. New competency requirements mandate new employee capabilities, skills, and behaviors, new psychological contracts, changes in human resource practices, and a culture that supports the new requirements. Teamwork, for example, takes work! People's attitudes and behaviors need to change, but so do the prevailing culture, reward systems, and managerial viewpoints that define what kinds of work are valued. The golden cord provides an indication of what that work will be.

The company wishing to transform is much more likely to succeed when it develops an unambiguous understanding of both the detailed people transformation issues and the overall strategic intent viewed from the "people change" perspective. When the people transformation requirements are large, it is imperative to assess desirability from the point of view of those who are to operate in the new environment.

■ Before papermaking machines adopted computer control systems, there was a long-running tradition of papermakers, with skills often passed down from father to son. It included a strong sense of identification with the machine, knowing its sounds and its smells, and even in some cases tasting the liquid to see if it were properly formulated. The adoption of computer controls put most of these people out of work; those remaining are largely in control rooms where they cannot even hear the machine, and where the skills and behavior requirements are completely different. Many people will not enthusiastically accept these kinds of changes; most craft workers will see them as undesirable.

The relatively high failure rate of business process reengineering projects may well be due to a lack of clear understanding of the linkages between the reengineering changes and the requirements for people transformation. Newly defined processes and systems require new skills and behaviors to operate them, as well as a new culture beyond the existing organizational definitions. When this does not occur, the transformation is not feasible. The issue is not that feasibility be determined by personal desirability. The important point is that, whatever the transformation objectives, one needs to determine the detailed people and new culture requirements in order to define the appropriate *change agenda for people*—and thereafter develop a set of plans that can in fact be achieved.

A related issue in desirability is the perceived urgency of a particular transformation effort. A lot can be done when employees believe the firm has its back against the wall, but this is not the case for most proactive transformation efforts. These need to be taken not when the company is in trouble, but precisely when it is not. There are more options open; the proactive choice alternatives are much greater; the alternatives are more pleasant; and the results can be more profound in terms of thereafter changing the game for everyone else. Proactive transformation requires the same degree of urgency as the "back against the wall" circumstances. This is a key challenge for managers, but it can be helped by the transformation model, which can show that the challenges are shared, and everyone can see the golden cord that connects those challenges to actions to competency requirements to infrastructure to change agenda.

Fostering People Transformation

When transformation is viewed not as a one-time event but as an ongoing process, there are some important implications for the people dimension. First, it is obviously desirable to have people who are more open to change, less resistant to new ideas, less tied to past practices and ideas, and more willing to participate and identify with the set of enterprise transformation objectives. Developing this mentality might be an overriding transformation objective, regardless of any particular transformation effort.

Some companies foster people transformation by the choices they make in plant locations. Thus the American Japanese auto transplant firms and General Motors' Saturn have chosen rural sites in farm communities where the population is more homogeneous than at Ford locations in England, for example, where many languages are spoken, Hindus work with Moslems, Arabs with Jews, and Serbs with Croats. People transformation is inherently more challenging when groups are diverse and have historical enmities.

Teams need to be put together to design, implement, and run new processes and systems. But the members of the teams in some places are more like Legos, which fit together ingeniously in any design, while in others we seem to have a few Legos, some miscellaneous puzzle pieces, some metric nuts and bolts, and some American screws and nuts. The

American screw does not easily fit the metric nut, so sometimes one just uses a hammer to make it work, but the functioning thereafter is not very good. Team design is the same way. Sometimes it is easy, sometimes hard, and other times impossible. Force fits may work temporarily, but there are limits.

No matter what the "raw material," however, companies increasingly need to acknowledge that the process of transformation is important, instead of just focusing on the day-to-day work. This implies devoting managerial attention to developing the context and culture that is most supportive of ongoing change, where people can understand the overall objectives as well as the golden cord leading all the way to the detailed change agenda to accomplish the objectives.

Figure 8.1 comes from a study done by the Boston Manufacturing Roundtable. It shows the relative deployment of overhead personnel in Japan and the United States. At the time of the study, the Americans had twice as many top managers, three times as many accountants, and 50 percent more materials managers as the Japanese. The Japanese had 50 percent more first-line supervisors, twice as many human resource man-

Figure 8.1

Overhead Deployment: Japan versus United States

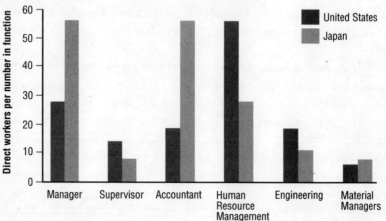

Source: Adapted from Miller and Roth, "Report on the 1986 North American Manufacturing Future Survey," and Nakano and Amano, "Report on the 1986 Japanese Manufacturing Future Survey."

agers, and 50 percent more industrial engineers. Clearly, the Japanese overhead deployment focuses on making the basic operations work flawlessly, as well as on continually improving them.

Although the data for Figure 8.1 are dated, there is a key point related to the management time issue. It is not enough to manage the day-to-day operations. Deployment of managerial resources must focus on creating a culture that supports *ongoing* transformation.

Culture Change Examples

The culture of an enterprise is largely a manifestation of "the way things are done around here." The culture serves to frame responses to initiatives or change mandates, because it defines the way that people will perceive and respond to various stimuli. In effect, culture is a critical part of a model for viewing the world and sifting information. Changing culture is then almost always a key part of organizational transformation. New ideas have to be learned, while old ones have to be unlearned. It is the new culture that allows changes in infrastructure to be seen in the right light, which is often counter to that prevailing under the old culture or environment.

Alps Electronics

At Alps Electronics, the overall paradigm shift was to "eliminate mass production," which was manifested in infrastructure changes to achieve a make-to-order approach with no stocks, very rapid changeovers, and reduced hidden factory transactions with customers. The culture change involves a new appreciation of the need for variety in customer demands, a focus on solving customer problems, a new class of customers (automotive) with new ways of thinking, and a focus on throughput time in the factory, with less attention paid to individual machine productivity. Achieving an overriding culture change was more important than the series of individual changes in processes and systems. It is the culture change that allows people to understand the need for the other changes. Moreover, it is the culture change that keeps people from going back to old ways—and focused on making the right decisions when unique new problems occur.

Achieving the necessary culture change at Alps required education and training of the workers, but the key is essentially to do so in terms of all the parts of the golden cord. The workers needed to understand the challenges the company was facing (such as internal discontinuities associated with lack of growth in its traditional markets, trade restrictions facing all Japanese electronics producers, the yen crisis, and customer needs for reduced inventories and just-in-time deliveries); why a new market segment, greater variety, and make-to-order manufacturing had to be a strategic response; why new competencies such as supply chain management, fast changeovers, and logistics were needed; the detailed infrastructure to support these competencies; how responses come together into an overriding strategy, and the attendant change agenda for the company.

Company XYZ

Company XYZ is a European subsidiary of an American Fortune 500 company that also needs to transform. At the time of our investigation, it found itself behind its competitors in all the activities associated with "world-class manufacturing" or "lean manufacturing." As a result, there was a top-down mandate for change. The mandate was programmatic: Implement statistical process control. Implement changeover time reduction. Implement empowerment in your factory. Implement total productive maintenance. Implement just-in-time manufacturing. Implement a new factory reporting system.

The results were interesting. When we visited the plants, we could see manifestation of compliance with these mandates, but closer examination revealed that it was only skin deep. Display boards set up in factory areas were as neat as a pin. Charts never had one greasy fingerprint on them. The main charts depicting progress were in a visitors' hall. But the plants were mostly old, dirty, and poorly laid out; equipment was antiquated. The vast majority of equipment stood idle, the work methods were ergonomically poor, and the spirit of the workers and management was one of resignation. Unfortunately, the response of the senior management, particularly in the U.S., was to increase pressure on the factories.

It is not an optimistic situation. To transform, the company needed a culture of proactive change, practice sharing, enthusiasm, and empowerment. Instead it had one of fear, resignation, sham compliance with corporate edicts, and an interest in holding on as long as possible—until the inevitable plant closure. One of the managers who was described as a great change driver indicated in private that he stayed only because he could not find another job.

Applicon

Applicon was a small U.S. manufacturer of computer-aided design/computer-aided manufacturing (CAD/CAM) terminals. It implemented a just-in-time manufacturing environment, which allowed it to decrease its time to manufacture from eighteen weeks to a few days. The more interesting part of the company operations, however, concerned its ability to build products routinely *at the same time* that it took on many other tasks. All engineering changes were processed routinely on the shop floor, as were the more usual additional tasks such as scheduling, quality, maintenance, and improvements. Applicon took an interesting approach to nonvalue-added work, which it called "coping mechanisms"—such as inspections to "cope" with the fact that the manufacturing was not being done well enough to do away with inspection. Workers were trained to do not only their own jobs but also to take on as many as four additional temporary workers if they had a large volume order; they were completely responsible for the output. Here is a culture focused on always doing more—and on devoting only part of the time to the routine day-to-day activities under most circumstances.

Company RST

Company RST was one of the first to integrate the time-based competition into its manufacturing operations. One of its best factories managed to do just about everything in the way of improvement programs. Inventories were exactly accurate; people never missed a shipment and could do some amazing things when customers got into trouble. The spirit in the plant was as good as in any plant I have ever seen. RST's approach to customer visits was unique: Customers were encouraged to take their own plant tour—asking *anyone* any question they could think of. The workers loved this and responded enthusiastically.

But the plant turned out to be too good for its own interests. It was able to increase its productivity much more quickly than the sales were going up. For a time, it took in work from other plants, but finally the plant was closed and the workers made redundant. The bottom-line question in this story is whether an excellent culture ingrained in an operating unit is supported at the top—when the hard decision making is required.

Company IJK

Company IJK is a division of a large conglomerate that decided to transform. The division was at the time the most profitable in the company, with close to 100 plant sites in several countries. A key issue for IJK was how to develop and maintain a culture of urgency when it was doing so well. When managers applied the transformation model, it became clear that they had plenty of potential problems on the horizon, and they communicated these to the plants. But there was still another communication mandate. Overall, the group saw the need to evolve from the "mass production" stage to "continuous improvement." Some plants were much farther along than others, but there was a general need to make this transformation, and implement the concomitant culture change. This implied significant reduction in the "command and control" managerial style and a deliberate shift toward empowerment and lower-level decision making.

IJK had a history of factories getting into serious financial trouble, only to be "restructured" using the meat ax approach, aided by a consulting company famous for this style of cost reduction. The resultant culture change message from the top was: "You have a choice—implement the move from mass production to continuous improvement, or face the music. Do it yourself, or have it done unto you." An interesting difference between Company IJK and Company XYZ is that IJK did not *mandate* any improvement programs. The choice of *what* to do was open. But the choice of whether to do anything was certainly not open. The choice of not doing anything would cost the plant manager his job.

One feature of the transformation and culture change at Company IJK is its newly adopted interest in practice sharing. The company's decentralized structure had made all the factories quite independent; they saw themselves as on their own. Comparison and competition on financial criteria leads to good ideas not being shared. The new culture of empowerment in fact intensifies decentralization, but the division is now very interested in practice sharing and is changing its culture to encourage practice sharing; an education session allowed the factory managers to see its advantages.

Opportunities—and Cultural Barriers

One question often associated with transformation in general—and the people part in particular—is what kinds of rewards in fact accrue to those who can implement the changes? How substantial are they? How long does change take? What is "best practice"? Are the benefits just marginal, or are they truly significant? Is large-scale transformation driven only by capital investments? Further, if payoffs are so good, what keeps companies from achieving them?

Eliminating Output Restrictions

At age eighteen, I was hired as a machinist at Bell & Howell, a camera company in Chicago. I wanted to work hard to prove myself.

The work day was ten hours. The first day on the job, I worked only about eight hours because of new employee orientation. At the end of the day, I counted up my production and filled out a labor reporting ticket as instructed. The next morning I was greeted by the plant manager of this 2,500-employee factory, my foreman, the head of inspection, and the timekeeper. It seemed that I had turned in almost a 300 percent work performance for ten hours—when I had only in fact worked eight, an all-time record for the company.

The logical conclusion was that I did not know how to count, so the parts were counted. The count was correct. Ah, then the parts must be of poor quality—no, all perfect. The only conclusion left was that the standard time rate for the job must be wrong—but it had been in place for some years. About 10:00 o'clock that morning, an old-timer said: "Son, let's go have a cup of coffee." I had just ruined a good job.

Transforming is not about incremental improvements. I learned to live within the system, but at the same time I developed considerable interest in work measurement, productivity, and a culture that kept me from making twice as much money—and the company from being driven out of business. I have since observed that work is artificially restricted in most places—even more so in offices than in factories—and that the difference between the best and the average is not 10 percent; it is 100 percent. There are many reasons output may be artificially restricted, but the key issue for companies is how to close this gap. How can output be doubled with no significant capital investment? How do we create the culture to make this a reality? How do we foster the mutual trust necessary for productivity improvements to be seen as desirable for everyone?

■ One chemical industry executive in Manufacturing 2000 expressed it as follows: "We believe that at most of our sites we have a 'hidden plant'—an extra one that we have paid for but do not even know we have. We have achieved this 'hidden plant' production in several instances—but only with the right approach—by focusing explicitly on the culture change that will support these objectives."

Focusing on the Right Costs

A U.S. corrugated box producer recently proposed to deliver in a forty-eight hour lead time exact quantities needed to a large furniture manufacturer. This allows the manufacturer to virtually eliminate cardboard box storage and the associated handling of the materials. The manufacturer pays a slightly higher price per box than other suppliers charge, but its overall cost is reduced considerably because it is able to dramatically reduce inventory holding, handling, stock outs, transactions, and obsolescence. At the same time, the furniture manufacturer can afford to provide "just-in-time payments" for the just-in-time deliveries. All invoicing is electronic, with instant payment. This is a big plus for the box manufacturer: Its working capital requirements are significantly reduced—offsetting the additional costs associated with the fast response offered to the customer.

SMED

SMED stands for "single-minute exchange of dies." The term was coined by Shigeo Shingo, and it has a very special meaning.[4] It applies to changeovers, and the mandate is that no changeover will take more than single minutes—nine minutes is the maximum. Shingo did his most famous work at Toyota, where changes from stamping out one car part to the next might take ten to twenty hours. Changeovers now are all done in single minutes. The key point is that a reduction of 25 percent is just not at all adequate. Shingo also states that *any* setup can be reduced by 75 percent, and most can be cut by 90 percent or 95 percent. Reductions of this magnitude are indeed possible and are made every day. Virtually *all* SMED benefits are achieved by shop floor workers, with minimal support and minimal investment in new equipment. Workers have this ability, but the climate for using it needs to be right. Managers need to create an *expectation* of improvements in the 90 percent order of magnitude, create the proper empowerment culture, provide the necessary tools to get the job done, and not be satisfied with anything less than perfection. The company that cultivates only a modest rate of productivity improvement is in serious danger.

The right SMED culture empowers teams to achieve excellence—and recognizes them when they do. There is a key learning point here that applies to more than SMED. Managers must indeed not be satisfied with less than major improvement, but in the most successful cases these improvements are not achieved by top-down mandates or command/control approaches. In fact, in many situations, SMED included, it is getting out of the way that is important. In the right culture, people will outperform the expectations of managers.

Working with the Customers and Suppliers

Some of the truly great opportunities for reducing costs and increasing value involve working across the supply chain. In "virtual integration," two or more firms develop mutual synergy as if they were in the same company. There are many well-known examples. One is the Wal-Mart–Procter & Gamble liaison to reduce distribution and stocking costs and smooth manufacturing and shipping cycles through "cross docking" and "everyday low prices," where artificially high demands placed on suppliers due to sales promotions are eliminated.[5] We know a European consumer products company that worked with its customers to reduce product lines significantly, while maintaining the same amount of shelf space in the stores, and while giving the customers a lower price. Similar win-win benefits are being achieved by working with suppliers. The key to achieving these benefits is to develop a culture that focuses on developing *and maintaining* the necessary trust to achieve the win-win benefits.

Making It Happen

People transformation is not easy. It never was, and it is not getting easier over time. In fact, both the size and the frequency of people changes become tougher all the time. Enterprise transformation requires concomitant transformations in organizational cultures and the ways in which people do their work. A primary implication is that companies need to spend more time improving their change mechanisms (transformation engines) instead of focusing exclusively on the next change itself. That is, they must focus on the underlying process, rather than the result.

The Manufacturing 2000 companies have shown a keen interest in understanding the change processes of other companies. This includes auditing of change engines, benchmarking of change processes, understanding culture changes, comparing human resource practices, establishing new approaches to psychological contracts, and forming supply chain alliances. Increasingly, firms realize that changing the organizational culture is often the hardest part of transformation. It is too easy to focus on the technological bells and whistles instead of on the people who will have to ring those bells and toot those whistles—all playing the same tune.

Starting Selectively

Organizations change at different rates and have differing degrees of resistance to change. Figure 8.2 illustrates the range of change acceptance. Depicted are five groups of people: the innovators, the early adapters, the early majority, the late majority, and the laggards. Each of them is shown

Figure 8.2

Change Acceptance

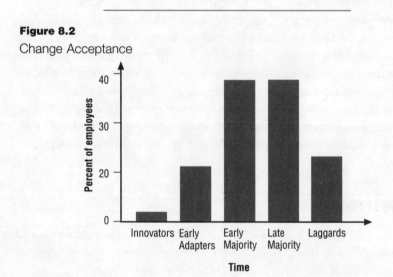

as adopting change at different points in time. Successful change likely involves forgetting about the laggards and probably the late majority, and perhaps even the early majority to some degree. The change efforts and resources need to focus on the early adapters. The innovators will usually need only minimal encouragement. After the early adapters are up and running, the others will follow, fairly naturally.

■ A packaging company implementing SMED has seen the advantage of selective application very clearly. In several locations, the original team for SMED was selected on the basis of who was most enthusiastic about the concept. The team was given the necessary encouragement, tools, and support to implement SMED. In most cases, its performance was duplicated by other teams in the same factory—usually in less overall time—*after* it became clear that SMED works and that the company was willing to support it.

A related selectivity approach that successful change managers use is to develop an elite group that takes upon itself the implementation of significant changes. These groups are often cross-functional, informal, highly motivated, willing to take risks, and inclined to ask forgiveness rather than permission. These groups recognize—either implicitly or explicitly—that many times transformation requires behaviors and attitudes that are inconsistent with the existing norms. The group develops and implements selectively the "outside-the-box" thinking that is needed. When it works, new groups of converts are added. The elite group becomes a role model for others, and the overall culture shifts to support the kinds of activities undertaken by this group.

Selective change will not always work. Sometimes the ideas may in fact be wrong. At other times, the magnitude of the change is grossly underestimated. Moreover, if change proceeds with no failures, the speed of change is probably too slow. Managers must be able to recognize a failure for what it is, learn from it, make necessary adjustments, and resist the temptation to punish those who are willing to risk failure. Adjustments to failure are much different from just admitting failure and returning to the status quo. Good companies often learn from a failure, but immediately go after the same objectives as before—with a different approach. Returning to the status quo will inevitably lead to greatly increased reluctance to experiment and to take chances.

Changing the Metrics

We have mentioned that making transformation happen requires a change in the way performance is measured. In the traditional way of doing things, the company tends to get what is *inspected* not what is *expected.*

Changing from a command and control culture to one of empowerment will be extremely difficult if top-down financially driven measures and narrow focus on "making the numbers" are the rule of the land. We can talk all we like about the difference between drivers and passengers, and the need to focus on the former, but it is essential that at some point the measures of effectiveness reflect this shift. This requires not only a change in measures—it also requires a change in the behaviors of those at the top. They must believe in the drivers.

■ A European company selling a commodity product to suppliers to the auto industry faced a tough market situation early in the decade. There was significant industry overcapacity, prices were low, and all the competitors were experiencing losses. This firm went to its customers and asked one fundamental question: What can we do to sell you more? The answers were quite varied, but in essence each customer had somewhat different problems that could be ameliorated by developing *and continually enhancing* unique product specifications and service enhancements for each major customer. This required teams focused on particular customers, different approaches in each factory, and the overall empowerment to make this approach work. Teamwork was the critical requirement, as was a culture that supported teamwork.

The management made the commitment to teamwork, but it also made the commitment to changing the personal measurement for managers to reflect the shift to teamwork. Teamworking metrics were developed and thereafter refined. Metrics that inhibit teamwork were explicitly discarded. Most, but not all, managers were able to make the necessary change in attitude. The firm increased its overall worldwide market share by two percentage points and returned to prior levels of profitability. A few of its competitors went out of business.

Summary

A fundamental issue in transformation is that transformation requires *people* to *do* it. The need to change behaviors, attitudes, and the underlying culture is paramount to actually achieving transformation.

☐ Transformation is about different ways of working. There will be major changes in the ways in which work is managed and accomplished, as well as in the culture that establishes work practices.

☐ Each transformation has its own unique characteristics, which need to be reflected in the ordering of priorities, the choice of methodology, the selection of people to drive it, and perhaps even in the establishment of objectives.

☐ Major changes in human resource management practices and the development of new psychological contracts need to be an explicit part of developing the culture required to support transformation.

☐ People capabilities development must be focused on transformation—as well as on continually improving the current jobs as defined. This is not an either/or choice.

☐ The model for integrated strategic transformation is useful to provide insights into the underlying people transformation requirements.

☐ The culture change examples illustrate good and poor practice. They also demonstrate that managers have an inherent mandate to drive the changes and live with the results.

☐ The payoffs in people transformation are not at all trivial. A doubling of productivity is quite common, and marginal improvement goals well may inhibit the necessary people transformation steps. But achieving these results requires a culture based on mutual trust.

☐ It is absolutely incumbent upon top managers wishing to transform an enterprise to rethink their performance measures.

9 So What?

Throughout my work, my main question has always been: So what? What does this mean to the business executive? What is the bottom line? What are managers supposed to *do*? I hope to answer these questions in three sections:

☐ What is enterprise transformation, and why is it different from the usual changes and challenges models?

☐ How can the model for integrated strategic transformation help your company as it tries to implement true transformation?

☐ How good are the "engines" for enterprise transformation in your company, and how do you go about improving them?

Enterprise Transformation

Your company needs to see enterprise transformation as more than today's buzzword to describe working smarter. It has to be more than empowerment, managing change, strategic planning, and a host of other improvement programs that are necessary but not sufficient. Fundamentally, enterprise transformation is concerned with renewal of the business; doing better things as well as doing things better; changing basic paradigms; a culture of urgency and proaction. It has to be integrated, consistent, feasible, and desirable. "Integrated, consistent, feasible, and desirable" means that your enterprise transformation has both a well-thought out strategic direction—one that addresses the key challenges faced—as well as the necessary detailed infrastructure that directly supports the strategic direction. The overall transformation has to be doable, and it has to be consistent with the values of those who must carry it out. These are tough imperatives, but they are essential nonetheless.

Key Concepts

"Dominate or die" is the message on which we started. Whether its manifestation is "transform or die," or "learn or die," the death alternative is always the consequence of inaction. Dominance implies being especially good at something—better than your competitors in at least some aspects of the product or some segments of the market. Transformation, however, implies that being good is not permanent. Competition is ever unfolding, and the rules are constantly changing. Your objective needs to be establishment of new rules, ones that lead to dominance. Learning, then, carries the argument still one step farther. Transformation is ongoing, and the dominant enterprise transforms more rapidly, more fundamentally, and more effectively than its rivals. To do this, your company must learn *faster*—and it must learn the right things.

Dominance is indeed the goal, but, by itself, "dominate or die" has a normative connotation. The more operative question is the "how." "Transform or die" moves us much closer to the "how" question, particularly when you use one or more of the models for the transformation journey. The integrated strategic transformation model has worked well for many companies, and there is no reason why it cannot be useful for you as well.

Finally, the concept of "learn or die" recognizes explicitly that your transformation journey must continue. You *must* work very hard on maintaining both the speed at which your transformation is accomplished and, perhaps even more important, the direction for the learning. Getting better at yesterday's game is decidedly not what either you personally or your company should be doing.

There are "false trade-offs" in how to define and achieve dominance. Your company need not be trapped by the classic trade-offs that firms have traditionally made. Dominance requires that your company achieve *both* low costs and higher quality, faster response and higher productivity, a low level of inventories and a high level of customer service, and a host of other "and" conditions. You and your colleagues need to identify any explicit trade-offs you are now making—and determine how you can break out of these constraints—perhaps by examining how other firms are doing it.

Enterprise transformation requires adopting a new model. Old winning ways often need to be unlearned, and your changes need to be proactive, not wait until your company is in serious trouble. The reactive changes associated with downsizing might be necessary in some cases, but your running room is much greater when a transformation does not require this kind of drastic change. All too often, you lose capabilities when you discard people. If you must downsize, however, do it—and do it quickly. Do it so that it will not be necessary to do it again. Then do your utmost to move from the crisis mode to the transformative mode—where you can get on with proactive pursuit of dominance.

You can use the eight viewpoints or facets to examine your enterprise, and your enterprise transformation needs to assess the change in each of these facets, with a goal of consistency and integration. In these facets, the essence of the enterprise is described according to the person doing the describing. One might say: "The essence of the company is its strategic intent—everything else flows from the real mission and reflects it." This is true, but so is another statement: "A company is essentially defined by its bundle of competencies. Everything else supports and builds on them." Equally true is: "A company is essentially its value-adding resources: people, information, and technology. Everything else is dependent on them, and the company is as strong or weak as they are." So which one of these statements is true? They all are. The usefulness of the eight-facet view is that you can enter the process through the facet that most closely accords with your viewpoint.

The master key, however, is that whichever door you enter through is the door to the *whole enterprise*. It gives you access to all other rooms. Enter enterprise transformation through processes, for example, and immediately you must visit challenges, strategic intent, strategic response, competencies, and the rest. If not, then you are merely flushing the pigeons. Processes do not stand alone.

The implication, therefore, is that there is no formula for transformation. That the model shows challenges at the top, and actions at the bottom, is only because we happened to choose the drivers of change as our starting point. Enter from any starting point, *but* touch eight facets:

☐ The strategic intent viewpoint is concerned with setting directions for your company, and your transformation necessarily must examine the extent to which your basic objectives need to be altered.

☐ The competencies viewpoint recognizes that your transformation will require you to be able to do some things much differently, and that you will need to attain new competencies to achieve dominance.

☐ The processes viewpoint focuses on the necessary changes you will need to make in infrastructure to achieve distinctive competence. Your company cannot afford to improve any and all processes; you must reengineer those processes critical to achieve distinctive competencies.

☐ The resources viewpoint explicitly focuses on the necessary modifications you will need to make in people, information, and technology to achieve your critical processes and competencies.

☐ The strategic response viewpoint characterizes your company by the set of changes and action programs it undertakes. In order to be dominant, your firm will not only undertake *more* action programs, but will also integrate them to achieve a strategic intent, and your actions will define the changes in your competencies, processes, and resources.

☐ The challenges viewpoint of your enterprise is the particular set of internal and external discontinuities and changes in customer expectations that your company faces. It is successful responses to your set of challenges that form the basis for dominance.

☐ The learning capacity viewpoint provides direction to your enterprise transformation journey in two ways. First, learning should be the "driver" of your transformation, not the "passenger." Second, your learning necessarily will be highly concentrated in infrastructure—it takes a lot more than good ideas to transform a company.

Implications

Transformation has to be accepted as a maxim for virtually every business. If your company does not have transformation high on its list of priorities, it well may be on the death path. Dominate or die needs to be made operational: Precisely where is your company *really* good? Why? What do you need to do to be even better? How is your company developing a distinctive competence in transformation? What kind of change would redefine your industry? What could you do that would make life very hard for your competitors? What could you do that would be difficult to copy? What might someone else do that would present serious problems for you?

The dominant company anticipates and causes change—proactively. Surprises are for birthdays. You need to envision a different competitive world, to identify the changes necessary to achieve it, and develop the "people transformation" necessary to implement it. The "golden cord" concept will help you link all concepts to component parts of your paradigm shifts and determine the necessary unlearning that must accompany them.

The eight viewpoints or facets of an enterprise provide a useful cross check to assess your enterprise transformation path. It is essential that managers take the trouble to articulate the implications in all facets in their individual transformations, see where there are shortcomings in the transformation planning, and use this cross check as a means to learn more about the process and journey of transformation.

Every manager needs to be challenged and to challenge. Every employee needs to use his or her brain to accelerate transformation. Enterprise transformation is much too essential for survival to leave to chance, and you cannot afford the luxury to always be polite. Every checklist you can find on enterprise transformation is worth looking at. Even if the result is only confirmation of your existing plans, you will often find that making these cross checks increases commitment, your comfort level in each transformation, and your learning about "transformation engines."

When going through your checklist, remember that you are not just operating from the past. You are not just saying: "Given that these are the competencies we have, what do we do?" Ask stretching questions. Transformation may involve a step in the dark—very frightening. But it may equally be discovering that one of your business units is doing · something quite innovative. You must pick up on that change—bottom-up instead of top-down. Be prepared to reject complacency and open your eyes.

You and your colleagues need to focus the enterprise energy on true transformation. It is far too easy to confuse indiscriminant actions with integrated, consistent transformation. You must be on the lookout for it.

Finally, transformation needs to be seen as an ongoing process of the way you manage, integral to the way your company needs to be run, and a part of your professional development. It is not a one-time happening; it is not something that consultants can do for you; it is not ever finished; and it is never done as well as it might have been. There is always room for improvement, and there is always a chance to learn what the lessons are, and how to do it better next time. *Never* assume there will not be a next time for transformation.

The Integrated Strategic Transformation Model

Our work with companies undergoing fundamental change has lasted several years. The Manufacturing 2000 project itself is now five years old, and the fundamental research effort has always been in what we now call enterprise transformation. A key focus of this research has been to develop the integrated strategic transformation model. We now know it works. We know that the journey is as important as the destination, and you can learn a lot by using the model.

Key Concepts

The most basic advantage of the model is that it is completely consistent with the eight-facet view of enterprise transformation, and its use strongly supports the "golden cord" linkages among them. Consistency, integration, feasibility, and desirability in your company can be achieved by having the managers with the responsibility for defining the transformation in your enterprise use the model. The model helps to ensure that your strategic intent is focused on the right set of issues, that your action programs are consistent with the discontinuities/expectation changes, that your new competencies are correctly identified, and that your efforts on new process development are targeted on the *right* process improvements rather than on just any improvements.

The "Post-it Note process" starts with identifying your discontinuities and the changes in expectations of your customers and other stakeholders. By listing all that you and your colleagues can think of, and then grouping and prioritizing them, your group reaches consensus. Moreover, the people also reach a comfort level with the analytical process, having made some reasonable selections. The same comfort level and consensus comes from the strategic responses to the discontinuities/expectations, as well as from the competencies and competence mapping. Every time we have conducted one of these sessions, we have found a special feeling of camaraderie among the group participants.

The model is best approached in two halves; the top one sets your strategic direction, and the bottom half delineates the detailed infrastructure necessary to implement your strategy. The key intersection between the two halves is competencies. Being explicit about the new competencies mandated for your company by the transformation is essential for enterprise transformation. Perhaps even more essential is division of your competencies into their required capabilities, processes, systems, and resources. Far too many grand ideas for enterprise transformation become precisely that when the true infrastructure implications become well-understood.

It is also easy to think that, because your firm is engaging in a large series of action programs to improve its operations, it is in fact transforming. Without some clearly articulated and *operational* definition of overriding strategy, the two halves of the model are not integrated. It is only when you fully develop both the strategic direction and the infrastructure—in an integrated consistent way—that you will achieve effective transformation in your firm.

The concept of "distinctive competence" is particularly useful. Understanding which competencies will allow your company to differentiate itself from its competitors is basic to achieving dominance. The progression of natural competencies—usually from distinctive to essential to routine to outsourcing—can also lead to important priority setting. In the long run, it is *creating* distinctive competence that should be your goal for enterprise transformation.

Managerial Imperatives

The primary managerial imperative of the integrated strategic transformation model is that since it works—you should use it! You should also use other models, such as the four-stage Boynton model, as a cross check. In several Manufacturing 2000 companies, Boynton's model has helped managers recognize the need for a profound change, rather than continue on their past direction to improvement. The integrated strategic intent model can help you to bring about consensus on enterprise transformation, to prioritize the work that follows, and to communicate the wisdom of your vision and choices throughout the enterprise.

If you deal with "soft" issues in an open forum, people may more readily understand the relative importance of your nontechnical competencies, and the set of your key competency requirements (and underlying infrastructure) may become more apparent. The overall feasibility of your transformation can be better analyzed, as well as the subsequent resource requirements. Still another benefit comes from making the issue of "desirability" more transparent. The competence maps and supporting processes, systems, and resources make your necessary changes in personnel fairly obvious. This in turn can lead to open discussions of implications for particular people: the transformations they will need to undergo, the training and other reskilling requirements, and an earlier view of those who will be made redundant—which should foster more humane treatment of any outplaced workers.

Transformation Engines

Enterprise transformation is far too important to leave to chance. Processes or "engines" for transformation should be institutionalized. Dominance requires that companies explicitly identify, study, and continuously improve their transformation engines. Making sure that the engines always represent the state-of-the-art is a critical enterprise objective, although not so easily achieved.

Key Concepts

Learn or die is basic to developing and improving the transformation engines. The direction for transformation—as well as integration of the various aspects—is supported by the enterprise transformation models. The ways in which transformation takes place in your company, your ongoing evaluation methodology, your detailed tool kit, the practices your management uses to support and guide transformation, your development of individuals for implementing transformation, your in-house support groups for making transformation a reality, your use of external consultants and other help, and the dissemination of lessons learned throughout your company are all key aspects of the transformation engines that you should continually study and improve.

If your company is committed to dominance through ongoing enterprise transformation, it must develop an explicit mechanism for evaluating and improving all parts of its transformation engine. This learning is in many ways more essential than the dictates of any particular transformation. It is not enough to make one transformation successfully. You must ask: How could you have done it better? What will you change next time? What are the lessons you have learned? How do you disseminate them, to minimize reinvention of the wheel in your company?

We have seen the need for individual leadership in enterprise transformation, particularly in smaller companies. But even in the larger ones, leadership at the business unit level is critical. In far too many large firms, there can be a fear of attempting anything radical; this fear needs to be recognized at a top level in your company and a means found to encourage experimentation. Almost every enterprise transformation requires some fairly radical thinking, as well as a need for your firm to "unlearn." Your tool kit for enterprise transformation needs to include methodologies to foster this "outside-the-box" thinking—both on an individual basis and for group decision making.

Finally, the concept of benchmarking needs to be clearly integrated into the structure of your transformation engines. Comparisons are always possible and if done right can lead to breakthrough thinking. One key is to focus your benchmarking on practices much more than on metrics. Another is to learn the benchmarking methodology well—no "recreational" benchmarking in your company! Benchmarking must be an integral part of your tool kit for enterprise transformation and extended to benchmarking other engines. Several of the Manufacturing 2000 companies are doing precisely this. They are looking very carefully at *how* transformation is institutionalized in other companies. The focus is less on the benefits or outputs of particular transformations, but instead on the engines to guide and support enterprise transformation—and the potential lessons for improvement of their own engines. You need to do this as well.

Implications

You *must* focus on how to make your enterprise transformation process better, faster, and more frequent. This mandates careful examination of transformation engines—and their continuous improvement. The transformation journey needs to be sized up early on. When you are looking at a particular business unit, you must quickly develop a sense of proportion: What is the optimum size for this unit after transformation? Does this represent a major reduction in personnel? If so, the action probably needs to be taken sooner rather than later; the choice of tool kit needs to reflect this decision.

Similarly, your choice of tool and approach to specific transformation efforts needs to be seen as a key design issue. Several transformation efforts have an overall focus, such as time-based competition, implementation of TQM in one of its forms, cost reduction, or customer value maximization. Adopting a particular theme or focus helps in tool kit selection and approach, but the actual processes used and the reactions of people to your transformation are always unique. There are lessons to be learned from these reactions. When you are working on a specific transformation project, you should not be so focused on it that you do not take the time to learn about implications or results of the overall transformation process.

Every indication is that companies must transform *before* crisis conditions are reached. The options available to a company—both in terms of alternatives and timing—are much more agreeable. The unpleasant decisions that often take out muscle along with fat are all too necessary when costs are out of control, losses are being posted, markets have been lost, products are out of date, the organization is bloated, or the competitive game has fundamentally changed. It is hard to get people's attention when the company is in good condition, but in fact that is precisely what you need. "If it ain't broke, don't fix it" is fundamentally wrong, and you must reject it. You need to instill in your people a constant sense of urgency; complacency in any form has to be rooted out.

Enterprise transformation is much too important to be done by some small group of experts. A select group may indeed take on the leadership role—and the role of continually improving the engines—but the actual work needs to involve as many people as possible. You need to develop transformation skills in, again, as many people as possible. Managing the transformation engines in your company has to include a general call to mobilization: not once, but constantly.

Notes

Chapter 1

1. Henry Goldblatt, "Bill Gates and Paul Allan Talk," *Fortune,* 2 October:1995, 56.

2. Ira Sager, "The View from IBM," *Business Week,* 30 October:1995, 41.

3. "When the Going Gets Tough, Boeing Gets Fouchy-Feely," *Business Week,* 17 January:1994.

4. Richard Tanner Pascale, *Managing on the Edge: How Successful Companies Use Conflict to Stay Ahead* (New York: Simon and Schuster, 1990). The fourteen companies are: Allen Bradley (Rockwell), Disney, Boeing, DEC, Emerson, Frito-Lay, IBM, Intel, Johnson & Johnson, Mars, Maytag, McDonald's, Merck, and Wal-Mart.

5. Roger Martin, "Changing the Mind of the Corporation," *Harvard Business Review,* (November–December 1993): 92.

6. Rosabeth Moss Kanter, "Transcending Business Boundaries: 12,000 World Managers View Change," *Harvard Business Review* (May–June 1991): 151–164.

Chapter 2

1. Hamel and Prahalad use the term "strategic intent" also to encompass long-term "stretch" objectives and a sense of where a company needs to be in order truly to be competitive. Strategic intent conveys a sense of direction, a sense of discovery, and a sense of destiny. See Gary Hamel and C.K. Prahalad's "Strategic Intent," *Harvard Business Review* (May–June 1989): 63–76; "Strategy as Stretch and Leverage," *Harvard Business Review* (March–April 1993): 75–84; and *Competing for the Future* (Boston: Harvard Business School Press, 1994).

2. For more information on the SKF transformation, see Sandra Vandermerwe, *From Tin Soldiers to Russian Dolls* (Oxford: Butterworth-Heinemann, 1993).

3. Benjamin Porter, "The IT Value Imperative: Delivering Results from Information Technology Investments," Andersen Consulting, 1994.

4. Some authors distinguish between "redesign" and "reengineering," where the former relates to "the best existing practice," and the latter describes "what could conceiv-

ably be done." For further information, see Everett Shorey, "Process Redesign," *Executive Excellence* (October 1993); L.N. Masonson, "Reengineering is Here to Stay," *Healthcare Financial Management* (November 1993); or *Industry Week* (February 10, 1995).

5. For more information, see A.J. Nanni, J.R. Dixon, and T.E. Vollmann, *The New Performance Challenges: Measuring Operations for World Class Competitiveness* (Homewood, Ill.: Dow Jones-Irwin, 1990).

Chapter 4

1. If an outside facilitator is not used, it is best not to name a facilitator on the basis of authority. An alternative is to ask the person whose first name is first in the alphabet to be the facilitator. The task should be rotated so that no one person is perceived as "in charge." A good place to change facilitators is after the entire process described in this chapter, but before taking on the strategic response exercise described in Chapter 5.

2. The Pareto Principle states that 80 percent of one's results come from 20 percent of one's efforts.

3. For further information on this subject, see F. Szekely, T.E. Vollmann, and A. Ebbinghaus, *Benchmarking Environmental Performance* (Cheltenham, England: Stanley Thornes, 1996).

4. Sandra Vandermerwe, *From Tin Soldiers to Russian Dolls* (Oxford: Butterworth-Heinemann, 1993), 67.

Chapter 5

1. For more information, see A.J. Nanni, J.R. Dixon, and T.E. Vollmann, *The New Performance Challenges: Measuring Operations for World Class Competitiveness* (Homewood, Ill.: Dow Jones-Irwin, 1990).

2. George Stalk, Jr., and A.M. Webber, "Japan's Dark Side of Time," *Harvard Business Review* (July–August, 1993): 93–102.

3. There are several publications that describe this model. Two that explain some critical managerial implications are B.J. Pine, B. Victor, and A.C. Boynton, "Making Mass Customization Work," *Harvard Business Review* (September–October 1993): 108–119, and A.C. Boynton, "Achieving Dynamic Stability through Information Technology," *California Management Review* (Winter 1993): 58–77.

4. R. Morgan Gould, "Revolution at Oticon A/S (A): Vision for a Change Competent Organization," IMD case study OB 229, May 24, 1994.

Chapter 6

1. There are several *Harvard Business Review* articles written by Gary Hamel and C.K. Prahalad on core competence. "The Core Competence of the Corporation" appears

in the *Harvard Business Review* (May–June 1990): 79–91. Other articles appear in the May–June 1989 and January–February 1989 issues of the same journal. See also their book, *Competing for the Future* (Boston: Harvard Business School Press, 1994).

2. Richard A. Bettis, Stephen P. Bradley, and Gary Hamel, "Outsourcing and Industrial Decline," *Academy of Management Executive* (February 1992): 7–22.

3. Benjamin Porter, "The IT Value Imperative: Delivering Results from Information Technology Investments," Andersen Consulting, 1994.

4. Sandra Vandermerwe, *From Tin Soldiers to Russian Dolls* (Oxford: Butterworth-Heinemann, 1993).

Chapter 7

1. David Garvin, "Beyond Buzzwords: A Realistic Approach to Total Quality and the Learning Organization," *European Quality J* (February 1994): 22.

2. Tom Peters, *The Tom Peters Seminar: Crazy Times Call for Crazy Organizations* (London: Macmillan, 1994): 11.

3. Peter F. Drucker, "The New Society of Organizations," *Harvard Business Review* (September–October 1992): 95–104.

4. Roger Martin, "Changing the Mind of the Corporation," *Harvard Business Review* (November–December 1993): 81–94.

5. Julia King, "Reengineering Slammed," *Computerworld* (June 13, 1994): 1, 14.

6. For more on the Oticon Story, see R. Morgan Gould, "Revolution at Oticon A/S (A): A Vision for a Change Competent Organization," IMD case study OB 229, May 24, 1994.

7. The Siemens TOP transformation initiative is profiled in the *Manufacturing 2000 Business Briefing*, no. 3 (Autumn 1994): 2–3.

Chapter 8

1. Chris Argyris, "Organizational Effectiveness Under Stress," *Harvard Business Review* (May–June 1960): 137–146; Paul Sparrow and Jean-Marie Hiltrop, *European Human Resource Management in Transition* (London: Prentice Hall International, 1994).

2. Jean-Marie Hiltrop, *Managing People in International Organizations*, (London: Prentice Hall International, forthcoming).

3. See, for example, Charles W. Ginn and Donald L. Sexton, "A Comparison of the Personality Type Dimensions of the 1987 Inc. 500 Company Founders/CEOs with Those of Slower-Growth Firms," *Journal of Business Venturing* (September 1990): 313–326. The Myers-Briggs Type Indicator (MBTI) of founders-chief executive officers of fast-growth firms were compared with those of slow-growth firms under the assumption that differences in psychological preferences would have an impact on the strategic or

growth orientation of the firm. Kevin Costello explores the use of the MBTI since 1989 in the education and development department of Saint Luke's Hospital (Kansas City, Missouri) as an instrument to show nurse managers how their behavior affects other people in, "The Myers-Briggs Type Indicator—A Management Tool," *Nursing Management* (May 1993): 46–51. The use of the Belbin Self-Perception Inventory (SPI) is explored in Tony Glaze's "Cadbury's Dictionary of Competence," *Personnel Journal* (November 1989): 72–78.

4. Shigeo Shingo, *A Revolution in Manufacturing: The SMED System* (Cambridge, Massachusetts: Productivity Press, 1985).

5. Cross docking calls for the retailer to communicate its exact product sales from each store to the supplier, which in turn ships the right replenishment quantities of products to the warehouses. Materials thus are never put into inventory; they go "across the dock" and out to the stores.

Index

About the Author

Thomas E. Vollmann is a professor of manufacturing management and associate director of the Manufacturing 2000 Project at IMD International in Lausanne, Switzerland. His current research focuses on enterprise transformation, benchmarking, and supply chain management. Professor Vollmann consults to various firms on manufacturing, information systems, and enterprise transformation as well as to several schools on operations management curricula. He also serves as the series editor for the Dow Jones Irwin Series in Integrated Resource Management. Professor Vollmann has written more than seventy-five articles in journals such as the *Harvard Business Review, California Management Review, Management Science*, and *Journal of Operation Management*. He has also written eleven books, including *The New Manufacturing Challenge: Measuring Performance for World Class Competition* and *Benchmarking Environmental Performance*.